Mary J Pulte

Domestic cook book

Mary J Pulte

Domestic cook book

ISBN/EAN: 9783744785884

Printed in Europe, USA, Canada, Australia, Japan

Cover: Foto ©Lupo / pixelio.de

More available books at **www.hansebooks.com**

A COMPANION TO

Pulte's Domestic Physician.

Being a practical guide in the preparation of food for the well and the sick, and containing also useful hints for the household,

BY

MRS. DR. J. H. PULTE.

"Good Cheer Brings Content."

"If dinner has oppressed one
I think it is perhaps the gloomiest hour
Which turns up out of the whole twenty-four."
—*Byron.*

GEO. W. SMITH,
CINCINNATI,
1888.

To that
Noble Charity,
The Ohio Hospital
For Women and Children,
This Work is Cordially
Inscribed by its
Friend and Well-
Wisher,
The Author.

PREFACE.

This work was originally a suggestion of the late Dr. Pulte, and was intended as a companion to PULTE'S DOMESTIC PHYSICIAN, to be a practical guide in the preparation of food for the well and the sick; for the former that he might remain well, and for the latter that he might be aided to recover his health.

It is a fact, too little understood, that many of the ills that afflict mankind are directly traceable to the use of poorly prepared and unsuitable food.

The poor cook is the modern Pandora, and her kitchen is the box from which are issuing dyspepsia, gout, rheumatism and a host of other evils.

Your energetic business man, of happy mood and contented at home and abroad, will be found to have a good digestion; whereas, your sour, morose and irritable man for whom "there is no music in this life," will as surely be found to be a miserable dyspeptic.

Every recipe in this book has been carefully tested by the author, and directions for preparing them so plainly and accurately written down, that even the most inexperienced housekeeper, by following them may be so successful that her cooking "will shine with reputation."

Attention is called particularly to the diet for the sick; every article of which was tested, tried and approved by Dr. Pulte, in memory of whom this work is published; not with any desire or expectation of profit, but in further aid to a cause to which my late husband had devoted his life and talents.

A part of the net proceeds from the sale of the work are to be devoted to the uses of that excellent charity—THE OHIO HOSPITAL FOR WOMEN AND CHILDREN. MRS. DR. PULTE.

JUNE 1st, 1888.

CONTENTS.

BREAD AND BREAKFAST CAKES.

Baking, Bread, Yeast, Bread, Biscuit, Biscuit, Buckwheat, Buckwheat Harrison's, Buckwheat, Cinnamon Cake, Coffee Cake, Doughnuts, Doctor's Cake, Corn Griddle Cakes, Corn Mush, Corn Mush Fried, Corn Bread, Corn Muffins, Flannel Cakes, Graham Gems, Muffins, Muffins,, Pan Cakes, Pan Cake Rolls, Puff Balls, Potato Cakes, Rolls, Rusk, Strawberry Short Cake, Waffles.................................. 1–17

EGGS AND OMELETS.

Eggs in Stand, Eggs Soft, Eggs Hard, Eggs Poached, Eggs Scrambled, Omelet, Omelet Souffle, Omelet, Omelet with Cheese, Omelet with Ham, Omelet with Herbs 18–22

COTTAGE CHEESE—OAT GROATS—WHEAT AND RICE.

Cottage Cheese, Cottage Cheese Wine, Oat Groats, Hulled Wheat, Rice to Boil....... 23-25

COFFEE AND CHOCOLATE.

Coffee Pot, Coffee to Make, Coffee the Best, Chocolate, Cocoa, Baker's. Cocoa, Tea, Mock Cream................................. 26-29

SOUPS.

Beef, Beef Clear, etc., Bean, Bouillon, Chicken, Corn, Crab, Dumplings for Beef, Dumplings for Chicken, Dumplings for Oyster, Gumbo, Mock Turtle, Mutton, Noodles, Noodles to Make, Noodles as a Vegetable, Ox Tail, Oyster, Oyster Pea, Pea without Meat, Tomato, Veal, Vegetable................................. 30-48

FISH.

Codfish Boiled, Codfish Cakes, Eels Stewed, Eels Boiled, Eels Fried, Halibut Smoked, Herring Dutch Pickled, Mackerel Fresh Broiled, No. 1 Mackerel Salt Boiled, No. 1 Mackerel Salt Broiled, Perch and Bullheads Fried, Salmon Canned, Salmon Boiled, Shad Fresh Baked, Stuffing for

FISH.—Continued.

Shad, Shad Fresh Boiled, Shad Fresh Fried, Trout Boiled, White Fish Baked, Stuffing for White Fish...................... 49–59

SHELL FISH.

Crabs Deviled, Crabs Deviled, Oyster Soup, Oysters Escaloped, Oysters Fricasseed, Oysters Fried, Oyster Patties, Oysters Raw, Shrimp Salad, Shrimp Stewed, Terrapin 60–66

BEEF.

Beef Roast, Beef Steak, Beef Steak & Onions, Beef, a la mode, Beef Corned and Cabbage, Beef Tripe Stewed, Beef Corned Hash, Spiced-Pickle for Beef Venison and Rabbits, Beef Spiced, Beef Tongue Spiced, Beef Tongue Fresh, Sauce for Beef Tongue.................................... 67–75

VEAL.

A la mode Veal, a la Strasburg Veal, Cutlet Veal, Fricassee Veal, Fricandean, Fricassee with Sweet Breads, Hash Veal, Roast Veal, Sweet Breads Fricassee Sweet Breads Fried, Liver Calves......... 76–84

LAMB AND MUTTON.

Lamb and Turnips Stewed, Leg of Lamb Roasted, Leg of Lamb Roasted, Lamb Chops Fried, Leg of Lamb Boiled, Mutton Chops Broiled............................ 86–89

PORK.

Ham Boiled, Ham Roasted, Pig Roasted, Pig Stuffing, Pig's Feet Soused, Pork and Beans, Sausages, Spare Ribs Stuffed, 90–94

POULTRY.

Chicken Boiled, Chicken Fricassee, Chicken Fricassee, Chicken Pie, Chicken Spring, Ducks Roasted, Duck Stuffing, Goose Roasted, Goose Stuffing, Turkey Boiled, Turkey Roasted, Turkey Stuffing, Turkey and Chicken Stuffing, Turkey how to know a Young one........................96–105

GAME.

Hazenpfeffer, Quails Roasted, Quail and Bird Stuffing, Rabbit Spiced, Venison Saddle Roasted, Venison Saddle Spiced, Venison Steak..........................106–111

SAUCES FOR FISH AND MEAT.

Cape, Drrawn Butter, Egg, Hollandish, Horseradish, Mayonaise, Mayonaise, New Oyster, Parsley, Pickle, Tomato, Tomato 112–117

CONTENTS.

PICKLES—CATSUP AND MUSTARD.

Beans, Beets, Cabbage, Cucumbers, Onions, Tomato Catsup, Mustard..................118–123

SALADS.

Bean, Cabbage Cold Slaw, Celery, Chicken, Corn, Cucumber, Dressing No. 1, Dressing No. 2, Endive, Fish, Fish Dressing, Herring, Italian, Lettuce, Oyster, Oyster Dressing, Potato, Potato Dressing, Shrimp Shrimp Dressing, Tongue...............124–136

CROQUETTES—MACARONI.

Chicken, Chicken Sauce, Oyster, Oyster Sauce, Tongue, Tongue Sauce, Macaroni with Herb Cheese, Macaroni with Tomatos..................................138–142

VEGETABLES.

Asparagus, Beans Marrowfat, Beans Lima, Beans Yellow Wax, Beets Young, Cabbage White, Cabbage Red, Cabbage Curled Savoy, Carrots, Cauliflower, Corn Boiled, Corn Oysters, Corn Stewed, Greens Wild, Kale, Kale with Bacon, Kohlrabe, Leek, Onions Stewed, Parsnip Cakes, Parsnips Fried, Parsnips Stewed, Peas Green, Peas and Carrots,

VEGETABLES.—Continued.

Potatoes Boiled, New Potatoes, Potatoes Mashed, Potatoes Dresden, Potatoes Fried, Potatoes Baked, Potatoes Fried, Potatoes Mashed, Saurkraut to Make, Saurkraut, Saurkraut with Pork Ribs, Slaw Hot, Spinach, Succtash, Tomatoes, Turnips................................144–165

PASTRY—PIES AND TARTS.

Puff Paste No. 1, Puff Paste No. 2, Pie Crust, Apples for Pies, Apple, Cranberry, Curd, Custard, Currants to Wash, Lemon, Mince Meat, Peaches for Pies, Peach, Pumpkin........................166–174

PUDDINGS AND FRITTERS.

Almond, Apple and Rice, Apple Dumplings, Batter, Bread and Butter, Bread, Cocoanut, Corn Starch Baked, Corn Starch Boiled, Egg German Eierkase, Fruit, Marmalade, Peach, Plum Baked, Plum Boiled, Prune, Quince Tapioca, Quince Sauce, Rice Flour Boiled, Rice Baked, Rusk, Sago, Tapioca, Fritters Apple, Fritter Batter, Fritter Bread...............175–194

CONTENTS.

SWEET SAUCES FOR PUDDINGS.

Apple, Apricots, Butter Sauce, Chocolate, Cider, Cranberry, Cream, Cream, Custard, Hard, Milk, Peaches, Prunes, Raspberry, Strawberry, Vanilla, Wine German, Wine Sherry..195–204

CUSTARDS.

Almond, Apple, Chocolate, Cocoanut, Corn Starch, Corn Starch Snow Balls, Pumpkin, Raspberry, Snow Ball, Wine.........205–211

CREAMS—SYRUPS AND ICE CREAMS.

Almond, Chocolate, Cincinnati, Raspberry, Strawberry, Vanilla, Wine. to make Ice Cream, Chocolate, Lemon, Raspberry, Strawberry, Vanilla, Vanilla without Cream, Syrups for Ice Creams, Jellies and Sauces, Raspberry, Strawberry...........212–223

JELLIES WITH GELATINE.

Calfs' Foot, Cider, Lemon, Raspberry, Strawberry, Wine...........................224–228

CHARLOTTE RUSSE AND BLANC MANGE.

Charlotte Russe, Almond Blanc Mange, Blanc Mange.....................................229–231

CONTENTS.

CAKE MACAROONS MERINGUE.

Almond, Almond Jumbles, Almond Macaroons, Almond Macaroons 2, Almond Sponge, Almonds to Blanch and Grind, Bride's, Cake, Chocolate Macaroons, Citron, Cocoanut, Cocoanut Jumbles, Cocoanut Macaroons, Cocoanut and Raspberry Mixture, Cookies Berlin, Cookies Grandmother, Cookies Sugar, Cream Cincinnati, Cream Filling, Cup Cake, Currant, Fruit, Fruit, Gingerbread Soft, Gingerbread White, Golden, Groom's, Icing, Icing Chocolate, Jelly, Marble, Meringue, Pound, Silver, Snow, Sponge, Sponge Almond, Sponge Muffins, Sponge White, White 233-257

BEVERAGES.

Apple Wine, Cider to keep sweet, Cider Syrup, Milk Punch, Mulled Cider, Mulled Wine, Roman Punch, Raspberry Vinekept Sweet, Egg Nog Warm, Egg Nog Cold, Lemonade, Lemon Punch, Lemongar, Raspberry Shrub.................... ... 258-265

CANNED VEGETABLES.

Asparagus, Beans Lima, Beans String, Cauliflower, Corn, Peas Green, Tomatoes 286–289

DIET FOR THE SICK.

Apple Water, Apple Water, Arrowroot Gruel, Arrowroot Jelly, Blackberry Syrup, Barley Water, Barley Boiled, Beef Broth, Beef Tea, Broth and Milk, Bread and Milk Poultice, Cranberry Water, Chicken Broth, Cracker Panada, Cocoa, Crisped Ham, Dry Toast, Egg Nog, Farina Gruel, Flaxseed Tea, Ice its preservation, Iceland Moss Tea, Iceland Moss Jelly, Koumiss, Lemonade warm, Lemonade cold, Milk Porridge, Milk Toast, Milk Punch, Mulled Wine, Mutton Broth, Mustard Plaster, Mustard Poultice, Oat Meal Gruel, Oat Meal Porridge, Oat Groats Boiled, Pap, Panada, Raspberry Water, Raspberry Vinegar, Rice Water, Rice Boiled, Rice Jelly, Rusk Panada, Roasted Apples, Sago Gruel, Slippery Elm Tea, Slippery Elm Poultice, Tamarind Water, Toast Water, Tapioca Gruel, Tapioca Jelly, Tea, Whey 1, Whey 2, Wine Whey, Wine Cottage Cheese 291–313

CANNED FRUITS—MARMALADE—JELLIES AND PRESERVES.

Cherries, Peaches Clings, Peaches Freestones, Pears Seckel, Plums Damson,

CANNED FRUITS, MARMALADES, JELLIES, ETC.—Continued.

Plums Green Gage, Quinces, Raspberries, Strawberries, Marmalade, Peach, Quince, Raspberry Red, Strawberry, Jellies to make, Apple Siberian Crab, Cranberry, Currant, Green Gage, Quince, Raspberry Red, Green Gages, Peaches, Peaches Brandy, Quince, Strawberry...266–285

REMEDIES.

Arnica Tincture, Bruises, Burns, Cough, Cut, Felon, Scalds, Sprains..............316–319

HOUSEHOLD RECEIPTS.

Blankets to Wash, Black Satin and Silk, Black Lace Renewed, Bed Bugs Destroyed, Butter Kept Sweet, Cool House, Cloths to Soak, Cloths to Wash, Carpet Cleaning, Cockroaches Destroyed, Chapped Hands Prevented, Cashmere Shawl or Dress to Wash, Disinfectant, Eggs Kept Fresh, Flannels to Wash, Fresh Paint Removed, Flour Paste, Fruit Stains Removed, Grease Removed, Glove Paste, Gloves to Clean, Gray Gloves Colored, House Cleaning, Chamber, House Cleaning and Parlor, Housekeeping, Hair Prevented from Turning Gray, Lard Kept

Sweet, Lisle Gloves Cleaned, Lawn Dress Washed, Mucilage, Paintings Cleaned, Paintings Restored, Pile on Velvet Raised, Bats and Mice Destroyed, Rancid Butter Restored, Rancid Oil Restored, Starch to Cook, Starch Cold, Spots Removed from Furniture, Sink Pipe to Clear, Spermacetic and Sterrine removed, Satin and Silk Ribbons Cleaned Spots on Light Ribbons Removed, Spots from Rust Removed, To Clean Busts, To Clean Brass and Copper Kettles, To Clean Chandeliers, To Clean Marble, To Wash a Table Cover, Varnish for Furniture, Velvet Cloak to Clean, Water to Clear, White Wash, Whitening for Ceilings, Water Closet to Clean, White Dresses and Lawns, White Goods Kept, Wrinkles on Velvet Taken Out......................336–345

Bread and Cakes.

BAKING OVEN TO HEAT.

To ascertain the right heat of the oven, put a piece of writing paper into it, and if it is a chocolate brown in five minutes it is the right heat for biscuits, muffins and small pastry. It is called a quick oven. If the paper is dark yellow it is the right heat for bread, pound cake, puddings and puff paste pies. When the paper is light yellow it is right for sponge cake.

BREAD.

Peel and wash as many medium sized potatoes as you intend to have loaves of bread and boil them in water enough to cover them. Cut up fine a two cent cake of compressed yeast in half a cup full of luke warm water with one teaspoonful of white granulated sugar in it. Sift the flour, and when the potatoes are done put them into a colander, mash them fine and rub them through. Then mix enough flour with the potatoes and the scalding hot potato water as will make a sponge a little thicker than flannel cakes. When it is luke warm stir in the yeast and salt. Then set the pan with the sponge into a pan with luke warm water and put it where the water will keep at a uniform heat until the sponge is very light. Then put in one tablespoonful of melted lard, and stir in flour enough to make a soft dough. Put it on the bread board and knead it twenty or thirty minutes. Then make it into loaves and set it where it will rise again. Then bake it.

YEAST.

After the hops have been boiled in water, strain them out and whilst the hop water is still scalding hot stir in flour enough to make it as thick as griddle cakes; then put in cold water until you can hold your finger in it; then put in some yeast, cork it tight and set it in a cool place. It will keep a week or more in Summer.

BREAD.

Peel four large potatoes and boil them in water until they are soft; then mash them up fine and press them through a colander and mix them with the flour; then take the water that the potatoes were boiled in scalding hot and stir it into the flour and potatoes; then put in cold water till you can hold your finger in it; then put in the yeast and salt and set it in a warm place over night.

BISCUITS,—(EXCELLENT.)

Two pints of unsifted flour; three heaping teaspoonfuls of baking powder sifted in the flour; one and a half ounces of butter rubbed into the flour; one and a half ounces of lard rubbed into the flour; one teaspoonful of salt, two-thirds of a pint of cold sweet milk. Mix quick, roll out half an inch thick; cut with a cake cutter and bake twenty minutes. If the oven is a little hotter in the bottom than it is on top, the biscuits will be lighter, and when done they should be a light brown.

BISCUIT.

One heaped quart of sifted flour; four teaspoonfuls of baking powder; three gills of rich sweet milk; four ounces of fresh butter, or two ounces of butter and two of lard, and one teaspoonful of salt. Mix the flour and baking powder together; put the milk, butter and salt over the fire, and as soon as the butter is melted stir the whole into the flour. The milk must not be scalding hot, only warm enough to melt the butter. Make it into a soft dough as quick as possible. Roll it out half an inch thick. Cut it with a small cake cutter and bake in a quick oven fifteen or twenty minutes.

BUCKWHEAT CAKES.

One quart of buckwheat flour; half a cup of corn meal scalded; two cent cake of Fleischmann's compressed yeast; two tablespoonfuls of brown sugar; one teaspoonful of salt, and warm water enough to make a thin batter. Beat all well together and set to rise in a warm place.

HARRISON'S

Self raising buckwheat flour; mix with cold milk or water enough to make a thin batter and bake immediately on a hot griddle.

BUCKWHEAT CAKES.

One quart of flour; one teaspoonful of salt; one quart of warm water and a two cent paper of Fleischmann's compressed yeast. Cut the yeast up in a cup half full of warm water taken from the quart and let it dissolve. Put the flour and salt into a stone crock and stir in the warm water until it is a smooth batter. Then add the yeast and set it in a warm place to rise. If they are for breakfast make them up just before going to bed, for Fleischmann's yeast rises quicker than any other that I have used. When you are ready to bake, stir in two teaspoonfuls of baking powder. It makes them sweet and tender. Have the griddle hot, grease it with a piece of fat pork and bake. Have ready some fresh butter that is soft enough to spread, and butter the cakes well. Send them to table hot, a few at a time.

CINNAMON CAKE.

One cent cake of Fleischmann's compressed yeast cut up in half a cup full of luke warm water; one quart of flour; half a pint of warm sweet milk, half a pint of white sugar dissolved in the milk. Then make a hole in the flour and stir in the milk, sugar and yeast. Stir it into a batter and set it in a warm place to rise over night. In the morning make it into a thicker batter and let it rise again. Then stir in two ounces of soft butter. Then put in one egg and beat it in with your hand. Then put in another egg and beat it in the same manner. Then pour it into a baking pan and let it rise half an hour longer. Then put it into the oven and when it has baked ten minutes spread some soft butter over it and then strew powdered sugar and cinnamon on it and let it bake five minutes longer.

COFFEE CAKE

One pound of sifted flour with two teaspoonfuls of Royal baking powder in it, half a pound of white granulated sugar, four ounces of butter, four fresh eggs beaten separately, half a teaspoonful of cinnamon, beat the sugar and butter to a light cream, beat the yolks and stir them into the sugar and butter, then beat the whites with two teaspoonfuls of white sugar to a stiff foam and stir them in, then add the cinnamon and mix in the flour and baking powder last, roll it out, put it into a baking pan and bake it a yellow brown.

DOUGH NUTS.

One pint of rich sweet milk made warm, four

ounces of fresh butter melted in the milk, one pint and a half of white granulated sugar, two teaspoonfuls of grated nutmeg and one teaspoonful of salt all put into the milk, four yolks beaten with one tablespoonful of sugar and stirred into the milk, two quarts and one pint of sifted flour with seven teaspoonfuls of baking powder mixed with it, four whites beaten with one tablespoonful of sugar to a stiff foam, make a hole in the centre of the flour and stir in the milk with the other ingredients until it is as thick as batter cakes, then stir in the whites and the remainder of the flour, make the dough quick and as moist as possible, roll out half an inch thick and cut with a cake cutter. The lard should be hot enough to brown when the cakes are put in, and only cakes enough to cover the top of the lard should be put in at a time. They will rise in two minutes, then turn them and fry two minutes longer.

DOCTORS' CAKE.

One pint of sweet milk, two ounces of fresh butter, one teaspoonful of grated nutmeg, one teaspoonful of salt, half a pint of white granulated sugar, four fresh eggs beaten separately, one quart of flour, four teaspoonfuls of Royal baking powder. Put the milk, butter, nutmeg, salt and sugar into a sauce pan over the fire, and when the butter is melted and sugar dissolved, set it on the side of the range where it will keep warm, but not hot. Beat the yolks and stir them into the milk, beat the whites with one tablespoonful of white sugar to a stiff foam, mix the flour and baking powder together. Stir the milk into the flour until it is as thick as batter cakes, then stir in the whites and the rest of the flour.

CORNMEAL GRIDDLE CAKES.

Stir one pint of sweet milk boiling hot into one pint of sifted meal, then stir in one tablespoonful of fresh butter and one even teaspoonful of salt, beat the yolks of four fresh eggs with one tablespoonful of cold milk, and when the meal is not scalding hot stir them in, then stir in one heaped tablespoonful of flour and two teaspoonfuls of baking powder; beat the whites with one tablespoonful of white granulated sugar to a stiff foam and stir them in last; set the pan of cakes into a pan of warm (not hot) water whilst they are being baked; it will make them very light. Bake as soon as the whites are in.

CORN MUSH.

Put three pints of boiling water into an iron pot over the fire, sift one full pint of corn meal into a large bowl and stir into it one pint of rich sweet milk boiling hot, and stir into the boiling water, then put in one tablespoonful of fresh butter, two tablespoonfuls of white granulated sugar and one teaspoonful of salt. Stir it constantly and boil it thirty minutes; pour it into a flat bottomed dish; it cuts out better when cold if it is to be fried.

FRIED CORN MUSH.

Cut the cold mush in slices half an inch thick and of equal lengths. Have ready on the fire a frying pan containing one tablespoonful of fresh butter and one of fresh lard, and when it is hot enough lay in the slices of mush and fry them on both sides a light brown.

CORN BREAD.

Take one pint and a half of sifted corn meal and stir into it one pint of boiling sweet milk, then put in one teaspoonful of salt and one tablespoonful of butter. Beat the yolks of four eggs with one tablespoonful of white granulated sugar and stir them in, then beat the whites with one tablespoonful of sugar to a stiff foam, then stir in three teaspoonfuls of baking powder and the whites last. Put it into the oven as soon as the whites are in and bake it thirty minutes.

CORNMEAL MUFFINS.

Half a pint of sweet milk boiling hot, half a pint of sifted meal, one tablespoonful of fresh butter, half a teaspoonful of salt, two teaspoonfuls of white granulated sugar, two fresh eggs separated, one heaped tablespoonful of flour and two teaspoonfuls of baking powder; stir the boiling milk and meal together, then put in the butter, salt and sugar, beat the yolks and stir them in when the meal is not scalding hot, then stir in the flour and baking powder, beat the whites with one teaspoonful of white sugar to a stiff foam and stir them in last. Put them into muffin pans that have been greased, and bake them twenty minutes in a quick oven.

FLANNEL CAKES.

One pint of boiled sweet milk, one pint of sifted flour, one teaspoonful of salt, one tablespoonful of fresh butter, four fresh eggs separated, one tablespoonful of white granulated sugar beaten with the whites to a stiff foam, one tablespoonful of sugar beaten with the yolks, and two teaspoonfuls of baking powder. Put half of the milk into the pan that the cakes are to be made in and stir in the flour; stir it until it is a smooth batter, then stir in the other half of the milk with the salt and the batter, then stir in the yolks and the baking powder. Put the whites in last and bake as soon as they are in.

GRAHAM GEMS.

Two cups of Graham flour; one cup of white flour; one teaspoonful of salt; one heaped tablespoonful of lard; two and a half cups of warm sweet milk; three eggs beaten separately; three teaspoonfuls of baking powder; mix the graham and white flour, salt and lard together; then add the warm milk and beaten yolks; then beat the whites with two teaspoonfuls of white sugar to a stiff foam and stir them in, and last, add the baking powder. Heat the gem pans, grease them, put in the batter quickly and bake in a quick oven.

MUFFINS.

One quart of sifted flour, with three teaspoonfuls of baking powder in it, and one teaspoonful of salt, one pint of milk with three ounces of fresh butter, and one tablespoonful of white sugar melted in the milk, but not hot, six fresh eggs separated, one tablespoonful of white sugar beaten with the whites to a stiff foam; beat the yolks and stir in the milk, butter and sugar; then stir in half of the flour, mix it well together and then stir in the whites with the other half of the flour. Put them into the oven as soon as they are mixed; they bake in twenty minutes.

MUFFINS.

One pint of cold sweet milk; one teaspoonful of salt; one pint of flour with two teaspoonfuls of baking powder sifted with it; two eggs beaten separately; beat the whites with one teaspoonful of white sugar to a stiff foam, beat the yolks in the pan that you make the muffins in, then stir in the milk, salt, flour and baking powder, and last, stir in whites. Grease the muffin pans, fill them half full, put them into a quick oven and bake twenty minutes.

PAN CAKES

Three quarters of a pint of sifted flour, with two teaspoonfuls of baking powder in it, one pint of milk, warm, but not hot, one teaspoonful of salt, one tablespoonful of fresh butter melted, four fresh eggs separated, and one tablespoonful of white granulated sugar beaten with the whites to a stiff foam. Put the yolks into the pan that the cakes are to be mixed in and beat them a minute or two, then stir in the melted butter and salt, then half of the milk and the flour; beat it until it is smooth and then add the other half of the milk; stir in the whites last and bake immediately. Put a small quantity of butter or lard into the baking pan, and when it is hot enough to brown put in two large kitchen spoonfuls of the batter and let it spread all over the pan.

PANCAKE ROLLS.

Are made according to the preceding receipt, with this exception that five eggs are used instead of four, and two tablespoonfuls of white sugar with half a teaspoonful of grated nutmeg is put into the milk. Bake them a light brown, then put them on to a napkin and spread them with strawberry marmalade. Roll them up, trim off the ends and lay them in a warm dish until all are done. Serve them with a wine sauce.

PUFF BALLS.

One pint of rich sweet milk; two tablespoonfuls of fresh lard; two tablespoonfuls of white granulated sugar; one teaspoonful of grated nutmeg; one teaspoonful of salt; six ounces of sifted flour with two teaspoonfuls of baking powder mixed with it;

six fresh eggs beaten separately. Put half of the milk, lard, sugar, nutmeg and salt into an iron skillet over a slow fire and let it come to a boil. Mix the flour and baking powder with the other half of the milk until it is a smooth batter, then stir it into the boiling milk and keep stirring it until it is a smooth dough, then take it off the fire to cool and beat the yolks, and stir them in, then beat the whites with one tablespoonful of white sugar to a stiff foam and stir them in last. Have ready on the fire a skillet with hot lard and drop in half a tablespoonful of the dough at a time, fry them a light brown, sift powdered sugar over them and send them to table warm.

POTATO CAKES.

Peel a quarter of a peck of the best potatoes, wash them in cold water and put them into a colander to drain, then grate them on a horseradish grater. When they are all done put them into a linen cloth and squeeze out all the water; then put the grated potatoes into a pan with two teaspoonfuls of salt and the yolks of five fresh eggs; beat them together a few minutes and then stir in one pint of rich sweet milk; beat the whites to a stiff foam and stir them in when you are ready to bake. Bake them in fresh lard and send them to table in a warm chapping dish.

ROLLS.

Three pints of unsifted flour; three ounces of butter melted; one pint of sweet milk scalded and then used lukewarm; half a cake of Fleischmann's compressed yeast dissolved in half a cup full of the warm milk taken out of the pint, two tablespoonfuls of white granulated sugar; one teaspoonful of salt; sift the flour and put into a large bowl, make a hole in the centre of it and stir in all the ingredients until you have a thin sponge; cover the bowl, set it in a warm place and let it rise three and a half hours, then make it into a dough and put it on the bread board with half a pint more flour and knead it five minutes, then let it rise again one hour, then roll out half an inch thick, cut with a cake cutter, rub a little melted butter over the tops, fold one half over and let them rise half an hour; bake twenty-five minutes.

RUSK.—DOUBLE BAKED.

One pint of sweet milk scalded and then used lukewarm; half a cake of Fleischmann's compressed yeast dissolved in half a cup full of the warm milk taken out of the pint; three ounces of fresh butter melted; two tablespoonfuls of white granulated sugar; one teaspoonful of salt; three pints of unsifted flour; sift the flour and put it into a large bowl, make a hole in the centre of it and stir in all the ingredients until you have a thin sponge, cover the bowl, set it in a warm place and let it rise three and a half hours; then make it into a dough and put it on the bread board with half a pint more flour and knead it five minutes, then let it rise again one hour, then make it into a loaf and bake it. When it is done and cold cut it into slices half an inch thick and bake them on both sides.

STRAWBERRY SHORT CAKE.

One heaped pint of sifted flour; two teaspoonfuls of baking powder; two ounces of fresh butter; half a teaspoonful of salt; one gill and a half of rich sweet milk; one quart of strawberries, and half a pint of fine powdered white sugar; mix the flour and baking powder together; put the milk, butter and salt into a sauce pan over the fire, and when the milk is warm enough to melt the butter stir it into the flour. Make it quickly into a soft dough, divide it in two parts, roll them out half an inch thick and large enough to cover the bottom of two tin pie plates. Bake in a quick oven fifteen minutes. When done split them whilst hot and butter them with fresh butter. Mash the strawberries and sugar together, then put a layer of cake crust down and a layer of strawberries, then another cake crust down and strawberries, and so on, finishing with the strawberries. Sift powdered sugar over the top and serve with sweetened cream or a custard sauce; both are excellent.

WAFFLES.

Five fresh eggs separated, the yolks put into the pan the waffles are to be mixed in, one pint of milk warmed, but not hot, one tablespoonful of fresh butter melted, one teaspoonful of salt, one heaped pint of flour, with three teaspoonfuls of baking powder mixed with it, and one tablespoonful of white sugar beaten with the whites to a stiff foam; beat the yolks and stir in the milk, butter and salt, then stir in the flour, and last, the whites. Bake as soon as the whites are in.

Eggs and Omelets.

EGGS IN A STAND SOFT BOILED.

It takes twelve eggs twelve minutes to cook in the winter and ten minutes in the summer. It takes six eggs eight minutes to cook in the winter and seven minutes in the summer, and three eggs takes seven minutes in the winter and six minutes in the summer. Wash the eggs and place them in the stand. Then be sure that the water is boiling before it is poured on, and it must be half an inch deep over the eggs. Close the can as soon as the water is in and look at the time. If the eggs are small it takes one minute less time to cook them.

SOFT BOILED EGGS.

A soft boiled egg takes just four minutes to cook it. The water must be boiling when the eggs are put in.

HARD BOILED EGGS.

It takes just eight minutes to boil an egg hard. The water must be boiling fast when the eggs are put in.

EGGS POACHED.

Put boiling water half an inch deep (with a little salt in it) into a frying pan and set it on the range where it will stand perfectly even and keep boiling hot, but not boil; then break the eggs one at a time in a saucer and put them into the water. When all are in if the water does not cover the whites add a little more boiling water with a large spoon. As soon as the whites are set divide them with a cake turner and lift carefully.

EGGS SCRAMBLED.

Take twelve fresh eggs and break them one at a time into a saucer and put them into a deep dish, then put one tablespoonful of fresh butter into a large frying pan and set it over a good fire. As soon as the butter is melted put in the eggs and sprinkle over them one even teaspoonful of salt. Break the yolks with a spoon and as soon as the whites begin to harden turn them up from the bottom of the pan in large flakes. They must not be stirred together like mush, it spoils the taste and looks bad. They must be soft when done and lifted immediately. It takes less than five minutes to cook them. Serve in a warm chafing dish. When served half a teaspoonful of swiss herb cheese sprinkled over them is very fine.

OMELET.

Six fresh eggs beaten separately; half a pint of rich sweet milk; one tablespoonful of flour mixed with a little cold milk; one tablespoonful of fresh butter; half a teaspoonful of salt; one pinch of pepper; one teaspoonful of Royal baking powder; mix the flour with a little of the cold milk. Put the rest of the milk, butter, salt and pepper into a saucepan over the fire, and when it comes to a boil stir in the flour paste and let it boil two minutes; then take it off the fire, then beat the yolks and stir them in, then beat the whites with one teaspoonful of white sugar to a stiff foam and stir them in, then add the baking powder and put it quickly into a warm baking pan that has a spoonful of melted butter in it and set it in the oven and bake it a yellow brown. A gas oven bakes them beautifully.

SWEET OMELET SOUFFLE.

Six fresh eggs beaten separately; half a pint of rich sweet milk (with enough taken out to make the corn starch;) one tablespoonful of corn starch; one tablespoonful of fresh butter; four tablespoonfuls of white granulated sugar; one pinch of salt; one tablespoonful of lemon extract or grated nutmeg; one teaspoonful of Royal baking powder. Put the milk, sugar and salt into a sauce pan and set it into a pan of boiling water over the fire; mix the corn starch with a little cold milk and stir it until it boils three minutes, then take it off the fire and put in the butter and flavoring. Beat the yolks well and stir them in when the milk is not scalding hot; then beat the whites with one tablespoonful of white sugar to a stiff foam and stir them in quickly, and last, add the baking powder. Put it into a well buttered pan, set it into a quick oven and bake it a light yellow brown.

OMELET.

Three fresh eggs; two tablespoonfuls of cream; half a salt spoonful of salt; one ounce of fresh butter; beat the eggs, cream and salt together lightly until the froth begins to rise; have a brisk clear fire, then set the omelet pan on the range and grease it with beef suet, then take one ounce of fresh butter, cut it into small pieces and put it into the pan. As soon as it is melted and begins to bubble, pour in the beaten egg, distributing it evenly over the pan and when it begins to set, put a spoon under the edge and fold it over. The moment it is done place a plate over the pan and turn the omelet on to it. It should be a light yellow when done.

OMELET WITH CHEESE

Has two tablespoonfuls of grated Swiss herb cheese and two tablespoonfuls of crushed double baked rusk.

OMELET WITH HAM

Has two tablespoonfuls of grated sugar-cured ham.

OMELET WITH HERBS

Has one tablespoonful of chopped parsley, one tablespoonful of lives or onion, and one teaspoonful of crushed celery seed.

Cottage Cheese, Oat Groats, Rice and Wheat.

COTTAGE CHEESE.

Put one quart of rich sweet milk into a porcelain saucepan over the fire, and when it is just hot enough to drink stir into it two tablespoonfuls of cider vinegar; stir the milk fast whilst you put the vinegar in slowly, cover the saucepan and keep it where it will keep hot but not scalding. In four hours the curd will have formed, then put it into a linen cloth, hang it up until the whey has run out, then put the curd into a bowl with one gill of sweet cream and rub it together with the back of the spoon against the bowl until it is very fine, then stir in one tablespoonful of white granulated sugar and serve with cream, sugar and powdered cinnamon or a cream sauce. Milk can be turned with rennet, sour wine, lemon and vinegar.

WINE COTTAGE CHEESE.

Put two quarts of rich sour unskimmed milk with half a pint of sherry wine into a porcelain saucepan, cover it and set it where it will be quite warm, but not scalding hot. When the curd has formed put it all into a linen cloth, hang it up, and when the whey has run out put the curd into a bowl with one gill of thick sweet cream and rub it together with the back of the spoon against the bowl until it is very fine, then put in two even tablespoonfuls of white granulated sugar and serve with sweetened cream. Cottage cheese made by this receipt is very fine; the wine gives it a delicious flavor, and the whey with the addition of a little more wine and sugar makes a fine healthy drink.

OAT GROATS.

Half a pint of Groats; one pint of cold water; half a teaspoonful of salt. Pick the groats carefully, wash them in cold water and put them with the pint of water and salt into a tin saucepan that has a steam pipe through the lid and set it into a pan of boiling water over the fire and boil it three quarters of an hour; don't stir it until it is done. The water should be all boiled down before it is lifted. Serve with powdered white sugar and cream or with rich sweet milk.

HULLED WHEAT.

Hulled wheat is prepared in the same manner as oat groats and is cooked the same length of time and served in the same way.

RICE, TO BOIL.

One pint of rice; one pint of cold water; one even teaspoonful of salt. Cook the rice in a tin saucepan that has a steam pipe through the centre of the cover. After the rice is picked and washed put it into the saucepan with the water and salt, cover it and set it into a larger saucepan containing boiling water, enough to be even with the rice, but it must not boil into it. Don't put any more water into the rice nor stir it until it is done. Boil it three quarters of an hour, then set it on the side of the range where it does not boil, for thirty minutes, then stir it up with a fork and every grain will be separate. Serve with a milk sauce.

Coffee, Chocolate, Cocoa, Tea.

COFFEE POT.

My coffee pot has a close fitting cover and a cap attached to a chain to shut up the spout to prevent the aroma from escaping. Inside is a narrow hoop pierced with holes, to which I attach a bag made of double white crinoline which reaches to within a quarter of an inch of the bottom, into which the coffee is put.

COFFEE, TO MAKE.

Half a pint of browned coffee beans before they are ground; three pints of boiling water. After the coffee is ground put it into the bag and pour the boiling water on it; then set the coffee pot on the range where it will keep hot (but not boil) for half an hour.

THE BEST COFFEE.

To ascertain which was the best coffee, I made three different kinds and then invited three connoisseurs to pass judgment on them. The three kinds were the following: first, three parts Java, one part Mocha; second, three parts Java, one part Golden Rio; third, Santos. Now the connoisseurs all decided that Santos was the best.

CHOCOLATE, (BAKERS).

Three ounces of chocolate; half a pint of cold water; half a pint of boiling water; one quart of rich sweet milk boiling hot; three ounces of white granulated sugar. Scrape the chocolate up fine and put it into a saucepan with the half pint of cold water and set it into a pan of boiling water over the fire when it will be dissolved in ten minutes; then stir in the boiling water, milk and sugar; stir it constantly and boil it five minutes.

COCOA, (BAKERS.)

Three tablespoonfuls of cocoa; one pint of cold water; one pint of hot rich sweet milk; three tablespoonfuls of white granulated sugar. Put the cocoa and cold water into a saucepan over the fire, and when it is dissolved and hot, add the hot milk and sugar and boil it fifteen minutes.

COCOA

Can be made with water alone and is very good. Put three tablespoonfuls of cocoa into a saucepan with one pint of cold water and set it over the fire until it is dissolved; then add one pint of boiling water and boil it fifteen minutes. Serve it at table with cream or rich milk and sugar according to taste.

TEA.

When tea is drawn in a teapot the aroma escapes through the spout and half of the strength is lost by not having a uniform heat. Tea should be drawn in a close covered vessel that is used for no other purpose. Allow three teaspoonfuls of tea to one pint of boiling water, set it on the side of the fire for half an hour where it will keep hot without boiling, then put the tea strainer into the teapot and pour in the tea. Send it to table with a water pot of boiling water.

MOCK CREAM.

Put one pint of rich sweet milk into a porcelain saucepan and set it into a pan of boiling water over the fire, beat the white of one fresh egg with one teaspoonful of white granulated sugar to a stiff foam, then beat the yolk and stir the white into it and stir it quickly into the hot milk, (it must not boil) and take it off the fire. Beat it together a minute and then pour it into a cream pitcher. It is a good substitute for cream and gives the coffee a fine taste.

Soup.

BEEF SOUP.

The best beef soup is made from the leg of the beef that has been cut up into soup bones. Eight pounds will make two quarts of excellent soup. Six pounds will make three pints, and four pounds will make one quart. Wash the meat in cold water and put it into the soup kettle with cold water enough to cover it, and just before it begins to boil skim it as long as anything rises to the surface. Cover the kettle, set it over a slow fire and cook the soup five hours. If it boils down too low replenish with boiling water. When the soup has boiled three hours put in the following vegetables: one half of a celery root the size of an egg; two bunches of parsley and celery leaves; two small leeks and one tablespoonful of rice. Peel the celery root, cut it in thin slices then in strips as wide as a straw and then in squares and put it into the soup first. Wash the parsley and celery leaves in cold water and cut them up fine. Peel the leeks and cut them up fine. Pick and wash the rice and put it in last. When the soup has cooked five hours take out all the meat and bones, skim it carefully and put in salt and pepper to the taste. Put scant half a teaspoonful of grated nutmeg into the soup tureen, pour in the soup, stir it and send it to the table hot.

CLEAR BEEF SOUP WITH DUMPLINGS.

After the leg of beef has been cut into three or four pieces, wash them in cold water and take out the marrow for dumplings. Put the soup bones into the kettle with cold water enough to cover them, and just before it begins to boil skim it as long as anything rises to the surface. Keep it covered and boil it slowly five hours, then take the meat and bones out and skim off the fat, then add salt and pepper to the taste and put in the dumplings and cook them five minutes. Put half a teaspoonful of grated nutmeg into the soup tureen and pour in the soup. The dumpling must not be broken up in the soup.

DUMPLINGS FOR BEEF SOUP.

Four ounces of bread, without the crust, dipped in cold water and squeezed out quick; two ounces of marrow melted and strained; one yolk of an egg well beaten; one teaspoonful of celery seed; half a teaspoonful of grated nutmeg and half a teaspoonful of salt. Stir the whole well together, then add the white of one egg beaten to a stiff foam, flour the hands and make it into small balls the size of a pigeon's egg and cook them in the soup five minutes. They must be put into the soup as soon as they are all made or they will not be light.

BOUILLON.

The leg of the beef makes the best bouillon and six pounds will make three pints strong enough to become a jelly when cold. After the leg has been cut up into four or five pieces wash them in cold water and put them into the soup kettle with cold water enough to cover them. Just before the water begins to boil skim it as long as anything rises to the surface. Cover the kettle and set it over a slow fire to boil five hours. If the water boils down too low replenish with boiling water. When it is done take out with a skimmer all the meat and bones. Skim off all the fat and season with one even teaspoonful of salt to one pint of bouillon, then strain it through a fine wire sieve and add half a teaspoonful of grated nutmeg.

NOODLE SOUP.

Take one quart of beef bouillon that has two even teaspoonfuls of salt in it and put half a pint of noodles in it and cook them thirty minutes. Put a pinch of grated nutmeg into the soup tureen and four in the soup.

NOODLES FOR SOUP OR VEGETABLES.

Beat three eggs and three tablespoonfuls of sweet milk together. Sift some flour into a pan, make a hole in the centre of it, stir in the eggs and milk and make it into a stiff dough, then divide it into two parts and roll it out as thin as paper and let it lay two hours to dry, then roll them up close into a roll and cut them in fine rings as broad as a fine broom straw and shake them out loose. When dried they keep a long time.

NOODLES AS A VEGETABLE.

One quart of noodles; half a pint of rich sweet milk; half a teaspoonful of salt; three fresh eggs; three ounces of fresh butter; three ounces of grated Swiss herb cheese. Put the noodles into boiling water that has one teaspoonful of salt to each pint of water and boil them twenty minutes, (stir them up from the bottom to prevent them from sticking.) Then take them out with a skimmer into a colander to drain. Warm the milk and put the salt into it. Beat the eggs together and stir them into the milk. Melt the butter by itself. Take a deep tin pie-plate or small tin pudding pan and put in a layer of noodles and two or three tablespoonfuls of the milk and eggs; one tablespoonful of the butter and one tablespoonful of the grated cheese. Then another layer of noodles, and so on, until all are in. Put it into the oven in a pan that has a little boiling water in it and bake twenty minutes.

NOODLES AS A VEGETABLE.

Half a pint of rich sweet milk; three ounces of fresh butter; one teaspoonful of corn starch; three fresh eggs beaten with two tablespoonfuls of white sugar; half a pint of grated apples with two tablespoonfuls of sugar mixed with them; one teaspoonful of nutmeg, and one quart of noodles that have been boiled in salted water and drained in the colander. Melt the butter in the milk and stir in the corn starch, then take it off the fire and beat the eggs and sugar together and stir them into the milk. Mix the apples, sugar and nutmeg together.

Now take a small pudding pan and put in a layer of noodles and a layer of apples and two or three tablespoonfuls of the milk, then another layer of noodles, and so on, until all are in, finishing with the milk. Set it into the oven in a pan containing a little boiling water and bake thirty minutes.

MOCK TURTLE SOUP– (Very Fine.)

Six pounds of the leg of beef, cut up into soup bones; six bay leaves; six whole cloves and six whole pepper corns. Wash the soup bones in cold water and put them into the soup-kettle with cold water enough to cover them, and just before it begins to boil skim it as long as anything rises to the surface. Cover the kettle and boil it slowly five hours. If the water boils down too low replenish with boiling water. When it has boiled three hours put in the bay leaves, cloves and pepper corns. When it is done take out the soup-bones; strain it through a wire sieve and return the soup to the kettle. Put the calf's head on to boil at the same time that the beef is put on. One calf's head split open in the middle and the brains taken out; one celery root peeled, sliced thin, cut in strips and cross cut; three small leeks, peeled, split down and cut off; two tablespoonfuls of green parsley and two tablespoonfuls of celery leaves, cut up fine; one blade of mace the size of a five-cent piece. Wash the head in cold water and put it into a kettle with cold water enough to cover it, and just before it begins to boil skim it and boil it four hours. When it has boiled two hours put in the vegetables and mace. Half an hour before the soup is done take out the tongue, skin it and let it get cold. When the soup is done take out the bones, strain it through a wire sieve and pour it in with the beef soup. Now skim off all the fat, then put two tablespoonfuls of browned flour and two ounces of fresh butter into a skillet, and when it is hot stir into it a small ladle full of the soup and let it boil until it is thick and then stir it into the soup. Cut the tongue into slices half an inch thick, then in squares, and put it into the soup. Then put in salt and pepper to the taste. Pour the soup into the soup tureen and stir in one gill of sherry wine. There should be only two quarts of soup.

VEGETABLE SOUP.—(Julienne.)

Six pounds of the leg of beef cut up into soup bones; three tablespoonfuls of celery root; three tablespoonfuls of carrots; one pint full of cut up cabbage; three tablespoonfuls of white skinned onions; three small leeks; two tablespoonfuls of green parsley. After the soup bones have been washed in cold water put them into the soup kettle with cold water enough to cover them, and just before it begins to boil skim it as long as anything rises to the surface. Cover the kettle and boil the soup five hours. When it has boiled three hours put in the vegetables. First prepare the celery root, carrots and cabbage; it takes them longest to cook. Peel the celery root, cut it in thin slices and then cut it and cross cut it up fine. Scrape the carrots, split them down from the top, then cross split them the size of a fork prong, and then cut them off short. Take off the outside leaves of the cabbage, wash it in cold water, cut it in slices half an inch wide and an inch long. Peel the onions, slice them and cut them up. Peel the leeks, split them and cut them off an inch long. Wash the parsley and cut it up fine. Boil the vegetables two hours, then take out all the meat and bones and put in salt and pepper to the taste. There should be only three pints of soup. Grate one quarter of a teaspoonful of nutmeg into the soup tureen and pour in the soup.

OX TAIL SOUP.

Three ox tails cut in pieces three inches long; two ounces of fresh butter; three white skinned onions, peeled and sliced; one celery root peeled, sliced and cut up fine; two small carrots, scraped, split, cross split and cut small, two tablespoonfuls of green parsley, washed and cut fine; one leek peeled and cut up fine; four bay leaves and six whole cloves.' After the oxtails have been cut up and washed, fry them in the butter until they are brown on both sides. Then put them into the soup-kettle with one gallon of water and set it over the fire. Then fry the onions in the same butter until they are a light brown, and then put in a gill of hot water and stir them up from the bottom, and put the whole, butter and onions, into the soup kettle. Cover the kettle and let it cook slowly four hours. When it has boiled two hours put in the vegetables, bay leaves and cloves. Half an hour before the soup is done put one tablespoonful of browned flour and two tablespoonfuls of the fat from the top of the soup into a skillet and when it is hot add a few spoonfuls of the soup, stir it and let it boil a minute then stir it into the soup and let it cook thirty minutes. Then add salt and pepper to the taste and lift. Serve one piece of the ox tail with each plate of soup. When done there should be only one quart of soup.

MUTTON SOUP.

Six pounds of the leg of old mutton will make three pints of good soup. After it has been cut up into four or five pieces wash it in cold water and put it into the soup kettle with cold water enough to cover it. When it begins to boil skim it as long as anything rises to the surface. Cover the kettle and boil it slowly five hours. When the soup has boiled three hours wash three tablespoonfuls of barley and put it in. The barley must boil two hours. Then put in one tablespoonful of celery that has been washed, and cut up fine one tablespoonful of parsley and one leek. When the soup is done take out all the meat and bones, skim it and put in salt and pepper to the taste.

OYSTER SOUP.

Four pounds of the leg of veal cut into four pieces; one celery root peeled sliced thin and cut up fine; two tablespoonfuls of green parsley washed and cut up fine; one pint of middle sized oysters and the dumplings. After the veal has been washed in cold water put it into the soup kettle with cold water enough to cover it, and just before it begins to boil skim it as long as anything rises to the surface. Cover the kettle and boil slowly three hours. When the soup has cooked one hour put in the celery root (it takes the longest to cook) and then the parsley. Put the oysters into a porcelain saucepan with half a pint of cold water, and as soon as they are scalding hot (they must not boil) take them off the fire and pour them into a colander that has been placed over a porcelain dish, then take out the soup, meat and bones and put the liquor from the oysters into the soup kettle. Now put in salt and pepper to the taste and then put in the dumplings for oyster soup and cook them five minutes, then add the oysters and lift. The soup must not boil after the oysters are in. There should be three pints of soup when done.

CRAB SOUP.

Six pounds of the leg of beef cut into four pieces makes three pints of good bouillon. This is the quantity for this soup: two tablespoonfuls of cut up parsley leaves; two tablespoonfuls of cut up celery leaves, or half of a celery root cut up fine; two tablespoonfuls of leeks or white skinned onion; one quart of tomatoes measured after they are peeled and cut up; one tablespoonful of browned flour mixed with one tablespoonful of fresh butter; half a pint of crab meat. Wash the soup meat in cold water and put it into the soup kettle with cold water enough to cover it, and just before it begins to boil skim it as long as anything rises to the surface. Cover the kettle and let it boil slowly four hours. Put the crabs into boiling water for fifteen minutes or until the claws will come off, then take them out break them open and take out all the meat. When the soup has boiled three hours put in the parsley, celery and leeks and let it boil one hour longer, then take out all the soup meat when there should be three pints of soup in the kettle. Skim off the fat, then put in the tomatoes and cook them slowly three quarters of an hour. Put the browned flour and butter into a skillet and when it is hot stir into it a small ladle full of the soup and let it boil a few minutes, then stir it into the soup five minutes before the tomatoes are done, then put in the crab meat and as soon as it is hot take the soup off the fire. It must not boil after the crab meat is in. There should be two quarts of soup when it is done. I have made this soup with canned crab meat and it was excellent.

CORN SOUP.

Four pounds of the leg of beef, cut in four pieces; one pint of tomatoes, measured after they have been peeled and cut up fine; two tablespoonfuls of parsley leaves cut up fine; two tablespoonfuls of celery leaves cut up fine; six ears of sugar corn grated and scraped off the cob, and measured; there should be half a pint. Put the soup meat into the kettle with cold water enough to cover it, and just before it begins to boil skim it as long as anything rises to the surface. Then cover it and boil it slowly five hours. When it has boiled four hours put in the tomatoes, parsley and celery, and boil them three quarters of an hour, then take out the soup meat and put in the half pint of grated corn, and let it cook fifteen minutes after it begins to boil again. Then put in salt and pepper to the taste. There should be three pints of soup when it is done. This is an excellent soup and can be made in the winter with canned tomatoes and canned corn, but the corn must be put into a procelain mortar and made fine.

TOMATO SOUP.

Four pounds of the leg of beef, cut in four pieces; one celery root, peeled, sliced thin and cut up fine; one tablespoonful of parsley leaves, cut up fine; one tablespoonful of celery leaves cut up fine; two tablespoonfuls of white skinned onions cut fine; one quart of tomatoes measured after they are peeled and cut fine; one tablespoonful of browned flour; one tablespoonful of fresh butter. After the beef has been washed in cold water put it into the soup kettle with cold water enough to cover it, and just before it begins to boil skim it as long as anything rises to the surface. Then cover it, and let it boil slowly five hours. When it has boiled three hours put in the celery root, parsley, celery leaves and onions. When it has boiled four hours put in the tomatoes. Then put the browned flour and butter into a skillet, and when it is hot stir into it a small ladle full of the soup and let it boil until it is as thick as cream. Then take out all the soup meat and put in the flour and butter, with salt and pepper to the taste and let it boil a few minutes longer. There should be only three pints of soup when done.

CHICKEN SOUP.

An old, fat, yellow-legged hen makes the best soup. After the chicken has been dressed, washed and cut up, put it into the soup kettle with cold water enough to cover it, and when it begins to boil skim it as long as anything rises to the surface. Cover the kettle and cook it slowly four hours. When it has boiled two hours put in one celery root that has been peeled, sliced and cut up fine; one tablespoonful of green parsley and one tablespoonful of celery leaves that have been washed and cut fine; one tablespoonful of rice that has been picked and washed. When the soup is done take out the chicken, skim off the fat and add salt and pepper to the taste. Put scant half a teaspoonful of grated nutmeg into the soup tureen, pour in the soup, stir it up and send it to the table hot. This soup is excellent with dumplings or a pint of oysters put in just before lifting.

DUMPLINGS FOR CHICKEN AND OYSTER SOUP.

Two ounces of butter melted but not hot; one yolk of an egg beaten and mixed with the butter; one teaspoonful of celery seed crushed; half a teaspoonful of powdered mace; half a teaspoonful of salt and four ounces of bread without the crust, dipped in cold water and squeezed out. Mix the whole well together, then add the white of one egg beaten to a stiff foam, flour the hands and make into small balls and cook them in the soup five minutes. The dumplings must be put into the soup as soon as all are made.

GUMBO SOUP.

One large fat old hen, an old chicken makes the best soup; one tablespoonful of fresh butter; one tablespoonful of fresh lard; three quarts of boiling water, (it boils down one-half); one quart of green gumbo measured before it is sliced up fine; one celery root peeled, sliced thin and cut up fine; one pint of tomatoes measured after they are peeled and cut up fine; one tablespoonful of parsley leaves cut up fine; one tablespoonful of celery leave cut up fine; one even tablespoonful of browned flour. After the chicken has been dressed and washed in cold water, cut it up by the joints, split the breast and back down the middle, salt and pepper it and dredge it with flour. Have ready on the fire a frying pan with the butter and lard in it, and when it is hot enough to brown lay in the chicken and fry it a golden brown on both sides. Then put the chicken into the soup kettle with the three quarts of boiling water. Cover the kettle and let it boil slowly three hours. Set the frying pan with the fat in it on the side of the range until the soup is nearly done. When the soup has boiled one hour put in the gumbo, celery root, tomatoes and soup greens and let them boil two hours, then put the browned flour into the frying pan, and when it is hot stir in a small ladle full of hot water and let it boil a few minutes, stirring it up well from the bottom, then stir it into the soup with salt and pepper to the taste. Let it boil two or three minutes, then strain it through the colander into the soup tureen. There should be only two and a half pints of soup after it is strained.

OYSTER SOUP.

Put one quart of fresh oysters into a colander and let cold water run through them. Then put them into a porcelain saucepan with half a pint of cold water; one pint of rich, sweet milk, three ounces of fresh butter and one teaspoonful of salt or salt to the taste. Set them over a slow fire and then crush four double baked rusks fine, with the rolling pin, and just before the soup begins to boil stir in four large kitchen spoonfuls of the rusks. Now watch it closely. As soon as it begins to boil take it off the fire and pour it into the soup tureen. Serve it with crackers and celery, or cold slaw. If oysters boil one minute they become tough and tasteless. Therefore they must be watched closely and taken from the fire the moment they begin to boil.

PEA SOUP.

Take six pounds of the leg of beef that has been cut into four pieces, and wash it in cold water, put it into the soup kettle with cold water enough to cover it, and just before it begins to boil skim it as long as anything rises to the surface. Cover the kettle, and cook it slowly five hours. Measure one pint and a half of split peas after they have been picked. Wash them in cold water and put them into a saucepan with two quarts of cold water and cook them two hours and a half. Half an hour before the soup is done take out the soup bones, and put in two tablespoonfuls of green parsley that has been washed, and cut up fine. Then press the peas through a colander into the soup and cook half an hour. Then put in salt and pepper to the taste, and when ready to lift set the colander over the soup tureen and press the soup through. When done there should be only two quarts of soup.

BEAN SOUP.

Is made in the same manner as in the preceding receipt.

PEA SOUP—Without Meat.

Take one pound of split peas, and after they have been picked and washed in cold water, put them into the soup kettle with three quarts of cold water, and set it over a fire where it will cook slowly for three hours. Half an hour before the soup is done peel and slice up four raw potatoes and put them into the soup with two tablespoonfuls of green parsley, cut up fine, and salt and pepper to the taste. Then put half a tablespoonful of browned flour and three ounces of fresh butter into a skillet, and when it is hot put in one gill of hot water, stir it and let it boil five minutes. Then stir it into the soup and boil it a few minutes longer. Now place a colander over the soup tureen and press the soup through.

VEAL SOUP.

Four pounds of the leg of veal; one tablespoonful of rice; one small celery root peeled, sliced thin and cut up fine; one tablespoonful of celery leaves cut up fine; one small parsley root sliced thin and cut up fine; one tablespoonful of parsley leaves cut up fine; one tablespoonful of flour made yellow; one tablespoonful of fresh butter; half a teaspoonful of grated nutmeg. Wash the veal in cold water and put it into the soup kettle with cold water enough to cover it, and just before it begins to boil skim it well. Cover the kettle and boil it slowly two and a half hours. When it has boiled half an hour put in the rice, celery root, parsley root and soup greens. When the soup has boiled two and a half hours take out all the soup meat. Put the flour into a skillet over the fire, and when it has become yellow (not brown) put in the butter, then stir in a small ladle full of hot water and let it boil until it is as thick as cream, then stir it into the soup with salt and pepper to the taste. Let it boil five minutes longer, then put the nutmeg into the soup tureen and pour in the soup. There should be only one quart of soup.

Fish.

SALT CODFISH, BOILED.

Pound the codfish with a wooden mallet; it makes it tender and soaks quicker. If it is for breakfast put it into a pan with only cold water enough to cover it, at ten o'clock or just before going to bed. In the morning boil it in clear water thirty minutes. Serve with a drawn butter or an egg sauce.

CODFISH CAKES.

One pint of picked up codfish; two ounces of fresh butter; two yolks of fresh eggs; one pint of mashed potatoes. After the codfish has been pounded, soaked and boiled as in the preceding receipt, pick it up fine and measure it, then put the butter into a small saucepan and set it into a pan of boiling water, and as soon as it is melted put in the codfish and stir it together, then stir in the yolks and when it is scalding hot take it off the fire. Mash the boiled potatoes with butter alone, measure them and put them into a large bowl with the codfish and mix them well together, (this quantity makes seven cakes,) then flour your hands and make them into balls, then flatten them into cakes and fry them in butter, a golden brown.

STEWED EELS.

Take two large eels, skin them, dress them wash them in cold water, dry them off and cut them in pieces, three inches long. Put them into a stew pan or deep skillet, where they can all lay on the bottom, with cold water enough to be even with the fish. Then put in six bay leaves, an even teaspoonful of powdered mace, an even teaspoonful of salt, quarter of a teaspoonful of ground black pepper and three tablespoonfuls of cider vinegar Let the fish boil fifteen minutes from the time they begin to boil. Mix one heaped tablespoonful of browned flour with two ounces of fresh butter in a skillet, and when the butter is melted stir in four tablespoonfuls of the water the fish is cooking in and let it boil until it is as thick as cream. Then stir it in with the fish, and add two tablespoonfuls of crushed baked rusk.

BOILED EELS—(Cold.)

Take the largest sized eels, and after they are dressed and washed in cold water, put them into the fish kettle with cold water enough to cover them, that has in it one gill of cider vinegar, and one teaspoonful of salt to one quart of water. Then put in six bay leaves and let them boil slowly fifteen or twenty minutes, according to the size of fish. When cold garnish with sprigs of green, curled parsley, and serve with a new Mayonaise sauce that has three tablespoonfuls of my tomato catsup in it.

FRIED EELS.

After the eels are skinned, dressed, heads taken off and washed in cold water, cut them in pieces three inches long; salt and pepper them and dredge them well with flour. Have ready on the fire a frying pan with one tablespoonful of fresh butter and one of fresh lard in it, and when it is hot enough to brown lay in the eels, cover the pan and fry them a light brown. When they have fried ten minutes, turn them, baste them and fry them ten minutes longer. Then lift them into a warm chafing-dish, and put one gill of hot water into the gravy, let it boil a minute, stir it up from the bottom, then stir in three tablespoonfuls of my tomato catsup and pour it into the gravy dish.

SMOKED HALIBUT.

Smoked halibut makes a fine breakfast dish if prepared in the following manner: for a family of five or six persons take two pounds of halibut, score the skin through, wash it in cold water and put it into a pan with only enough cold water to cover it, at ten o'clock or before going to bed. In the morning put it into the fish kettle, skin side down, with cold water enough to cover it and let it boil forty-five minutes. Serve it with an egg sauce or a drawn butter sauce and poached egg.

DUTCH HERRING, PICKLED.

Take the smallest sized herring, as they are the youngest and fattest, wash them in cold water, scale them and skin them. The skin must all be taken off, then cut off their heads, take out the inside, wash them again and dry them off. Peel a quantity of small white skinned onions and slice them, then put into a glass jar a layer of herring and a layer of onions until the jar is full, finishing with a layer of herring. Fill the jar with good cider vinegar and close it. The vinegar must cover the herring. They are ready to use in twenty four hours and are an excellent relish with bread and butter. Serve some of the onions with the herring. They are also used as a salad with pea soup.

A No. 1 SALT MACKEREL, BOILED.

Wash the mackerel in two waters, and if it is for breakfast put it into a pan half full of cold water at six o'clock in the evening and change the water at ten o'clock, before going to bed. In the morning put it into a fish pan, skin side under, with water enough to cover it and boil it thirty minutes, then lift it whole into a warm chafing-dish, skin side under, and pour drawn butter over it.

SALT MACKEREL, BROILED.

After the mackerel has been washed and soaked the same length of time as in the preceding receipt take it out of the water, dry it off with a linen cloth, split it down the back and cut it across in pieces three inches long. Rub the gridiron with a piece of fat pork or a little lard on a cloth and lay on the mackerel, skin side under, and broil it thirty minutes. When it has broiled fifteen minutes turn it. Serve with drawn butter. A No. 1 mackerel prepared in this way and broiled by gas is excellent.

FRESH MACKEREL, BROILED.

Broiling is the best way of cooking fresh mackerel. After they are dressed and washed in cold water, dry them off with a linen cloth, then split them down the back and cut them across, in pieces three or four inches long; salt and pepper them, then rub the gridiron with a piece of fat pork or lard, place the mackerel on it and broil it thirty minutes. When it has broiled fifteen minutes turn it, and when it is done put it into a warm chafing-dish and serve with a parsley sauce

FRIED PERCH AND BULL HEADS.

Perch are our best river fish. Next comes the bull heads, salmon and bass. They are all good breakfast fish. After the fish have been scaled and dressed, wash them in cold water, and lay them on the meat board and dry them off. Then put a pinch of salt and pepper inside and out, and dredge the upper side with flour. Have ready on the fire a frying pan with a tablespoonful of fresh butter and one of lard, and when it is hot enough to brown lay in the fish with the flour side in the butter, and then dredge the other side. Cover the pan and cook them slowly. When they have cooked fifteen minutes, turn them, baste them and cook them fifteen minutes longer. When they are lifted put one teaspoonful of browned flour, one teaspoonful of anchovy paste and one gill of hot water into the gravy. Stir it up well from the bottom of the pan and let it boil five minutes.

CANNED SALMON.

Put the can of salmon into boiling water for thirty minutes. The water must not boil after the can is put in, but be kept at boiling heat. Then take the can out, wipe it off, and with the oyster scissors make a small hole in the top of the can, pour the juice out into a tin cup, and set it on the range where it will keep hot, but not boil. If there is not quite juice enough for the gravy add a tablespoonful of boiling water. Then mix one teaspoonful of fresh butter with half a teaspoonful of flour and stir it into the juice. Let it boil two minutes then add a pinch of salt and one tablespoonful of my tomato catsup. Cut the whole top out of the can and let the salmon out whole into a warm chafing-dish. Put the gravy into a gravy dish and send it to table hot.

BOILED SALMON.

A salmon weighing six pounds, if it is to be cooked whole, takes thirty minutes. After it is scaled, dressed and washed in cold water, put it into the fish kettle, with hot water enough to cover it, that has one teaspoonful of salt in it to a pint of water. When it begins to boil skim it and let it cook slowly thirty minutes. If the salmon is cut in slices one inch thick, boil them ten minutes in salted water. Serve with a Hollandish sauce.

STUFFING FOR FISH, (Shad.)

Five ounces of fresh butter; two tablespoonfuls of green parsley after it is washed and cut up fine; one teaspoonful of crushed celery seed; one teaspoonful of grated nutmeg; one teaspoonful of salt; half a teaspoonful of pepper; three fresh eggs beaten separately; three ounces of stale bread without the crust, dipped in cold water, taken out quickly and squeezed out. Put the butter into a skillet, and when it is melted put in the parsley, celery, nutmeg, salt and pepper, then take the skillet off the fire. Beat the yolks and stir them in with the butter, then stir in the bread, then beat the whites to a stiff foam, and stir them in when you are ready to fill the fish.

BAKED SHAD.

After the shad has been scaled and dressed, wash it in cold water and dry it off. Fill it with the stuffing, leaving room for it to swell, then sew it up with a small cord, sprinkle salt and pepper on it, and dredge it with flour. Have ready on the fire the fish pan with one tablespoonful of fresh butter and one of fresh lard in it, and when it is hot enough to brown lay in the fish, put it into the oven and bake it three quarters of an hour. Baste it often,

FISH RECIPES. 57

and when it is lifted put a gill of hot water into the gravy and one teaspoonful of anchovy sauce and two tablespoonfuls of my tomato catsup. Let it boil a minute, stir it up from the bottom of the pan and pour it into a gravy dish. Cut the cord the fish was sewed with in short pieces with a pair of scissors and draw it out carefully.

FRIED SHAD.

A fresh shad weighing two and a half pounds is the best size for frying and makes a most delicious breakfast dish. After the fish has been scaled and split down the belly, dressed and washed in cold water, dry it off with a linen cloth, then salt and pepper it inside and out and dredge it with flour on both sides. Have ready on the fire a frying pan with one tablespoonful of fresh butter and one of lard in it, and when it is hot enough to brown lay in the fish whole, cover the pan and fry it slowly forty minutes. When it has cooked twenty minutes turn it, and when done lift it into a warm chafing-dish and put one teaspoonful of browned flour and one gill of hot water into the gravy and let it boil five minutes. Stir it up well from the bottom and then put in three tablespoonfuls of my tomato catsup and pour it into the gravy dish.

FRESH SHAD BOILED

Is prepared in the same manner as in the preceding receipt, but it must be broiled forty minutes, it being a thicker fish, and it is best served with drawn butter that has three tablespoonfuls of my tomato catsup in it.

BOILED TROUT, (Cold.)

A lake trout weighing three pounds will take twenty minutes to cook. Scale it thin, dress it with the head on and wash it in cold water. Put it into the fish kettle with cold water enough to cover it that has one teaspoonful of salt to a pint of water. When it begins to boil skim it and cook it slowly twenty minutes. Sift it carefully and put it on the dish that is to be sent to table. When it is cold garnish it with sprigs of curled parsley and serve with a Mayonaise sauce.

BAKED WHITE FISH.

Take a six pound white fish and after it is scaled and dressed (leaving the head on) wash it in cold water and dry it off, then put a pinch of salt and pepper inside and fill it with stuffing, leaving room for it to swell; then sew it up with a small cord, salt and pepper the outside and dredge it well with flour. Have ready on the fire a fish pan with one tablespoonful of fresh butter and one of fresh lard in it and when it is hot enough to brown, lay in the fish put it into the oven and bake it three quarters of an hour. Baste it often and when it is lifted put one gill of hot water into the gravy; let it boil up a minute, stir it up well from the bottom and put in three tablespoonfuls of my tomato catsup; cut the cord the fish was sewed with in short pieces with a pair of scissors and draw it out carefully.

STUFFING FOR FISH.

One pint of sliced onions cut up fine, measured after they are cut up; five ounces of fresh butter, four ounces of bread without the crust, two fresh eggs separated, one tablespoonful of parsley after it has been cut up fine, one teaspoonful of grated nutmeg, one teaspoonful of salt, half a teaspoonful of pepper. Put the butter and onions into a skillet and cook them soft; dip the bread into cold water, take it out quickly, squeeze it out and stir it in with the onions and butter. Then put in the parsley, nutmeg, salt and pepper and mix it well together. Then take it off the fire and beat the yolks and stir them in, now beat the whites to a stiff foam and stir them in when you are ready to fill the fish. The stuffing should be warm when it is put in.

Shell Fish, Oysters, Crabs, Shrimps, Terrapin.

OYSTER SOUP.

Put one quart of fresh oysters into a colander and let cold water run through them. Then put them into a porcelain saucepan, with half a pint of cold water; one pint of rich sweet milk. Three ounces of fresh butter and one teaspoonful of salt, or salt to taste. Set them over a slow fire, and then crush four double baked rusks fine with a rolling pin, and just before the soup begins to boil stir in a few large kitchen spoonfuls of the rusks. Now watch it closely. As soon as it begins to boil take it off the fire and pour it into the soup tureen.

Serve it with crackers and celery or cold slaw. If oysters boil one minute they become tough and tasteless. Therefore they must be watched closely and taken from the fire the moment they begin to boil.

ESCALLOPED OYSTERS.

Three dozen large fresh oysters. One pint of crushed double baked rusk, made fine. One teaspoonful of salt. Quarter of a teaspoonful of pepper. One teaspoonful of dried summer savory, after it has been made fine and sifted. Two ounces of fresh butter, melted. Half a pint of rich sweet milk. Put the oysters into a colander and let cold water run through them, then let them drain. Put the rusk into a deep dish and mix the salt and pepper and summer savory with it, mix it well together. Take a deep tin pie plate and cover the bottom with the rusk, then put in a layer of oysters, then a layer of rusk, then part of the butter, then with a tablespoon part of the milk evenly over the rusk. Then another layer of oysters in the same manner until all are in, finishing with the rusk, butter and the remainder of the milk. Put it into a quick oven and bake twenty minutes.

FRICASSEED OYSTERS.

One quart of large fresh oysters; half a pint of water; one tablespoonful of green parsley washed and cut up fine; one teaspoonful of crushed celery seed; one gill of rich sweet milk; two teaspoonfuls of flour; three yolks of fresh eggs; three ounces of fresh butter; one teaspoonful of salt; half a teaspoonful of pepper; three tablespoonfuls of crushed double baked rusk. Put the oysters into a colander and let cold water run through them. Put the half pint of water, parsley and celery seed into a saucepan and let it come to a boil, then put in the milk. Mix the flour with a spoonful of cold milk, then beat the yolks and flour together and stir them in. Stir it until the yolks thicken, but it must not boil. Then put in the butter, salt, pepper and the oysters. As soon as the oysters are fringed and swollen, (they must not boil) stir in the rusk, take them quickly off the fire and put them into a warm chafing-dish.

FRIED OYSTERS.

One quart of large fresh oysters; one pint of oyster crackers; one teaspoonful of salt; quarter of a teaspoonful of pepper; one large kitchen spoonful of fresh butter. If they are canned oysters put them into a colander and let cold water run through them, let them drain only a minute, then put them into a porcelain dish. Put the crackers on to a clean paper and crush them fine with a rolling pin, then put them into a pie plate and mix the salt and pepper with them. Roll the oysters over (one at a time) in the crackers and lay them on a large plate. Have ready on the fire a frying pan with the butter in it hot enough to brown (try it first with one oyster) then lay in the oysters one at a time, let them fry one minute, then turn them, fry them another minute, then lift. Put them into a warm chafing dish and send to table hot. Oysters prepared in this way are much better than when they are dipped in eggs.

RAW OYSTERS.

If they are canned oysters put them into a colander and let cold water run through them. Then let them drain and then put them into china dishes with small pieces of clear ice strewn amongst them. Serve with tomato catsup made by my receipt, celery salad or cold slaw and Albert or English crackers.

OYSTER PATTIES.

Put some large fresh oysters into a colander and let cold water run through them, then let them drain. Rub the small patty-plates with fresh butter and line them with puff paste; fill the plates with oysters and put a very little salt on each oyster, cut up some fresh butter into small pieces the size of a hazel nut, roll them in powdered cracker and put six of them into each plate, or one to each oyster; cover with puff paste and bake in a quick oven.

DEVILED CRABS.

One pint of crab meat; half a pint crushed double baked rusks or bread crumbs; one gill of vinegar; two ounces of fresh butter; one teaspoonful of my made mustard; half a teaspoonful of salt; a quarter of a teaspoonful of pepper; one gill of rich sweet milk and three yolks of fresh eggs; put the vinegar, butter, mustard, salt and pepper over the fire to get hot, but not to boil. Beat the yolks and milk together and stir them into the vinegar and the other ingredients until it is thick, but it must not boil after the eggs are in. Now take a deep pie-plate and cover the bottom with a thin layer of rusk, then a layer of crabs, and rusk again, with a couple of spoonfuls of the sauce distributed over it, then another layer of crabs, rusks and sauce and so on until all are in, finishing with the rusk and sauce. Put it into a quick oven where it will brown lightly in ten minutes.

DEVILED CRABS. (Excellent.)

Half a pint of crab meat; half a pint of beef soup; half a pint of tomatoes; one tablespoonful of butter; one teaspoonful of my made mustard; half a teaspoonful of salt; one quarter of a teaspoonful of pepper; one gill of crushed double baked rusk; cook the tomatoes in the soup until they are all broken up. Then put in the butter, mustard, salt and pepper and take it off the fire, then put in the crab meat and rusk and mix it together. Then put it into a dish and set it in a quick oven for ten minutes and then serve.

SHRIMPS STEWED.

One quart of shrimps, that is two cans; two ounces of fresh butter with two teaspoonfuls of flour mixed in it; half a pint of hot rich sweet milk; half a pint of hot water; one teaspoonful of crushed celery seed; one pinch of nutmeg; one teaspoonful of salt; half a teaspoonful of pepper; four yolks of fresh eggs, mix the butter and flour together and put it into a stew pan and let it fry a minute, then stir in the milk and water and let it come to a boil, then add the celery, nutmeg, salt and pepper, and put in the shrimps, and when they are hot, but not boiling, beat the yolks with two tablespoonfuls of milk and stir them in, when they are scalding hot take them off the fire, they must not boil.

TERRAPIN.

Put the terrapin into boiling water and boil until the skin and toe nails come off easily. Then take it out, pull off the skin, take out the toe nails and wash it in warm water and boil it again in salted water until the flesh is tender; then take it out of the shell, remove the sand bag and gall which you must be careful not to break, as it will make the terrapin bitter and uneatable. Cut the terrapin into small pieces and save the juice that comes out in the cutting with as much of the water it was boiled in as will make half a pint. One quart of terrapin meat; half a pint of the juice and water it was boiled in; four ounces of fresh butter with two teaspoonfuls of flour mixed in it; four tablespoonfuls of cider vinegar; one teaspoonful crushed celery seed; one teaspoonful of my made mustard; one teaspoonful of salt; half a teaspoonful of pepper; three yolks of fresh eggs; four tablespoonfuls of rich sweet milk; mix the butter and flour together and put it in a stew pan and let it fry a minute, then stir in the juice and water and let it come to a boil, then add the vinegar, celery seed, mustard, salt and pepper and when it is hot put in the terrapin and let it boil five minutes. Then beat the yolks and milk together and stir them in, let it get scalding hot, but not to boil, and then lift.

Beef.

ROAST BEEF.

Have the oven hot before you begin to prepare the meat. Take six pounds of beef, wash it in cold water, dry it, salt and pepper it with two teaspoonfuls of salt and half a teaspoonful of ground black pepper. Dredge it well with flour, mix one tablespoonful of fresh butter and one of lard with one teaspoonful of flour and put it into the roasting pan and let it brown a minute. Then stir in half a pint of hot water and put in the beef the outside up. After it has roasted fifteen minutes begin to baste. When the water has boiled down in the gravy add a kitchen spoonful of hot water from time to time and baste often. Cook it one hour and a half. After it is lifted skim off part of the fat and put in half a pint of boiling water. Stir it up well from the bottom and let it boil a few minutes, then lift. Six pounds of beef take one hour and a half to roast. Ten pounds two hours.

BEEF STEAK BROILED BY GAS.

Since I have become the possessor of one of Mr. Thomas Gaussen's gas cooking stoves, we have had the most delicious beef steaks. Take a young porterhouse steak one inch thick, wash it in cold water, but don't let it lay in the water to soak the juice out, then lay it on the meat board, dry it off, pound it with a wooden mallet and then nick the out side skin to prevent it from curling. Salt and pepper it on both sides, then place the gridiron over the pan that is to catch the gravy, put the steak on it and set it into the broiler, then let on the gas, and in ten minutes turn the steak and broil it ten minutes longer. Lift it into a warm chafing-dish and pour the gravy over it. This is the real juice of the beef without butter or water.

BEEF STEAK SMOTHERED IN ONIONS.

Prepare a porterhouse steak in the same manner as in the preceding receipt, and whilst it is broiling put one pint of sliced onions, cut up, into a skillet with two ounces of fresh butter, half a teaspoonful of salt and a pinch of pepper, and fry them a light brown. When the steak is done and put into a warm chafing-dish with the gravy poured over it, cover the steak with the onions, close the chafing-dish and send it to table hot.

BEEF A LA MODE.

Four pounds of beef from the rump without bone and two inches thick; half a pound of fat bacon; two ounces of fresh butter; six bay leaves; half a tablespoonful of juniper berries; one teaspoonful of cloves; one gill of cider vinegar; two onions peeled and cut in quarters. Wash the beef in cold water, dry it off, pound it with a wooden mallet and lard it with fat bacon. Cut the bacon in slices, cut off the skin, trim off the edges and cut it in pieces wedge shaped. Make the incisions deep with a sharp pointed knife and press in the bacon, then salt and pepper it on both sides and dredge it with flour. Have ready on the fire a dutch oven with the two ounces of butter in it, and when it is hot enough to brown lay in the beef and brown it well on both sides, then put in hot water enough to half cover the beef and the bay leaves, juniper berries, cloves, vinegar and onions. Keep the oven covered and cook it slowly two hours if young, two and a half if old. When it has cooked one hour turn it, and if the water boils down too low replenish with a little boiling water. When the beef is done the water should be boiled down and there should be a brown gravy, then lift it, skim off part of the fat from the gravy, put in a gill or more of hot water, let it boil a minute, stir it up well from the bottom and pour it through the gravy strainer into the gravy dish. It is good warm or cold served with the gravy.

CORNED BEEF AND CABBAGE.

Take five pounds of the brisket piece of sugar cured corned beef that is fat, wash it in cold water and if it is too salt let it lay in cold water for an hour or so. Put it into a pot with cold water enough to cover it, and when it begins to boil skim it as long as anything rises to the surface, then set it where it will cook slowly for three hours. The cabbage should be the Dutch flat heads and of the smallest size. Trim off the outside leaves, cut off the stalk and cut the cabbage in two if it is very small, if not, quarter them. Put them into a large pan of cold water for half an hour, examine them carefully, shake them up and down in the water and then put them into the colander to drain. As soon as the corned beef is well skimmed put the cabbage in with it and cook it slowly two and a half hours. If the water boils down too low replenish with a little boiling water, but there must not be much water in the pot when it is done or the cabbage will not be rich enough.

CORNED BEEF HASH.

One quart of fine chopped corned beef from the brisket piece; four middle sized onions peeled, sliced and chopped fine; two raw potatoes peeled, sliced and chopped fine; half a pint of water; half a teaspoonful of pepper. The beef is salt enough without any extra salt. Put the whole into a frying pan and cook it half an hour. Just before lifting stir in scant half a teaspoonful of grated nutmeg and the yolks of two eggs. It must be almost dry when it is lifted.

TRIPE, STEWED.

Tripe must be cooked five hours; take five pounds of tripe, cut it in pieces half an inch wide and two inches long. Wash it in warm water, put it into a stew pan with boiling water enough to cover it and boil it three hours. If the water boils down replenish with boiling water, then put it into a colander, drain off the water and return the tripe to the stew pan with boiling water enough to cover it. Now put in six bay leaves and two blades of mace as large as a five cent piece and boil it one hour and a half, then put in one tablespoonful of fresh butter, half a teaspoonful of ground black pepper, two teaspoonfuls of salt and half a pint of good cider vinegar. Now put two tablespoonfuls of browned flour and one tablespoonful of fresh butter into a frying pan with as much liquor from the tripe as will mix it together, and let it boil two or three minutes, then stir it in with the tripe, then add two tablespoonfuls of crushed double baked rusk and let it simmer twenty minutes.

SPICED PICKLE FOR BEEF, VENISON AND RABBITS.

One gallon of good cider vinegar; one quarter of a pound of bay leaves; two tablespoonfuls of cloves; two tablespoonfuls of whole pepper; three large spoonfuls of juniper leaves; two tablespoonfuls of salt. Put the whole together into a porcelain kettle and let it boil five minutes. Have ready four large onions sliced and put them into the pickle as soon as it is taken off the fire. Keep it covered closely. It is ready for use as soon as it is cold. It is very fine for beef, venison and rabbits. Six pounds of beef should lay in the pickle eight days, six pounds of venison six days and a rabbit three days. This pickle can be used three times in the winter by adding a little more vinegar the last time.

SPICED BEEF A LA MODE. (Very Fine.)

Take six or seven pounds of beef without any bones in it and four or five inches thick, (the butchers have it ready cut for this purpose) wash it, wipe it and pound it well. Then lard it with one pound and a half of fat bacon, cut the bacon in slices half an inch thick, take off the skin and cut the bacon wedge shaped, then take a strong sharp pointed knife and make the incisions deep; lard it close on both sides and stick a clove in each piece of bacon. Now take part of the bay leaves out of the pickle, lay in the beef and put the bay leaves on top, the pickle must cover the beef and the kettle must be close covered. When the beef has been in four days turn it, when it has been in eight days take it out and put it into an iron dutch oven with hot water enough to come half way up to the top of the beef, cover the oven and cook it slowly three hours. When it has cooked two hours turn it, brown it on both sides and when it is lifted stir into the gravy half a tablespoonful of browned flour and half a pint of hot water, let it boil a few minutes, stir it up well from the bottom and skim off part of the fat before sending it to table. It is excellent cold, served with the gravy and when chopped up makes nice sandwiches. Mashed potatoes, stewed carrots, parsnips or turnips should be served with spiced beef.

BEEF'S TONGUE, SPICED.

Prepare a fresh beef's tongue in the following manner: Wash it in two waters, trim off the back part and put it into a sauce pan with cold water enough to cover it and boil it two hours.

Then take it out on a platter and take off the skin and cut out the meat from underneath the tongue, Then put it into my spiced pickle for beef and game, and let it remain in it eight days, then take it out and put it into a dutch oven with cold water enough to half cover the tongue and boil it two hours. Keep the oven covered and when it has cooked one hour turn it, then mix one tablespoonful of fresh butter with one tablespoonful of browned flour and put it into a skillet with a small ladle full of the water from the tongue and let it boil until it is as thick as cream, then stir it in with the tongue. When the tongue is done there should be about half a pint of gravy. It is good either warm or cold, is very nice for lunch and makes fine sandwiches.

BEEF'S TONGUE, FRESH.

Take a young fresh beef's tongue and wash it in two waters with a coarse linen cloth, then let clear water run over it and put it into a sauce pan with cold water enough to cover it, and when it begins to boil skim it well, then put in six bay leaves and a teaspoonful of salt, cover the sauce pan and let it cook slowly four hours. When it has cooked two hours turn it and if the water has boiled down too low, replenish with a little boiling water, when it is done take off the skin, trim off the back part and cut out the meat from underneath the tongue. Send it to table whole or cut it in slices and lay it in rows. Serve it with the following sauce:

SAUCE FOR BEEF TONGUE.

Put one tablespoonful of browned flour into a skillet and when it is hot put in two ounces of fresh butter and half a pint of the water that the tongue was cooked in, poured through a gravy strainer, then put in half a teaspoonful of powdered mace, half a teaspoonful of powdered cloves, one quarter of a teaspoonful of ground black pepper and two tablespoonfuls of good cider vinegar. Stir it together and let it boil slowly fifteen minutes.

Veal.

VEAL A LA MODE.

Four pounds of veal cut two inches thick (from the round); one pound of fat bacon; two ounces of fresh butter; six bay leaves; half a teaspoonful of powdered mace; half a teaspoonful of powdered cloves; four tablespoonfuls of cider vinegar; two teaspoonfuls of browned flour. Wash the veal in cold water, dry it off, cut the outside skin to prevent it from curling, and pound it well on both sides. Cut the bacon in slices, take off the skin, trim off the outside edges and cut it in pieces wedge shaped, then make the incisions deep with a sharp pointed knife and lard it half an inch apart. Have ready on the fire a dutch oven with two ounces of fresh butter in it, and when it is hot enough to brown, salt, pepper and dredge the veal with flour on the upper side and lay it in, flour side down, then season and dredge the other side, cover the **oven close, and brown** it on both sides a yellow brown, then put in the bay leaves and hot water enough to reach half of the veal. Cover the oven and cook it slowly one hour. Baste it often and when done lift it into a warm chafing-dish, skim off part of the fat from the gravy, then put in two teaspoonfuls of browned flour, half a pint of hot water, the mace, cloves and vinegar. Let it boil a few minutes, stir it up from the bottom, put in salt and pepper to the taste and pour it through the gravy strainer into the gravy dish.

CINCINNATI PÄTËS A LA STRASBOURGH.

One pound of young calf's liver weighed after it is cooked; six bay leaves; half a teaspoonful of salt; one gill of the water the liver was cooked in; half a teaspoonful of powdered cloves; half a teaspoonful of powdered mace; half a teaspoonful of pepper; half a teaspoonful of salt; four ounces of fresh butter with one teaspoonful of browned flour mixed with it. Wash the liver in cold water and put it into a stew pan with cold water enough to cover it, and when it begins to boil skim it as long as anything rises to the surface, then put in the bay leaves and half a teaspoonful of salt, boil it until it is very tender; it takes about two hours. When done put it into a deep porcelain dish, pour the water and bay leaves over it and let it stand until cold. The water should have boiled down to about half a pint. Strain the water through a gravy strainer or wire sieve, put one gill of it into a skillet, add all the spices and seasoning, set it over the fire, mix the browned flour and butter together, stir it in, let boil a minute and take it off. Weigh the liver, cut it in to thin small pieces and grind it in a porcelain mortar to a fine paste, moistening it each ime with two tablespoonfuls of the sauce. It can be put into small molds or one large one, and cut in slices when served. It is very nice for lunch or tea.

VEAL CUTLET.

A veal cutlet should be cut from the thickest part of the round and should be one inch and a half thick. After it is washed in cold water and dried off, cut the outside skin to prevent it from curling, then pound it on both sides, salt and pepper it and dredge it with flour on the upper side. Have ready on the fire a frying pan with a tablespoonful of fresh butter and one of lard, and when it is hot enough to brown lay in the cutlet, flour side down, then salt, pepper and dredge the other side. Cover the frying pan close, (the steam makes the veal tender) and cook it slowly twenty minutes, then turn it and cook it twenty minutes longer. When it is done lift it into a warm chafing-dish, put two teaspoonfuls of browned flour and a gill of hot water into the gravy. Let it boil a few minutes, stir it up well from the bottom, then pour it over the cutlet.

VEAL FRICASSEE.

Take four pounds of the breast of veal and cut it up according to the bones. Wash it in cold water and put it into a flat iron dutch oven that has a cover to it, and put in cold water enough to cover it. Just before it begins to boil skim it well, then put in one tablespoonful of fresh butter, six bay leaves, and a blade of mace the size of a ten cent piece. Keep it covered and cook it one hour and a half. When it has cooked one hour put in pepper and salt to the taste, then take two tablespoonfuls of browned flour, and whilst it is hot stir into it one tablespoonful of fresh butter and as much of the liquor from the veal as will mix it well together and stir it in with the veal, then stir in two large spoonfuls of crushed double baked rusk and let it simmer half an hour longer. Before sending to table remove the bay leaves and mace.

VEAL FRICANDEAU, (Excellent.)

Take two pounds of veal that is cut from the thickest part of the leg and is one inch and a half thick, wash it in cold water, dry it off, cut the outside skin to prevent it from curling, and pound it well on both sides, then lard it with two dozen anchovies. The anchovies that I used for this purpose were rolled up in a coil the size of a silver quarter of a dollar and were put up in olive oil. Make the incisions in the cutlet deep with a sharp pointed knife and wide enough to insert the anchovy (coiled up) without breaking. The anchovies are salt enough to season the cutlet; sprinkle a little pepper over it and dredge the upper side thickly with flour. Have ready on the fire a deep skillet with one gill of olive oil in it, and when it is hot enough to brown lay in the cutlet flour side down, then pepper and dredge the other side with flour; cover the skillet close and cook it a yellow brown, then turn it carefully, baste it often and cook it slowly thirty minutes longer. Keep the skillet covered and when it is done lift it into a warm chafing-dish, then put in one teaspoonful of browned flour, one gill of hot water and three tablespoonfuls of cider vinegar into the gravy; let it boil up a few minutes, stir it up well from the bottom and if required add a pinch of salt and pepper, then pour it over the veal.

VEAL FRICASSEE. (With Sweet-breads.)

Take three pounds of the breast of veal an

cut it up according to the bones. Wash it in cold water and put it into a flat iron dutch oven with a cover to it. Put in cold water enough to cover the veal, then take one sweet-bread for each person you are to have at table. Trim them, wash them and put them in with the veal; set it over a slow fire and before it begins to boil skim it well, then put in one tablespoonful of fresh butter, six bay leaves and a blade of mace the size of a five cent piece. Keep it covered and cook it one hour and a half. When it has cooked one hour take out the sweet-breads on a porcelain plate and set them where they will keep warm; now put in salt and pepper to the taste. Take two tablespoonfuls of browned flour and while it is hot stir in one tablespoonful of fresh butter and as much of the liquor from the veal as will mix it well together, then stir it in with the veal, then stir in two large spoonfuls of crushed double baked rusk, now put in the sweet-breads without breaking them and let the whole simmer half an hour longer. Before sending to table remove the bay leaves and mace.

ROAST OF VEAL. (The Kidney Piece.)

Wash the veal in cold water and dry it off, salt and pepper it on both sides with an even tablespoonful of salt and half a teaspoonful of black pepper; dredge it well with flour. Have ready on the fire an iron dutch oven with one tablespoonful of fresh butter and one. of fresh lard in it, and as soon as it is hot enough to brown put in the veal, the out side down, and cover the oven. Let it cook slowly until it is nicely browned, then turn it over and brown the other side; then put in two or three tablespoonfuls of hot water and baste after. Keep the oven covered, the steam makes the meat tender and juicy. Five pounds of veal take one hour and a half to cook. After the veal is lifted put half a pint of hot water into the gravy and stir it up well from the bottom, let it boil a few minutes, then pour it into the gravy dish.

VEAL HASH. (Very fine.)

One quart of fine chopped, cold roast veal; four middle sized onions; peeled, sliced and chopped fine; two raw potatoes, pared, sliced and chopped fine; and half a pint of water; put the whole into a frying pan with the gravy that was left from the roast of veal; if there is no gravy, mix one tablespoonful of fresh butter, and one tablespoonful of lard, with two teaspoonfuls of browned flour and stir it in; then add salt and pepper to the taste, and cook it half an hour; just before lifting stir in scant half a teaspoonful of grated nutmeg, and the yolks of two eggs; it must be almost dry when it is lifted.

SWEET-BREADS FRICASSEED.
(Very fine.)

Six sweet-breads of equal size; one pint of beef broth; six bay leaves; two blades of mace, the size of a five cent piece; half a teaspoonful of salt; one pinch of pepper; two tablespoonfuls of fresh butter; one tablespoonful of browned flour; one tablespoonful of crushed double baked rusk; wash the sweet-breads in cold water and boil them in salted water thirty minutes; there should be water enough to cover them, that has one teaspoonful of salt in it to one pint of water. Then take them out, trim them off nicely and put them into a deep skillet with the beef broth, bay leaves, mace, salt and pepper; cover the skillet and let them cook slowly thirty minutes longer. Mix the butter and flour together, then add to it three tablespoonfuls of the liquor from the sweet-breads and stir it into the gravy without breaking the sweet-breads; then stir in the rusks and let it simmer ten minutes longer. Remove the bay leaves and mace before sending them to table.

SWEET-BREADS, FRIED.

Wash them in cold water and put them into a stew pan with cold salted water enough to cover them, and when it begins to boil skim it; then put in one bay leaf and one blade of mace the size of a bean for each sweet-bread and boil them thirty minutes, if large size, forty minutes; then take them out and save the water they were boiled in for the gravy. Trim them off nicely, salt and pepper them and dredge them well with flour. Have ready on the fire a frying pan with a large kitchen-spoonful of fresh butter in it, and when it is hot enough to brown put in the sweet-breads, cover the pan; fry them a light brown, baste them and cook them slowly thirty minutes. When lifted put some of the spiced water they were boiled in into the gravy, let it boil a minute, stir it up well from the bottom and then pour it over the sweet-breads.

CALF'S LIVER.

A young calf's liver is light red, and an old one is dark red, and not fit to eat. Take a young calf's liver, wash it in cold water, dry it off and lay it on the meat board, cut it in slices half an inch thick, sprinkle a pinch of salt and pepper over them and dredge them thickly with flour. Have ready on the fire a skillet with one tablespoonful of fresh butter and one of fresh lard in it and when it is hot enough to brown lay in the liver, flour side in the butter; then sprinkle the other side with salt and pepper and dredge it with flour; cover the skillet and cook it slowly ten minutes, then turn it and cook it ten minutes longer. Lift it into a warm chafing-dish and put half a pint of hot water into the gravy; let it boil a few minutes, stirring it up well from the bottom, and add another pinch of salt and pepper. The gravy should be rich and plenty of it.

Lamb and Mutton.

LAMB AND TURNIPS.

Three pounds of the breast of fat lamb is enough to cook with one quarter of a peck of turnips. Peel the turnips and chip them up in thin pieces as you do apples for pies. Wash them in cold water and put them into a colander. Mix one tablespoonful of fresh butter with one teaspoonful of flour and put it into a stew pan and let it boil a minute, then put in a pint of boiling water and the turnips with one teaspoonful of salt. The water must cover the turnips and they must cook slowly three hours. Wash the lamb, dry it off and sprinkle it with salt and pepper. When the turnips have cooked one hour put in the lamb, skin side down, and cook them together two hours longer. If the lamb is very fat omit the butter. There must be very little water in the stew pan when the lamb and turnips are done.

LEG OF LAMB, LARDED.

Wash the lamb in cold water and dry it off with a linen cloth, then lard it with small pickled button onions. Make the incisions deep with a sharp pointed knife and put the onions in out of sight. Salt and pepper it and dredge it with flour. Put one tablespoonful of fresh butter and one of fresh lard into a dutch oven, and when it is hot enough to brown lay in the lamb and brown it on both sides. Put in a tablespoonful of hot water from time to time and baste often. Cover the oven to keep in the steam and cook it slowly one hour. When lifted put into the gravy one teaspoonful of browned flour and one gill of hot water. Let it boil five minutes, stirring it up well from the bottom, then put in three tablespoonfuls of my tomato catsup and lift.

LEG OF LAMB, ROASTED.

Take a leg of young lamb that weighs three and a half pounds, wash it in cold water, dry it, salt and pepper it with a teaspoonful of salt and scant half a teaspoonful of pepper. Dredge it well on both sides with flour; put one tablespoonful of fresh butter and one of lard into a dutch oven and when it is hot enough to brown lay in the leg of lamb; brown it on both sides and baste often; put in a tablespoonful of hot water before basting, and keep the oven covered. Cook it slowly for one hour; after it is lifted put in one gill of hot water; let it boil a minute, stir the gravy up well from the bottom and lift. Serve with young turnips, green peas and new potatoes.

LAMB CHOPS, FRIED.

Wash the lamb chops in cold water and dry them off, then salt and pepper them and dredge them with flour; have ready on the fire a skillet with one tablespoonful of butter and one of lard, and when it is hot enough to brown lay in the chops; cook them ten minutes, then turn them and cook them ten minutes longer, then lift into a warm chafing-dish, pour one gill of hot water into the gravy, let it boil a few minutes, stirring it up well from the bottom, then put in three tablespoonfuls of my tomato catsup and lift.

A LEG OF SOUTHDOWN MUTTON, BOILED.

Cut the knuckle from the leg, then wash the mutton in cold water and put it into a kettle with cold water enough to cover it that has one tablespoonful of salt in it; just before the water begins to boil skim it well; cover the kettle and let it boil slowly one hour and a half if young, if old, two hours. If the water boils down too low replenish with boiling water. Serve with caper, mint or tomato sauce.

SOUTHDOWN MUTTON CHOPS, BROILED BY GAS.

After the chops have been washed in cold water and dried off pound them with the beef steak pounder, then salt and pepper them; rub the gridiron with a piece of fat pork or some lard tied in cloth and lay the chops on it; place the gridiron over the pan that is to catch the gravy and set it into the broiler, then let the gas on and in ten minutes turn the chops and broil them ten minutes longer.

Pork.

BOILED HAM.

Take a sugar cured ham weighing ten pounds, cut off the end bone, scrape off the underside, wash it in warm water and put it into a large kettle with cold water enough to cover it and let it heat slowly until it begins to boil, then boil it three hours from the time it begins to boil. When it is done take it out on to a large platter, skin side down and trim off all the outside and put the trimmings on to another plate, then turn the ham upside down and take off the skin. Spot it with black pepper and wind fringed paper around the bone.

ROASTED HAM.

After the ham has been boiled, trimmed off and skinned, put it into a roasting pan (skin side up) with half a pint of sherry wine, one gill of hot water and three tablespoonfuls of white granulated sugar, then put it into an oven that is hotter on top than it is in the bottom and baste it with the wine every five minutes. Roast it a yellow brown. It takes about thirty minutes if the oven is right. When it is done lift it into a warm chafing-dish and skim off all the fat in the pan, then mix a teaspoonful of browned flour with a little water and stir it into the pan. Let it boil a few minutes, then add a little more wine, water and sugar. Put it into a gravy dish and serve it with the ham.

ROAST PIG.

Take a young pig four weeks old that has been well cleaned, wash it in cold water, lay it on the meat board and dry it off. Make a stuffing with the following ingredients: Put two quarts of peeled and sliced sour apples into a saucepan with one gill of cold water, and when they are cooked soft put in three tablespoonfuls of white granulated sugar, then mix two teaspoonfuls of corn starch with a tablespoonful of cold water and stir it in. Let it boil five minutes and then take it off.

STUFFING.

Pick and wash one pound of dried German prunes and put them into a saucepan with cold water enough to just cover them. Cook them until they are soft but not to break. Fifteen minutes before they are done put in three tablespoonfuls of white sugar, and when they are done measure them without the juice and put them into a large bowl, then measure the same quantity of apples and mix it with the prunes, then take one tablespoonful of anise seed to one quart of fruit. Rub the anise seed through the hands to take off the stems and then sift it and mix it with the apples and prunes and then stuff the pig, sew it up with a small cord, put a small block of wood in its mouth to keep it open; salt and pepper it and dredge it with flour. Put two tablespoonfuls of fresh butter with two teaspoonfuls of flour mixed with it into the baking pan and let it fry one minute, then put in half a pint of hot water and the pig. After the flour on the pig is browned baste often, putting in a spoonful of hot water from time to time. Brown it well and cook it two hours and a half. When it is lifted put half a pint of water into the gravy, stir it up from the bottom, put in salt and pepper to the taste and let it boil a few minutes. Cut the cord in short pieces with a pair of scissors and draw it out. Take the block out of its mouth and put in a red apple. Garnish with green parsley.

PIGS' FEET, SOUSED.

Select the smallest pigs' feet, they are the youngest; wash them in cold water and put them into a kettle with cold water enough to cover them, and when they begin to boil skim off whatever rises to the surface. If the water boils down replenish with boiling water; the feet must be covered with water until they are done; cook them four hours, or until they are very tender. Then take them out onto a large platter, split them open between the hoofs and take out the large bones; now take a large flat stone crock and put in a layer of the pigs feet, cut side up, and sprinkle over them a pinch of salt and pepper and a teaspoonful of cloves; then another layer with salt, pepper and cloves, and so on until all are in. Then fill the crock with good cider vinegar and cover it close. They will be ready to use in twenty-four hours; they can be eaten cold or warm, but they are better warm. Put them into a skillet with some of the congealed vinegar and cloves, and when they are hot if they are too sour add a little water and salt if required.

PORK AND BEANS.

The white marrow beans are the richest and easiest cooked. Take one quart of beans, pick them, wash them in two waters and put them into a pan that holds two quarts and a half, then take one pound of fat, pickled pork, wash it in warm water and trim off the parts that are not fresh cut, then cut the skin in cross-bars and put the pork down in the middle of the beans, leaving only the skin in sight. Now put in one teaspoonful of salt and one tablespoonful of white granulated sugar and fill up the pan with cold water to within half an inch of the top; put it into the oven and bake them three hours and a half. Replenish with hot water from time to time, keeping the water even with the beans until half an hour before they are done; then let the water cook down and if they are browned a little on top remove them before sending to table.

SAUSAGES.

Wash the sausages in cold water, then separate them and put them into a skillet with half a pint of hot water and boil them ten minutes; then turn them and prick them with a fork and boil them until the water is boiled down; then brown them on both sides in their own fat. They are done in thirty minutes.

SPARE RIB, STUFFED.

Take a whole young spare rib that has small bones, and after it is washed in cold water lay it on the meat board and dry it off, then crack the bones exactly in the middle with a hatchet, but they must not be cut clear through, then fold the two edges together, trim off the ends to make it even and sew it up with a small cord leaving the largest end open for the filling. Fill it with the following ingredients: Half a pint of cooked sour apples that have two teaspoonfuls of sugar in them, half a pint of cooked prunes with two teaspoonfuls of sugar in them and two teaspoonfuls of anise seed. Put the apples and prunes into a bowl and mix them together, then stir in the anise seed, fill and sew up, salt and pepper it on both sides and dredge it with flour. Put two ounces of fresh butter into the roasting pan with half a pint of water and lay in the spare rib. Brown it on both sides, baste it often, putting in a spoonful of hot water from time to time. Keep the oven closed and cook it two hours. When it is lifted cut the cord in short pieces with a pair of scissors and draw it out. Put half a pint of hot water into the gravy, stir it up well from the bottom and let it boil a few minutes.

Poultry.

HOW TO KNOW A YOUNG TURKEY.

If the lower joints of the legs are a dark red it is a young turkey. If they are white it is an old one. This is a sure sign. I never knew it to fail.

ROAST TURKEY.

Take a young hen turkey that weighs six or seven pounds and wash it inside and out with cold water and dry it with a clean napkin. Rub the inside of the turkey with half a tablespoonful of fresh butter and a pinch of salt and pepper. Stuff it, sew it up and sprinkle a little salt and pepper on it. Put some small pieces of butter on the outside of it, put it into the roasting pan with half a pint of water and a tablespoonful of fresh butter. Baste it often. It takes one hour and a half to roast a young turkey of this size in the range. Put the giblets on to boil when the turkey is put into the oven. Cook them until they are soft, then cut them up and mash the liver. After the turkey is lifted skim off part of the fat from the gravy and stir in half a tablespoonful of browned flour, then put in the giblets with the water they were cooked in which should be half a pint, then add salt and pepper to the taste and stir it up well from the bottom of the pan. Let it cook a few minutes and lift.

TURKEY STUFFING.

One quart of fresh oysters; eight ounces of fresh butter; eight ounces of bread, without the crust, dipped in cold water and squeezed out quickly; three fresh eggs beaten separately; one tablespoonful of green parsley leaves cut up fine; one tablespoonful of celery leaves cut up fine; two teaspoonfuls of dried summer savory after it has been made fine and sifted; one teaspoonful of salt; half a teaspoonful of pepper. Put the oysters into a saucepan and let them scald, but not boil, then pour them into a colander to drain. Put the butter into a deep skillet and set it where it will melt, but not get hot, beat the yolks and stir them in with the butter, then put in the parsley, celery, summer savory, salt and pepper and then stir in the bread. Beat the whites to a stiff foam, stir them in then put in the oysters and fill quickly. The stuffing should be warm when it is put into the turkey.

STUFFING FOR A TURKEY OR CHICKENS.

One quart of sliced onions, cut up fine, measured after they are cut up; eight ounces of fresh butter; eight ounces of bread without the crust; four fresh eggs beaten separately; two tablespoonfuls of parsely after it has been washed and cut up fine; two teaspoonfuls of grated nutmeg; two teaspoonfuls of salt; one teaspoonful of pepper. After the onions are peeled and sliced, cut them up fine, then put them into a skillet with the butter and cook them soft, but not brown. Dip the bread into cold water, take it out quick, squeeze it out and stir it in with the butter and onions, then put in the parsley, nutmeg, salt and pepper and mix it well together. Then take it off the fire and beat the yolks and stir them in, now beat the whites to a stiff foam and stir them in when you are ready to fill. The stuffing should be warm when it is put in.

BOILED TURKEY.

Choose a young hen turkey, and after it has been dressed and washed in cold water dry it off with a linen cloth, then take half a pound of fat pickled pork trim off the outside, that is not fresh cut, wash it in warm water and put it inside of the turkey. Tie the legs fast to the body, turn the wings behind and tie them, then put the turkey into a porcelain kettle with cold water enough to cover it, and just before it begins to boil skim it, then set it where it will boil slowly for two hours, if it is an old one two and a half hours. When it has boiled one hour turn it and if the water boils down too low replenish with boiling water. Serve with oyster or egg sauce. Save the water the turkey was boiled in for soup next day. Skim off the fat, it is good to fry potatoes with.

BOILED CHICKEN.

Take a young full grown yellow legged chicken and after it has been dressed and washed in cold water dry it off with a linen cloth, take one quarter of a pound of fat pickled pork, trim off the outside edges, wash it in warm water and put it inside the chicken, then tie the legs fast to the body, turn the wings behind and tie them, then put the chicken into a large saucepan with cold water enough to cover it, and when it begins to boil skim it, then set it where it will boil slowly one hour. If the water boils down too low replenish with boiling water. Serve with oyster or egg sauce.

CHICKEN FRICASSEE.

Select a young full grown chicken and after it is dressed, cut up and washed, put it into a stew pan with cold water enough to cover it and just before it begins to boil, skim it. Peel four celery roots, slice them thin, wash them and put them in with the chicken, then put in one tablespoonful of fresh butter, and when the chicken has cooked one hour put in two tablespoonfuls of green parsley leaves cut up fine, one teaspoonful of salt and a quarter of a teaspoonful of pepper. Now mix one tablespoonful of fresh butter with one heaped tablespoonful of flour and stir it in with the chicken. Let it simmer slowly fifteen minutes then put in two dozen fresh oysters and as soon as it begins to boil again take it off the fire and lift.

CHICKEN FRICASSEE.

After the chicken has been dressed, cut up and washed, put it into a stew pan with cold water enough to cover it and just before it begins to boil skim it; then take three quarters of a pound of pickled pork, trim off all the outside that is not fresh cut, wash it, cut it in slices and put it in with the chicken; then put in six bay leaves and two blades of mace the size of a five cent piece. When the chicken has cooked one hour, or until it begins to be tender, add one quarter of a teaspoonful of pepper and salt if required, then roll out some pastry dough a quarter of an inch thick, cut it in squares, put it in with the chicken and cook it slowly thirty minutes. Remove the bay leaves and mace before sending it to table.

CHICKEN PIE.

A young chicken that is not quite fully grown is the best for a chicken pie. After it has been cut up by the joints split the back in three pieces, cut out the wish bone piece and split the breast in two, wash it in cold water and put it into a stew pan with just cold water enough to cover it. Just before it begins to boil skim it, then put in one tablespoonful of chopped parsley leaves, one blade of mace the size of a five cent piece, half a grated lemon peel, two tablespoonfuls of fresh butter with two teaspoonfuls of flour mixed in it, one teaspoonful of salt and a pinch of pepper. Cover the kettle and cook it until tender, then take the chicken out and boil the water down to half a pint and then strain it through a gravy strainer or wire sieve. Roll out some pastry one fourth of an inch thick and cut it in squares. Line a deep well buttered dish with some of the pastry and then put in a layer of chicken cut side up and a layer of pastry squares, with two large spoonfuls of the broth, then another layer, and so on, finishing with the chicken and broth. Cover with pastry and cut a few slits in it with a sharp knife, put it in the oven and bake thirty minutes.

SPRING CHICKENS, COOKED WHOLE.

Yellow legged chickens are the best and the best way to cook them is in a dutch oven with a cover to it and in the following manner: After they are picked and dressed light a paper and singe them. Wash them in cold water, dry them off, salt and pepper them with one teaspoonful of salt and a pinch of pepper to each chicken. Dredge them well with flour. Put one tablespoonful of fresh butter with one of fresh lard into the dutch oven, and when it is hot enough to brown put in the chickens. Brown them on both sides. Put in from time to time a kitchen spoonful of hot water and baste them every fifteen minutes. Let them cook slowly and keep the oven covered. The steam makes them tender and juicy. If the chickens are full grown cook them one hour, if not full grown three quarters of an hour. After the chickens are lifted put half a pint of boiling water in the gravy. Let it boil a few minutes, stir it up well from the bottom and lift.

ROAST DUCKS. (Young ones.)

After the ducks have been dressed and washed in cold water, dry them off with a soft linen cloth then rub the inside of each duck with a teaspoonful of fresh butter and a pinch of salt and pepper; now fill them, sew them up, put a pinch of salt and pepper over them, dredge them with flour and put them into the roasting pan with half a pint of water, a large spoonful of fresh butter and a double baked rusk. When the flour on the ducks has browned baste them from time to time and cook them one hour; when lifted put half a pint of hot water into the gravy, let it boil up a minute, stir it up well from the bottom and pour it into the gravy dish. Serve with currant or cranberry jelly.

STUFFING FOR DUCKS. (One pair.)

One quart of sliced white onions cut up fine; six ounces of fresh butter; eight ounces of stale bread without the crust, dipped in cold water and squeezed out quick; three fresh eggs beaten separately; one teaspoonful of grated nutmeg; one teaspoonful of salt; half a teaspoonful of pepper. Put the butter and onions into a deep skillet and cook the onions soft, then put in the bread, nutmeg, salt and pepper and mix it well together, then take it off the fire and beat the yolks and stir them in, then beat the whites with one teaspoonful of white sugar to a stiff foam and stir them in when you are ready to fill.

YOUNG GOOSE. ROASTED.

A young goose has yellow feet and red joints of the leg and an old one has red feet and white joints. After the goose has been picked light a paper and singe it off, then dress it, wash it in cold water and take out the fat and save the giblets for the gravy; cut off part of the neck and tie the skin over it with a small cord; cut up half a tablespoonful of fresh butter in small pieces and put it inside of the goose, then fill and sew it up with a small cord; tie the legs to the body with the cord, salt and pepper the outside and dredge it with flour, mix one tablespoonful of fresh butter with one teaspoonful of flour and put it into the roasting pan and let it brown two minutes, then put in half a pint of hot water and the goose; baste often, putting in a little hot water from time to time; keep the oven closed and cook it one hour and a half. Put the giblets on to boil when the goose is put into the oven, boil them until they are very tender, then cut them up and put them in with the gravy; then put in half a pint of the water the giblets were cooked in, stir it up well from the bottom of the pan, let it boil a few minutes and put in salt and pepper to the taste. Cut the cord the goose was sewed with with a pair of scissors in short pieces and draw it out. A young goose takes one hour and a half to cook, and an old one two hours and a half.

STUFFING FOR A GOOSE.

Take one pound and a half of dried prunes, wash them in cold water and put them into a saucepan with cold water enough to cover them, and cook them until they are soft, but not soft enough to break. Fifteen minutes before they are done stir in three tablespoonfuls of white granulated sugar. Put two quarts of sliced sour apples (pippins are the best) into a porcelain saucepan with one gill of water and three tablespoonfuls of white sugar and cook them until they are soft, then mix two teaspoonfuls of corn starch with a little cold water and stir it in, let it cook four minutes. Then measure one pint and a half of the apples and one pint and a half of the prunes and put them together in a large bowl, then take one tablespoonful and a half of anise seed and rub off the little stems and then sift it and mix it with the apples and prunes.

Game.

HASENPFEFFER.

One rabbit, eight bay leaves, one tablespoonful of fresh butter, six onions the size of an egg with six cloves stuck in each onion, half a pint of hot cider vinegar, one teaspoonful of salt, half a teaspoonful of pepper, one tablespoonful of browned flour with one tablespoonful of fresh butter mixed in it, two tablespoonfuls of crushed double baked rusk. After the rabbit has been skinned, cut up and washed in cold water, put it into a dutch oven or flat stew kettle with cold water enough to cover it and just before it begins to boil skim it, then put in the bay leaves and one tablespoonful of butter and cover the kettle. Peel the onions and stick six cloves in each one; when the rabbit has cooked one hour put in the vinegar, onions, salt and pepper, put the browned flour and butter into a skillet and when it is hot stir in a few spoonfuls of the liquid from the rabbit and let it boil a minute or two, as soon as the onions are soft stir in the flour and butter, then stir in the rusk and let it simmer slowly twenty minutes, or until the gravy is thick enough. Remove the bay leaves before sending it to table.

QUAILS, ROASTED.

After the quails have been picked and dressed, wash them in cold water, dry them with a napkin and put a pinch of salt and pepper inside of each one. Put a large kitchen spoonful of fresh butter into a dutch oven or deep skillet over the fire, and when it is hot enough to brown, lay in the quails. Then put in six crushed juniper berries for each quail, cover the oven or skillet and brown them on both sides. Then put in a tablespoonful of hot water from time to time, and baste often. Cook them slowly thirty minutes, and when they are lifted, put a gill of hot water into the gravy, stir it up from the bottom, let it boil a few minutes, and then pour it through the gravy strainer.

GAME STUFFING FOR QUAILS, PIGEONS AND BIRDS.

One gill of rich sweet milk, four ounces of fresh butter, half a pound of crushed double baked rusk.

three fresh eggs beaten separately, two tablespoonfuls of green parsley leaves, cut up fine, two teaspoonfuls of crushed celery seed, one teaspoonful of powdered mace, one teaspoonful of salt, half a teaspoonful of pepper. Put the milk and butter into a deep skillet and let it get warm enough to melt the butter. Then put in the parsley, celery, mace, salt and pepper. Beat the yolks with a spoonful of cold milk and stir them in. Then put in the rusk and beat the whites with one teaspoonful of white sugar to a stiff foam and stir them in just when you are ready to fill.

RABBIT, SPICED.

Skin the rabbit, dress it and leave it whole with the head on, wash it in cold water, take out the eyes and lay it on the meat board and lard it with fat bacon, cut the bacon one quarter of an inch thick, cut off the skin, trim off the edges and cut it in wedge shaped pieces, make the incisions in the thick part of the rabbit with a sharp pointed knife and press in the bacon; put the rabbit into the pickle and let it stay in three days, then take it out, dry it off, sprinkle a little salt over it and dredge it with flour; have ready on the fire a frying pan containing half a tablespoonful of fresh butter and half a tablespoonful of lard, and when it is hot enough to brown lay in the rabbit, cover the pan, brown it on both sides, baste it from time to time and cook it slowly thirty minutes. When it is lifted put a gill of hot water into the gravy, let it boil a few minutes, stir it up from the bottom of the pan, then pour it into the gravy dish.

SADDLE OF VENISON, ROASTED.

A six pound saddle of venison should be larded with one pound of fat bacon. Wash the venison in warm water and dry it off with a linen cloth, then cut the bacon in slices half an inch thick, cut off the skin, trim off the outside edges and cut it in pieces wedge shaped, make the incisions deep in the venison with a sharp pointed knife and press in the bacon, then salt and pepper it and dredge it with flour. Have ready on the fire a dutch oven with two ounces of fresh butter in it and when it is hot enough to brown put in the venison and brown it on both sides, then put in half a pint of hot water, six bay leaves, half a tablespoonful of juniper berries, one teaspoonful of cloves, two onions peeled and cut in quarters and one gill of cider vinegar. Cover the oven and cook it slowly two hours; baste it from time to time, and if the water boils down too low replenish with a little boiling water. When it has cooked one hour turn it, and when it is done lift it into a warm chafing-dish and skim off part of the fat from the gravy, then put in one gill of hot water, let it boil up a minute, stir it up well from the bottom of the oven and pour it through the gravy strainer into the gravy dish. Serve with currant or cranberry jelly, mashed potatoes, sweet potatoes, celery or cold slaw.

SADDLE OF VENISON, SPICED.

Take six pounds of the saddle of venison, wash it in warm water and dry it with a clean linen cloth and lard it with one pound of fat bacon; cut the bacon into slices half an inch thick, take off the skin and cut it into wedge shaped pieces an inch and a half long. Make the incisions with a sharp pointed knife clear through the thick part of the venison and press the bacon into it a far as possible. After it is closely larded; put it into the pickle and let it remain in it six days. Then take it out dry it off and dredge it with flour; have ready on the fire a dutch oven with two tablespoonfuls of fresh butter in it and when it is hot, put in the venison and brown it on both sides as quickly as possible. Then put in a little hot water from time to time and baste often with the gravy, keep it covered and cook it slowly for two hours and a half. When it is lifted stir into the gravy half a pint of hot water and let it boil a few minutes stirring it up well from the bottom. Serve with stewed carrots, turnips and mashed potatoes, currant or cranberry jelly.

VENISON STEAK.

Take a venison steak one inch thick, wash it quickly in warm water, not letting it lay in the water. Then pound it with a wooden mallet nick the outside skin to keep it from curling; salt and pepper it and dredge it with flour. Have ready on the fire a frying pan with two tablespoonfuls of fresh butter in it, and when it is hot enough to brown put in the steak. Brown it on both sides, cover the pan and cook twenty minutes. Then lift it into a warm chafing-dish and put one gill of hot water into the gravy; let it boil up a minute, stir it up from the bottom of the pan, then put in one tablespoonful of currant jelly and pour the gravy over the steak. Venison is such a lean, close meat the gravy should be rich and plenty of it.

Sauces for Fish, Fowls and Meat.

HOLLANDISH FISH SAUCE, (Warm,)—(Excellent.)

Half a pint of the water the fish has been boiled in, one teaspoonful of flour, three yolks of fresh eggs, three ounces of fresh butter, one saltspoonful of salt, half a saltspoonful of pepper; four tablespoonfuls of my tomato catsup. Put the water into a saucepan and set it into a pan of boiling water over the fire and let it get hot, but not boiling. Mix the flour with a little cold water then beat the yolks and flour together and then stir them into the water, stir it until it is thick (but it must not boil) then take it off the fire and stir in the butter, then add the salt, pepper and last the catsup.

MAYONAISE SAUCE, FOR FISH OR SALAD.

Three yolks of hard boiled eggs; one yolk **raw**; four tablespoonfuls of olive oil; two teaspoonfuls of my made mustard; one teaspoonful of grated white onion; one salt spoonful of salt; half a spoonful of pepper; four tablespoonfuls of good vinegar. Slice the boiled yolks up fine into a porcelain bowl and mix the raw yolk with them. Then rub them together until they are fine and smooth; then put in the oil a little at a time, and rub it in with the back of the spoon. Then add the mustard, onion, salt and pepper, and last add the vinegar.

NEW MAYONAISE SAUCE, FOR FISH OR SALAD, (Excellent.)

One gill of cider vinegar, two teaspoonfuls of my made mustard, two teaspoonfuls of grated white onion, one teaspoonful of salt, half a teaspoonful of pepper, six yolks of fresh eggs, two tablespoonfuls of olive oil, one gill of rich sweet milk; put the vinegar, mustard, onion, salt and pepper into a skillet over the fire and let it get **hot but not boil**; beat the yolks and oil together then **stir in the milk** and then stir it into the vinegar, stir it until it thickens but it must not boil. It can be used cold or warm.

HORSE-RADISH SAUCE.

One pint of beef broth, six tablespoonfuls of grated horse-radish, one tablespoonful of vinegar, one teaspoonful of pounded mace, two teaspoonfuls of white granulated sugar, one teaspoonful of salt, one tablespoonful of fresh butter, two tablespoonfuls of crushed double baked rusk. Put the beef broth and horse-radish into a saucepan over a slow fire, then put in the vinegar, mace, sugar, salt and butter, crush the rusk with a rolling-pin and put them in last; let it cook slowly for fifteen or twenty minutes. To be served with beef or veal.

OYSTER SAUCE.

One pint of oysters, half a pint of rich sweet milk, one tablespoonful of green parsley washed and cut fine, one even teaspoonful of crushed celery seed, one teaspoonful of flour, two yolks of fresh eggs, two ounces of fresh butter, one saltspoonful of salt, half a saltspoonful of pepper. Put the oysters into a colander and let cold water run through them, then let them drain; put the milk, parsley and celery into a saucepan and set it into a pan of boiling water over the fire and let it get hot, but not to boil, mix the flour with a little cold milk, then beat the yolks and flour together and then stir them into the milk, stir it until it becomes as thick as cream, but it must not boil, then add the butter, and when it is melted, put in the oysters and as soon as they are fringed and swollen (they must not boil) take them off the fire and add the salt and pepper, then pour it into a sauce tureen. Serve with boiled turkey and chicken.

DRAWN BUTTER SAUCE.

Four ounces of fresh butter; one teaspoonful of flour; one gill of hot water; one third of a teaspoonful of salt. Mix the flour and one tablespoonful of the butter together in a tin cup; then stir in slowly the hot water and set the tin cup into a tin pan that contains a little boiling water. Stir it until it becomes thick or begins to boil. Then take it off the fire and stir in the remainder of the butter and of one third of a teaspoonful of salt.

PARSLEY SAUCE

is made by putting two tablespoonfuls of chopped parsley into half a pint of drawn butter sauce.

EGG SAUCE.

Half a pint of drawn butter; two hard boiled eggs chopped up and one tablespoonful of parsley chopped fine. Beat the yolks of two fresh eggs with two tablespoonfuls of sweet milk and stir it in the drawn butter. Stir it until it is thick; then put in the hard boiled eggs, the parsley, and salt to the taste.

CAPER SAUCE.

Caper sauce is made by stirring three tablespoonfuls of capers and two tablespoonfuls of cider vinegar into half a pint of drawn butter sauce. Then add salt and pepper to the taste.

PICKLE SAUCE.

Take some small cucumber pickles that are made by my receipt; slice them thin and chop them up fine. Then put three tablespoonfuls of the pickles and two tablespoonfuls of cider vinegar into half a pint of drawn butter-sauce with salt and pepper to the taste and mix it well together.

TOMATO SAUCE.

One pint of canned tomatoes, one tablespoonful of fresh butter, one tablespoonful of chopped white onions, one tablespoonful of flour, three tablespoonfuls of cider vinegar, half a teaspoonful of ground allspice, half a teaspoonful of ground cloves, half a teaspoonful of my made mustard, half a teaspoonful of salt, one quarter of a teaspoonful of ground black pepper. Fry the onions in the butter until they are soft, then stir in the flour and let it cook two minutes, then put in the tomatoes and all the other ingredients, stir them well together and let them boil fifteen minutes, then strain it through the gravy strainer into the sauce tureen.

TOMATO SAUCE.

Put one tablespoonful of browned flour into a skillet and when it is hot put in two ounces of fresh butter and half a pint of beef broth, let it boil until it is as thick as cream, then stir in one gill of my tomato catsup.

Pickles. Catsup, Mustard.

WAX BEANS, PICKLED.

Beans for pickling must be young, round and full, string them carefully with a knife and let them remain whole, after they are washed in cold water put them into a kettle of boiling water over a brisk fire, and after the water begins to boil again cook them thirty minutes, then take them out and spread them on a table that is covered with a cloth. When they are cold put them into glass jars that hold one gallon; first put in a layer of beans then four bay leaves, then another layer of beans and bay leaves until the jar is within one inch of being full; then put in one tablespoonful of ground pepper, two tablespoonfuls of ground black mustard and three tablespoonfuls of salt. Fill the jar with cold cider vinegar to within half an inch of the neck, and then put in two tablespoonfuls of whole black pepper, close the jar with a ground glass stopper and pour a little melted beeswax around it. The vinegar must not touch the stopper.

PICKLED ONIONS.

Peel half a peck of small, white-skinned button onions without cutting off the tops. Put them into a porcelain kettle with one quart of cold water and one pint and a half of sweet milk. When they are hot, but not to boil, set them on the side of the range for fifteen minutes. Then take them out and spread them on a table that is covered with a cloth. When they are cold put them into half-pint, wide-necked glass jars. Then put in a blade of mace the size of a five cent piece, and one even teaspoonful of salt. Fill up with cold cider vinegar, cork tight and seal with wax.

PICKLED BEETS.

Put a tablespoonful of cloves into a pint of cider vinegar and set it over the fire for half an hour where it will get hot, but not boil. Then let it get cool. Take small dark red beets that have been boiled and skinned. Slice them and let them get cold. Then take some small white onions and cut them in thin slices. Take a glass or stone jar and put in first a layer of beets, then a few slices of onion, then a spoonful or two of the vinegar and cloves and a pinch of salt; then another layer in the same manner until the jar is almost full. Fill up with cold cider vinegar. They are ready to use in twenty-four hours.

RED CABBAGE PICKLED.

Take some small firm heads of dark red cabbage and trim off the outside leaves and cut the stalk off even with the cabbage. Then cut it in quarters lengthwise and then in half quarters; take a gallon jar and put in a layer of cabbage six bay leaves, three blades of mace each the size of a five cent piece, half a teaspoonful of whole cloves and half a teaspoonful of whole black pepper; then another layer of cabbage, bay leaves and spices until the jar is within an inch of being full. Then put in three tablespoonfuls of salt, two tablespoonfuls of whole cloves and two tablespoonfuls of whole pepper; then fill up the jar with cold cider vinegar until the vinegar and spices come into the neck of the jar, but they must not touch the stopper; close up with ground glass or stone stoppers and pour a little melted bees-wax around them.

PICKLED CUCUMBERS, (Very fine.)

Cucumbers for pickling should be small, and have the stems on; put them into cold water for half an hour, then wash them in two waters, rubbing them carefully with the hands. Put a double cloth on a table and spread the cucumbers on it to drain and dry; now assort them, putting each size by itself, and if there are any without stems, or broken, lay them aside. Pickles should be put into glass or stone jars; take a jar one gallon in size and put in a layer of cucumbers then five bay leaves, then another layer of cucumbers and five bay leaves; and so on until the jar is within an inch of being full, then put in one tablespoonful of ground black pepper, two tablespoonfuls of ground allspice and three tablespoonfuls of salt; fill up the jar with cold cider vinegar and put on the top two tablespoonfuls of whole black pepper and two tablespoonfuls of whole allspice. The vinegar and spice should come into the neck of the jar, but not touch the stopper. Close up with ground glass stoppers and pour a little melted bees-wax around them. If the vinegar is pure cider vinegar the pickles will be as hard and crisp at the end of a year as they were when first put up. The spices should be ground at home, you cannot depend upon what you buy at the groceries.

TOMATO CATSUP. (Excellent.)

One gallon of peeled tomatoes; four pods of cayenne pepper; (they are very small, about one inch long,) three tablespoonfuls of black pepper, ground at home; four tablespoonfuls of black mustard, made fine in the mortar; three tablespoonfuls of allspice, ground at home; three tablespoonfuls of salt; one quart of strong cider vinegar; one long root of horse-radish chipped up thin. Boil four hours. Two bushels of tomatoes make thirty bottles of catsup. After the tomatoes have boiled two hours put in all the spices—everything excepting the vinegar and horse-radish. (It must be stirred at the bottom all the time it is boiling.) Set the vinegar on the side of the fire where it will get hot, but not boil. Then chip up the horse-radish in thin chips. Half an hour before the catsup is done put in the vinegar, and when the catsup has boiled four hours stir in the horse-radish and take it off the fire. Put it into large wooden vessels or large stone crocks. Cover it closely, so that the aroma cannot escape, and let it stand over night. Then strain through a wire sieve, and with a wooden spoon press as much through as you can. What is left in the sieve take into your hands and squeeze it out. Bottle it. Drive the corks in with a wooden beetle, and put a strong twine over the corks and make it fast around the neck of the bottle. Then dip it into hot sealing-wax, and when it is cold tie a piece of cotton cloth over it to prevent the wax from being knocked off. This catsup will keep any length of time. It is excellent with raw oysters, fresh meats of all kinds, salads, sauces and gravys.

MUSTARD.

One pint of yellow English mustard flour, half a pint of white granulated sugar, one gill of fine salt, one gill of cider vinegar. Put the mustard flour into a porcelain bowl and pour in slowly boiling water enough to make it into a dough, stir it until it is all scalded and perfectly smooth. Then stir in the sugar and mix it well together, then add the salt and last the vinegar, mix it well together, then put it into small, wide mouthed glass jars, and cork it tight, it will keep good a long time. It is very fine for the castor and for salad dressing.

Salads.

SALAD DRESSING. (No. 1, th best.)

Three tablespoonfuls of cider vinegar, one tea spoonful of my made mustard, half a teaspoonf of salt, quarter of a teaspoonful of peppe three yolks of fresh eggs, one tablespoonful of oliv oil, three tablespoonfuls of rich sweet milk. Pr the vinegar, mustard, salt and pepper into a sma skillet and let it get hot, but it must not boil, bea the yolks and olive oil together and then st in the milk, then stir it into the vinegar; stir it ur til it is thick, but it must not boil. Put it into porcelain bowl and when it is cold mix it with th salad.

SALAD DRESSING. (No. 2.)

Three yolks of hard boiled eggs, one yolk raw egg, two tablespoonfuls of olive oil, one te spoonful of my made mustard, one teaspoonful of grated white onion, one saltspoonful of salt, half a saltspoonful of pepper, three tablespoonfuls of cider vinegar. Slice the yolks into a porcelain bowl, mix the raw yolk in with them and rub them together with the back of the spoon until they are very smooth, then put in the oil, a little at a time, rubbing it well together, then add the mustard, onion, salt and pepper and last the vinegar.

CABBAGE SALAD, OR COLD SLAW.

Two quarts of cut cabbage, one tablespoonful of fresh butter, with one teaspoonful of flour mixed in it; one gill of cider vinegar, one teaspoonful of my made mustard, one heaped teaspoonful of salt, (celery salt,) quarter of a teaspoonful of pepper, three yolks of fresh eggs, one gill of rich sweet milk. Mix the butter and flour together, put it into a skillet and let it fry one minute, then stir in the vinegar, mustard, salt and pepper and let it get hot, but it must not boil, then beat the yolks and milk together and stir them into the vinegar, stir it until it is as thick as cream, but it must not boil, pour it into a bowl, and when it is cold enough, mix it with the cabbage. Take a small flat dutch head of cabbage and trim off the outside leaves, cut it in halves, wash it in cold water, then cut it on the cabbage cutter, but not too fine, spread a clean napkin into the colander, put in the cabbage, take the four corners together and shake out the water, then measure and put it into the salad dish. When ready to serve mix the dressing and cabbage well together. It is excellent with **raw or fried oysters.**

LETTUCE SALAD.

Take the head of lettuce and strip off all the outside leaves; then separate the inside leaves from the stalk, and put them into cold water and let them remain in it half an hour. Then spread a clean napkin into the colander, pick the lettuce carefully over and throw it into the colander; then take the four corners of the napkin together and shake it to get the water off the lettuce. Put it into the salad dish, and when ready to serve, mix the dressing with it.

ENDIVE SALAD.

Only the yellow part of endive can be used for salad. After the green leaves have all been taken off, put the yellow part into cold water. Separate the leaves, pick it carefully and wash it in two waters. Cut the leaves off two inches long, put them in the salad dish with the curled ends on top. Serve with lettuce salad dressing.

CORN SALAD.

Corn salad is so small and grows so near the ground that it has to be carefully picked; examine every bunch closely, then take off the under leaves and cut off the root and wash it twice in cold water, let it remain half an hour in the last water. Then put it into the colander to drain, serve with lettuce salad dressing.

BEAN SALAD.

The yellow wax beans are the best for salad; string them and boil them whole, when they are boiled tender; take them out on to a table that is covered with a clean cloth and let them get cold then put them into the salad dish; mix one tablespoonful of olive oil, one saltspoonful of salt, half a saltspoonful of pepper and one teaspoonful of my made mustard together; then add four tablespoonfuls of cider vinegar.

CUCUMBER SALAD.

Cucumbers for salad should only be a little more than a finger length long and a little thicker than a thumb. They have a much finer taste than those large unwholesome cucumbers which are generally used for salad. Put them into cold water, peel them, **cut off** the stem end and throw them into a pan of cold water until it is time to serve; then slice them thin and send them to table with a separate plate of sliced small white onions; serve them at table to suit the taste, some prefer them with only vinegar, salt and pepper, whilst others prefer them with the addition of oil. When oil is used it should be put on first and mixed with the cucumber before the vinegar is put on.

CELERY SALAD.

Take the yellow stalks of the celery and wash them in cold water, spread a clean cloth on a table and put the celery on it to drain, then split the stalks down lengthwise in four or five pieces, cut them off half an inch long and put them into the salad dish, make a dressing with the following ingredients: Two yolks of fresh eggs, one tablespoonful of olive oil, three tablespoonfuls of rich sweet milk, three tablespoonfuls of cider vinegar, half a teaspoonful of my made mustard, half a teaspoonful of salt. Put the vinegar, mustard and salt into a small skillet and let it get hot, but not boil; beat the yolks and oil together, then stir in the milk and then stir it into the vinegar, stir it until it is the thickness of cream, (but it must not boil,) then put it into a bowl and when it is cold mix it with the celery. Garnish the top with the yellow leaves.

OYSTER SALAD.

One pint of small oysters measured after they have been scalded and drained, one pint of eels, or lake trout, after it has been boiled and cut up, one pint of celery measured after it is cut up, six small cucumber pickles the size of a little finger.

DRESSING.

Four tablespoonfuls of cider vinegar, one teaspoonful of my made mustard, one teaspoonful of salt, half a teaspoonful of pepper, four yolks of fresh eggs, one tablespoonful of olive oil, four tablespoonfuls of rich sweet milk. Put the oysters, with their own liquor, into a saucepan over the fire and just when they begin to boil take them off and pour them quickly into a wire sieve to drain; when cold put them into a salad dish. Boil the fish in salted water fifteen minutes, and when cold take out the bones, cut the fish into pieces the size of a five cent piece and put into the salad dish. Wash the celery in cold water, split the stalks lengthwise in four or five pieces, then cut them off half an inch long and put it with the oysters and fish. Cut the pickles lengthwise in quarters, then in thin slices, and mix the whole together. Put the vinegar, mustard, salt and pepper into a skillet over the fire where it will get hot, but not boil, beat the yolks and oil together, then stir in the milk and then stir it into the vinegar, stir it until it is thick, (it must not boil) then pour it into a bowl and when it is cold mix it with the salad.

ITALIAN SALAD.

One pint of shrimps, one pint of eels, measured after they are boiled and cut up, one quart of celery, after it is cut up, one gill of small cucumber pickles, after they are cut up, one gill of pickled button onions, after the outside is taken off, one gill of cider vinegar, two teaspoonfuls of my made mustard, two teaspoonfuls of grated white onions, one teaspoonful of salt, half a teaspoonful of pepper, six yolks of fresh eggs, two tablespoonfuls of olive oil, one gill of rich sweet milk. Put the shrimps into a colander, let cold water run through them, let them drain, then put them into a large bowl. Boil the eels in salted water fifteen minutes and when cold separate the bones from the fish, then cut the fish up in pieces as large as the shrimps and put them into the bowl. Wash the white stalks of the celery in cold water, split down lengthwise in four or five pieces, then cut them off half an inch long and put them with the fish; take the smallest cucumber pickles that are made by my receipt, split them lengthwise in quarters, then slice them up; take the outside layer off the pickled onions to make them small enough, then mix the pickles with the other ingredients, put the vinegar, mustard, onions, salt and pepper into a skillet where it will get hot, but not boil; beat the yolks and oil together, then stir the milk and stir it into the vinegar, stir it until it is thicker than cream, (it must not boil) then pour it into a bowl and when cold mix it with the salad; place some head lettuce leaves around the salad dish, put in the salad and garnish with young celery leaves.

CHICKEN SALAD.

One young full-grown chicken boiled till tender; half a pint of the water the chicken was boiled in; two ounces of fresh butter with two teaspoonfuls of flour mixed with it; one teaspoonful of crushed celery seed; one teaspoonful of powdered mace; one teaspoonful of salt; half a teaspoonful of pepper. When the chicken is done and cold remove the bones and cut the chicken up in pieces half an inch square and put them into a salad dish. Boil down the water the chicken was cooked in to about half a pint; measure it and pour it through the gravy strainer into a skillet over the fire; then put in the celery seed, mace, salt and pepper. Mix the butter and flour together and stir it in; stir it until it boils up as thick as cream; then pour it over the chicken and mix it together. The head butter lettuce is the best, and there should be an equal quantity of lettuce and chicken. Separate the leaves from the stalks, wash them in cold water; then drain it well, cut it in pieces, put it into a large bowl, and when ready to serve dress it with No 1 Salad Dressing and then mix it with the chicken.

SHRIMP SALAD.

One pint of shrimps, one pint of celery, after it has been cut up.

DRESSING.

Three tablespoonfuls of cider vinegar, one teaspoonful of my made mustard, half a teaspoonful of salt, quarter of a teaspoonful of pepper, three yolks of fresh eggs, one tablespoonful of olive oil, three tablespoonfuls of rich sweet milk. Put the shrimps into a colander and let cold water run through them, let them drain, then put them into a large bowl. Wash the white stalks of the celery in cold water, split them lengthwise in four or five pieces, then cut them off half an inch long, put them in with the shrimps and mix them together. Put the vinegar, mustard, salt and pepper into a skillet over the fire where it will get hot, but not boil; beat the yolks and oil together, then stir in the milk and then stir it into the vinegar; stir it until it is thick, but it must not boil, then put it into a bowl and when it is cold mix it with the salad. Place some head lettuce leaves around the salad dish, put in the salad and garnish the top with hard boiled eggs cut in quarters.

FISH SALAD. (Lobster and Trout.)

One pint of lobster, after it has been cut up, one pint of trout, after it has been cut up, one pint of celery, measured after it is cut up, one pint of the inside leaves of head lettuce. Cut the lobster and trout in pieces an inch long and put them into a large bowl. Wash the white stalks of the celery in cold water, split them lengthwise in four or five pieces, then cut them off an inch long and mix them with the fish. Wash the lettuce in cold water, let it drain and put it into the bowl.

DRESSING.

Four yolks of fresh eggs, two tablespoonfuls of olive oil, four tablespoonfuls of rich sweet milk, four tablespoonfuls of cider vinegar, one teaspoonful of my made mustard, one teaspoonful of grated white onion, one teaspoonful of salt, half a teaspoonful of pepper. Put the vinegar, mustard, onion, salt and pepper into a skillet over the fire to get hot, but not boil; beat the yolks and oil together, then stir in the milk and then stir it into the vinegar, stir it until it is thick, (it must not boil) then put it into a small bowl to get cold and when ready to serve mix it with the salad. Place some large head lettuce leaves around the salad dish, put in the salad and garnish with hard boiled eggs cut to suit the fancy.

TONGUE SALAD. (Excellent.)

One beef's tongue boiled four hours; six bay leaves; half a teaspoonful of salt; one tablespoonful of brown flour mixed with one tablespoonful of fresh butter; half a pint of the water the tongue was cooked in; half a teaspoonful of powdered cloves; half a teaspoonful of powdered mace; half a teaspoonful of salt; quarter of a teaspoonful of pepper; twelve small cucumber pickles the size of a little finger, cut up fine; an equal quantity of celery and tongue. Wash the tongue in three waters; then put it into a stew pan with cold water enough to cover it and when it begins to boil skim it. Then put in the bay leaves and salt and cook it slowly four hours. When it has cooked two hours turn it. The water should have boiled down to about half a pint when the tongue is done; then lift it on to a large platter, skin it carefully, trim off the back part and cut out the meat underneath the tongue. When it is cold cut it in slices half an inch thick, then in pieces half an inch square and put them in a salad dish. Put the flour and butter into a skillet and when melted, put in the half pint of water the tongue was cooked in. Then put in the cloves, mace, salt, pepper and vinegar, and let it boil until it is as thick as cream; then mix it with the tongue. Cut the pickles fine and put them in with the tongue. Wash the white stalks of the celery in cold water, split them down lengthwise in four pieces, cut them off half an inch long and put them into a separate bowl. Then dress the celery with Salad Dressing No. 1 and mix it with the tongue. Garnish with young celery leaves.

HERRING SALAD.

Two dutch herring, one quart of sliced cold potatoes that were boiled with the skins on, one saucer full of sliced white onions, young ones are the best, one saucer full of red pickled beets, four tablespoonfuls of cider vinegar, one teaspoonful of my made mustard, half a teaspoonful of salt, quarter of a teaspoonful of pepper, four yolks of fresh eggs, one tablespoonful of olive oil, four tablespoonfuls of rich sweet milk. Wash the herring in cold water, scale them, then skin them, cut off their heads and take out the inside; wash them again, dry them off and put them into a deep dish with vinegar enough to cover them, let them remain in the vinegar eight hours, then take them out, remove the bones, cut the fish up fine and put it into a salad dish. Boil the potatoes with the skins, and when cold peel them, cut them lengthwise in quarters, slice them up and put them in with the fish; cut up the sliced onions fine, then cut the beets half an inch square and mix the whole together. Put the vinegar, mustard, salt and pepper into a skillet to get hot, but not to boil. Beat the yolks and oil together, then stir in the milk and then stir it into the vinegar, stir it until it is thick, but it must not boil. When it is cold mix it with the salad.

POTATO SALAD.

One quart of sliced cold boiled potatoes, one saucer full of sliced white onions, one tablespoonful of green parsley leaves cut up fine.

DRESSING.

Three tablespoonfuls of cider vinegar, one teaspoonful of my made mustard, half a teaspoonful of salt, quarter of a teaspoonful of pepper, three yolks of fresh eggs, one tablespoonful of olive oil, three tablespoonfuls of rich sweet milk. Boil the potatoes with the skins on then peel them, cut them lengthwise in quarters, slice them and put them into the salad dish, cut the sliced onions up fine and put them in with the potatoes, then put in the parsley and mix it together. Put the vinegar, mustard, salt and pepper into a small skillet and let it get hot, but not to boil. Beat the yolks and oil together then stir in the milk and then stir it into the vinegar; stir it until it is as thick as cream (but it must not boil) then pour it over the salad and mix it well together.

Macaroni.

MACARONI WITH HERB CHEESE.

Half a pound of macaroni; four ounces of butter; four ounces of grated cheese. Put the macaroni into boiling water that has one teaspoonful of salt to a pint of water and cook it ten minutes, or until it is done. It must not break up. Then put it into a colander to drain; then take a deep porcelain dish and put first a layer of macaroni, then a tablespoonful of melted butter; then a tablespoonful of grated cheese, and so on until the dish is full. Then put it into the oven and bake it a light brown.

MACARONI, WITH TOMATOES.

Half a pound of macaroni, one pint of beef soup that has one teaspoonful of salt in it, half a pint of tomatoes, two tablespoonfuls of butter, a pinch of salt and pepper, two tablespoonfuls of crushed double baked rusk. Boil the macaroni in the soup fifteen minutes, or until it is soft, not broken; after the tomatoes are peeled, cut up and measured, put them into a stew pan with the butter, salt and pepper and cook them until they are all broken up, then stir in the rusk and mix them with the macaroni. Put it into a deep dish and set it into a quick oven for ten minutes.

Croquettes.

CHICKEN CROQUETTES.

Three quarters of a pound of chicken chopped fine and mixed with one tespoonful of salt, half a teaspoonful of pepper, half a teaspoonful of crushed celery seed and one tablespoonful of green parsley, chopped fine. Mix it well together.

SAUCE FOR CHICKEN CROQUETTES.

Half a pint of the water the chicken was boiled in into which stir one tablespoonful of butter and two tablespoonfuls (not heaped) of corn starch wet with a little cold water and stir it into the boiling chicken water, stir it until it becomes a thick sauce, then pour it over the chopped chicken and mix it well together, then spread it on a shallow plate to cool, then shape it into balls and let it stand half an hour longer in a cool place, then shape it into rolls. Take half a pint of crushed double baked rusk and roll them very fine, then take one egg, to which add two tablespoonfuls of cold water, and beat it together; now roll the croquettes, one at a time, first in the crumbs then in the beaten egg, then in the crumbs again. Have ready on the fire a frying pan with one tablespoonful of butter and one of lard in it and when it is hot enough to brown lay in the rolls, turn them quickly and lift in a minute.

OYSTER CROQUETTES.

Three quarters of a pound of oysters, put the oysters into a colander and let cold water run through them. Then put them into a saucepan with half a pint of sweet milk and let them scald, then take them out into a colander and let them get cold; then weigh them and chop them, not very fine.

SAUCE FOR OYSTER CROQUETTES.

Put half a pint of milk the oysters were scalded in, in a saucepan over the fire, two ouces of butter, one tablespoonful of flour, one teaspoonful of salt, one quarter of a teaspoonful of pepper, half a teaspoonful of summer savory after it is made fine and sifted, half a teaspoonful of crushed celery seed, five tablespoonfuls of crushed oyster crackers, rolled fine. Mix the flour and butter together and stir it in, then put in the salt, pepper, summer savory and celery seed; then put in the crushed oyster crackers and pour it over the oysters. Mix it well together and spread it on a shallow plate to cool, then make it into balls and let it stand half an hour in a cool place, then make it into rolls. Take half a pint of double baked rusk and roll them very fine, then take one egg, to which add two tablespoonfuls of cold water and heat it together, then roll the croquettes one at a time, first in the crumbs then the egg, then in the crumbs again. Have ready on the fire a frying pan with one tablespoonful of butter and one of lard in it and when it is hot enough to brown, lay in the rolls, turn them quick and lift in a minute.

TONGUE CROQUETTES.

Three quarters of a pound of tongue chopped, not very fine.

SAUCE FOR TONGUE CROQUETTES.

Half a pint of the water the tongue was cooked in, half a teaspoonful of powdered mace, half a teaspoonful of powdered cloves, one quarter of a teaspoonful of pepper, half a teaspoonful of salt, two tablespoonfuls of cider vinegar, two tablespoonfuls of flour, two ounces of butter, two tablespoonfuls of crushed double baked rusk. Put the half pint of water the tongue was cooked in into a saucepan over the fire, then put in all the spices and vinegar and mix the flour and butter together and stir it in, stir it until it becomes a thick sauce, then stir in the crushed rusk, then pour it over the chopped tongue and mix it well together, then spread it on a shallow plate to cool, then shape it into balls and let it stand half an hour longer in a cool place, then shape it into rolls. Take half a pint of crushed double baked rusk and roll them very fine, then take one egg, to which add two tablespoonfuls of cold water, and beat it together. Now roll the croquettes one at a time, first in the crumbs then in the beaten egg, then in the crumbs again. Have ready on the fire a frying pan with one tablespoonful of butter and one of lard, and when it is hot enough to brown lay in the rolls, turn them quickly and lift in a minute.

Vegetables.

POTATOES, BOILED.

Select potatoes that are nearly of the same size, peel them carefully, take out the eyes, wash them in cold water and put them into boiling water that has a teaspoonful of salt to a pint of water. The water must cover the potatoes and should begin to boil half an hour before you are ready to lift dinder and must be kept boiling until it is poured off. Cover the kettle and in twenty minutes try them with a fork (the time depends upon the size of the potatoes) and if they are almost done, pour off the water quick, set them on the side of the range and leave the cover a little open; shake them up two or three times to let the steam out and they will be floury and dry. They must be lifted as soon as they are done.

NEW POTATOES.

Must not be peeled, the skins must be scraped off, the potatoes washed in cold water and put into boiling water that has a little salt in it. The water must be kept boiling until the potatoes are done, then pour off the water, set them on the side of the range and leave the cover a little open to let out the steam. An excellent way of dressing new potatoes is to put some fresh butter with a tablespoonful of green parsley that has been washed and cut up fine into a saucepan and set it into a pan of boiling water and let it boil one minute, then pour it over the potatoes after they are lifted; serve with drawn butter from a sauce tureen.

MASHED POTATOES.

After one quarter of a peck of potatoes have been boiled in salted water, cut them open to see if any of them are hollow, then put them into a flat stone crock that has been made warm, and mash them fine with a wooden beetle, then put in half a pint of hot sweet milk or cream and four ounces of fresh butter cut up in small pieces; mash them until they are light and smooth, then put them into a warm deep dish with a cover to it, and send to table hot.

DRESDEN POTATOES. (Very Fine.)

Half a pound of pickled pork, half a pint of sliced onions, one tablespoonful of browned flour, two teaspoonfuls of salt, half a pint of vinegar, and three pints of sliced cold boiled potatoes. Cut the pork in thin slices, then cut in strips the size of the prong of a fork and then cut them up fine, put it into a frying pan and fry it brown and crispy, peel the onions, slice them, cut them up fine and put them in with the pork and cook them fifteen minutes, mix the flour with just water enough to make a thin paste and stir it in, then put in the salt, vinegar and potatoes last, stir it all together, but not to break the potatoes. As soon as it is hot lift.

FRIED POTATOES.

Potatoes can be fried either in fresh butter, veal gravy or the marrow from beef soup bones, or the fat that is skimmed from the top of the soup, they are all very good. Put two tablespoonfuls of fresh butter into a frying pan and when it is hot put in one quart of sliced cold boiled pototoes, and one teaspoonful of salt and one half a saltspoonful of pepper. Fry them a light brown and send to table hot.

MASHED SWEET POTATOES.

Take one quarter of a peck of yellow sweet potatoes that are of equal size; trim off the roots, wash them, put them into a pot of boiling water and cook them half an hour, then take them out, peel them and put them into a warm stone crock and mash them with a potato beetle, then add one quarter of a pound of fresh butter cut in small pieces and mash them until they are smooth. Send to table hot. They are excellent.

SWEET POTATOES, FRIED.

Boil the potatoes as in the preceding receipt, then take off the skins and when they are cold cut them in slices half an inch thick and fry them in butter a light brown.

SWEET POTATOES, BAKED.

Select potatoes that are of equal size and after they are washed and trimmed off put them into an oven hot enough to bake a yellow brown, and if they are of middle size they will be done in three quarters of an hour, large potatoes take longer, the time depends on the size of the potato and the heat of the oven.

KALE.

Take one peck of young kale, strip the leaves from the stalks and put them into cold water for half an hour, then pick it, wash it in two waters and put it into a saucepan with cold water enough to cover it, and let it boil two hours and a half. Then take it out into a colander to drain, then put it into a wooden bowl and chop it up fine. Now mix one tablespoonful of fresh butter and one of fresh lard with two teaspoonfuls of flour and put it into a large deep skillet and let it boil one minute, then put in the kale with two teaspoonfuls of salt and let it simmer slowly thirty minutes longer.

KALE WITH BREAKFAST BACON.

After a peck of kale has been in cold water half an hour then picked over and washed in two waters, put it into a large saucepan with cold water enough to cover it, and cook it two and a half hours. When it has cooked one hour, take one pound and a half of breakfast bacon, wash it in warm water, trim off the outside edges that are not fresh cut and cut the skin through half an inch wide, then put it down in the middle of the kale and cook it one hour and a half longer.

SPINACH.

Put one peck of spinach into cold water for half an hour then pick it carefully, wash it in two waters and put it into a large saucepan with cold water enough to cover it, and boil it three quarters of an hour. Then take it out into a colander and let the water all drain off, then put it into a wooden bowl and chop it up fine. Now mix two tablespoonfuls of fresh butter with two teaspoonfuls of flour and put it into a large deep skillet, and when it has boiled one minute put in the spinach with two teaspoonfuls of salt, and let it simmer slowly thirty minutes.

WILD, OR COUNTRY GREENS, WITH BREAKFAST BACON.

Dandelions, lambs-quarters, mustard and sour dock are all good greens, and are good all cooked together. Put them into cold water for half an hour, then pick them carefully over, take off the outside leaves, wash them in two waters and put them into a pot of boiling water and boil them two hours and a half. When they have boiled one hour take one pound and a half of breakfast bacon, trim off the outside edges that are not fresh cut, wash it in warm water, score the skin to keep it from curling and put it down in the middle of the greens and cook them one hour and a half longer. The water should be boiled down low when the greens are done.

ASPARAGUS.

Take three or four bunches of asparagus (the thickest is the best) and scrape off the white part and throw them into cold water, then tie them up in bunches, heads together, and put them into boiling water that has one teaspoonful of salt to a pint of water, and cook them thirty minutes, then take them out to drain. Have ready on the fire an iron skillet with half a pint of rich sweet milk in it, mix two tablespoonfuls of fresh butter and two teaspoonfuls of flour together and when the milk is hot stir in the butter and flour; take the strings off the asparagus and lay it into the milk and butter, heads together, and let it simmer slowly for thirty minutes.

CAULIFLOWER.

Trim off the outside leaves of a large cauliflower and cut off the stalks one inch from the branches, put it into cold water that covers it, and let it remain in it one hour, then wash it carefully and see that the sand is all out of it; tie a string around the stalks to lift it out with, and put it into boiling water that has one teaspoonful of salt to a pint of water. Let it boil thirty minutes, then lift it out carefully by the string. Have ready on the fire a skillet with one pint of rich sweet milk in it, mix two tablespoonfuls of fresh butter and two teaspoonfuls of flour together, and when the milk is hot stir in the butter and flour. Take the string off and split the stalk into four parts without breaking the flowers and lay it carefully into the milk and butter, baste it from time to time with the milk and butter and let it cook slowly thirty minutes.

GREEN PEAS.

Take one quart of shelled young green peas and, after they are picked and washed in cold water, put them into a colander to drain, then put them into a stew pan with one pint of cold water and let them boil thirty minutes, then put in one tablespoonful of chopped green parsley leaves, one tablespoonful of white granulated sugar and two teapoonfuls of salt, then mix two tablespoonfuls of fresh butter with two teaspoonfuls of flour and stir it in with the peas and let them simmer slowly thirty minutes longer. They must be almost dry when they are done. The best peas are those which have flat pods.

GREEN PEAS AND YOUNG CARROTS.

To one pint of shelled peas one pint of cut carrots; they are prepared in the same manner as in the preceding receipt. The carrots are scraped and cut lengthwise, the size of the prong of a dinner fork, and then cut off an inch long, wash them, drain them and put them into the stew pan at the same time the peas are put in, and cook them the same length of time.

KOHL RABI, OR TURNIPS ABOVE THE GROUND.
(Brossica Kohlrape.)

Take two dozen of young kohl rabi and peel them deep enough to reach the soft part of the turnip, then cut them in thin slices and wash them in cold water, mix one tablespoonful of fresh butter with one teaspoonful of flour and put it into a saucepan with one pint of boiling water and let it boil a minute, then put in the kohl rabi with boiling water enough to cover them and boil them two hours, then mix a tablespoonful of fresh butter with a tablespoonful of flour and stir it in, then add salt to the taste and cook them slowly thirty minutes longer. They are as fine as cauliflower.

YOUNG BEETS, STEWED.

Boil two dozen young beets from two to three hours (the time depends upon the size of the beets.) They must be very tender and when they are done put them in cold water, skin them and then slice them. Mix two tablespoonfuls of fresh butter with two teaspoonfuls of flour and put it into a large deep skillet and boil it one minute. Then put in three tablespoonfuls of cider vinegar, one tablespoonful of chopped green parsley leaves, two teaspoonfuls of salt, one pinch of pepper and the beets. When they have simmered fifteen minutes turn them carefully without breaking them and let them simmer slowly fifteen minutes longer.

TOMATOES, STEWED.

One quarter of a peck of tomatoes, not over ripe, pink color, three large white skinned onions, peeled sliced and cut up, two tablespoonfuls of fresh butter, one tablespoonful of white granulated sugar, two teaspoonfuls of salt, one pinch of pepper, one pint of bread cut up fine (measured after it is cut,) put the onions into a large deep skillet with half a pint of water and cook them twenty minutes; scald the tomatoes, peel, cut them up and put them in with the onions; then put in the butter, sugar, salt and pepper and let them cook thirty minutes. Then put in the bread and let it cook thirty minutes longer. Tomatoes without the onions, prepared in the same manner as in the preceding receipt, are very good.

CURLED SAVOY CABBAGE.

Take four small heads of savoy cabbage, remove the outside leaves, cut them in halves, wash them in cold water and put them into a saucepan with cold water enough to cover them that has one tablespoonful of salt in it, and boil them three hours. Then put them into a colander to drain and mix two large spoonfuls of fresh butter with two teaspoonfuls of flour and put it into a large deep frying pan with three large spoonfuls of hot water, or beef broth is better; then put in the cabbage, cut side down, and let it simmer fifteen minutes; then turn it and with a spoon pour the butter over it and let it simmer fifteen minutes longer.

LIMA BEANS.

Take one quart of young lima beans, wash them in cold water and put them into a stew pan with cold water enough to cover them, and cook them two hours; then put in two teaspoonfuls of salt, half a pint of rich, sweet milk, and two tablespoonfuls of fresh butter, with two teaspoonfuls of flour mixed with it, and let them simmer slowly for thirty minutes longer. The beans must not be broken when done.

BEANS STEWED. (Marrowfat.)

Some persons prefer dried beans cooked in this way: After one quart of beans have been picked and washed, put them into a pot with two quarts of cold water, four ounces of fresh butter, and two teaspoonfuls of salt, and cook them slowly three hours; if the water boils down, replenish with a little boiling water. The beans must be whole and almost dry when done. If soup is making at the same time, put a few spoonfuls from the top of the soup in with the beans; in that case, it will take a little less butter. One pint of beans is enough for a small family.

RED CABBAGE STEWED.

Take two small firm heads of dark red cabbage and remove the outside leaves and stalks and cut it in halves, wash it, cut it fine with the cabbage cutter, then wash it again in cold water and put it into a colander to drain. Now mix two tablespoonfuls of fresh butter with two teaspoonfuls of flour and put it into a large deep skillet and let it boil one minute, then put in half a pint of boiling water, two teaspoonfuls of salt and the cabbage, cover it and when it has cooked thirty minutes put in three large spoonfuls of cider vinegar, then take half a cup full of rich sweet milk and the yolks of three fresh eggs well beaten together and stir them in and let it simmer slowly thirty minutes longer. It must be almost dry when it is lifted.

SUGAR CORN TO BOIL.

Take young sugar corn that is in the milk, husk and silk it and remove the blemishes, then put it into a pot of boiling water and after it begins to boil again let it boil just five minutes, then take it out immediately. If it boils longer it will become hard and lose its sweetness.

SUGAR CORN, STEWED.

Put half a pint of rich sweet milk into a saucepan and set it over the fire to boil. Take one dozen ears of young sugar corn that is in the milk, cut it off the cob and put it into the boiling milk with one tablespoonful of white granulated sugar and one teaspoonful of salt, then mix two tablespoonfuls of fresh butter with two teaspoonfuls of flour, and stir it into the corn. When it begins to boil again after the butter is in, let it boil just five minutes.

CORN OYSTERS.

Take one dozen ears of young sugar corn that is in the milk and grate it off the cob into a pan, then mix with the grated corn one tablespoonful of flour and one teaspoonful of salt, then add the yolks of five fresh eggs and beat the whole mixture together. Have ready on the fire a frying pan in which you have put equal proportions of fresh butter and fresh lard, and when it is hot enough to brown, put in the mixture the size of an oyster and not quite half an inch thick. Fry them on both sides a golden brown and send them to table in a hot chafing-dish. They are very similar in taste to oysters and make a nice breakfast or supper dish.

STRING BEANS, YELLOW WAX.

Take one quarter of a peck of yellow wax beans, string them with a knife, break them in two, throw them into cold water and let them remain in it half an hour, then wash them and put them into a saucepan with cold water enough to cover them and boil them slowly three hours. If the water boils down too low, replenish with boiling water. When the beans have boiled two hours mix two tablespoonfuls of fresh butter with two teaspoonfuls of flour and stir it in with the beans, then add one teaspoonful of salt and cook them slowly one hour longer, or until they are very soft. The water should be boiled down low before they are lifted. Half a pint of beef broth adds very much to the taste.

SUCCOTASH, STRING BEANS AND CORN.

The beans are prepared in the same manner and cooked the same length of time as in the preceding receipt. Cut the corn off of six ears of sugar corn that is in the milk and stir it in with the beans, then put in one more tablespoonful of fresh butter with one teaspoonful of flour mixed with it and one salt spoonful of salt and let it boil five minutes from the time it begins to boil again after the corn is put in.

STEWED CARROTS.

Take one dozen and a half of full grown carrots, scrape them and split them lengthwise from the top down, then cross split them the size of the prong of a dinner fork and cut them off an inch long; wash them in cold water and put them into a stew pan with cold water enough to cover them and boil them two hours. If the water boils down too low replenish with boiling water. When the carrots have boiled two hours put in one tablespoonful of chopped green parsley leaves, one tablespoonful of white granulated sugar and two teaspoonfuls of salt, then mix two tablespoonfuls of fresh butter with two teaspoonfuls of flour, and stir it in and let it cook slowly thirty minutes longer. They should be almost dry before they are lifted. A few spoonfuls of beef broth adds very much to the taste. This is the best way to cook carrots. Red carrots are sweeter than yellow ones and don't require any sugar.

STEWED PARSNIPS.

Parsnips prepared in the same manner as in the preceding receipt are excellent. Only they require one more tablespoonful of butter.

ONIONS, STEWED.

Peel one quarter of a peck of white skinned onions that are of equal size, wash them and put them into a stew pan with cold water enough to cover them, and boil them one hour. Then mix together two tablespoonfuls of fresh butter and two teaspoonfuls of flour and stir it in with the onions. Then put in one gill of rich sweet milk, two teaspoonfuls of salt and half a teaspoonful of pepper, and let them simmer slowly thirty minutes longer.

LEEKS.

are prepared in the same manner and cooked the same length of time as onions.

PARSNIPS, FRIED.

Select parsnips that are of equal size and not too large; after they are scraped and washed, split them lengthwise in halves and put them into boiling water that has a little salt in it and boil them two hours, or until they are very tender, (the length of time depends on the size of the parsnips) then take them out and let them drain. Put one large spoonful of fresh butter and one of fresh lard into a large frying pan and when it is hot enough to brown lay in the parsnips, cut side down, brown them on both sides and leave them in the frying pan until ready to serve.

PARSNIP CAKES.

One quart of mashed parsnips, two tablespoonfuls of fresh butter, one teaspoonful of salt, one quarter of a teaspoonful of pepper. Scrape the parsnips and boil them until they are soft, then mash them, and while they are warm put in the butter, salt and pepper, mix it well together, then make it into cakes three quarters of an inch thick. Have ready on the fire a frying pan with equal quantities of fresh butter and fresh lard, and when it is hot enough to brown, lay in the cakes and brown them well on both sides.

SAUR KRAUT, HOW TO MAKE IT.

The Dutch flat head cabbage makes the best saurkraut and a lard barrel is the best to make it in. The barrel should be cleaned and filled with hot water two or three days before it is used. It takes one hundred heads of cabbage and two quarts and one pint of salt to make a large barrel full of saurkraut. Trim off all the outside leaves of the cabbage until you come to the white part, then cut off the coarse ribs and take out the stalk. It must be done carefully by an experienced kraut cutter. I have a very nice German woman who makes it for me every year. The cutting machine is placed over a clean tub and the cut cabbage falls into it. Then put a layer of cut cabbage about one inch deep into the barrel, with a handful of salt sprinkled over it, and pound it with a long handled wooden beetle that has two cross pieces as wide as your hand fastened onto the end of it. Pound it for a few minutes until the cabbage is wet, then put in another layer of cabbage with salt, and so on, until you have the barrel as full as you want it. Then take some of the best whole cabbage leaves, wash them in cold water and place them over the saurkraut Then take one half of a linen tablecloth that is out of use, double it, wring it out of cold water, put it over the cabbage leaves and tuck it down all around the sides of the barrel. Then put on the head of the barrel which has been made small enough to fit inside, lay two cross pieces on top and put on two or three large stones for weights. The water must stand half an inch deep on the boards after the stones are put on. Two weeks after it is made take all the water out, remove the weights, boards, cloth and leaves, wash them in cold water and replace them just as they were before; then put in sufficient water (that has a little salt in it,) to cover the boards half an inch deep. The saurkraut will be ready to use in three or four weeks from the time it is made. Every time the kraut is taken out of the barrel the things on top must be washed clean and replaced again with salt and water half an inch deep over the boards. Saurkraut that is made and kept in this manner has a different look and taste from what you get in the market.

SAURKRAUT, HOW TO COOK.

Put two quarts of saurkraut into a colander and set the colander into a pan of cold water and stir it half a minute, (it must not be longer in the water) then take it out and drain off the water; take one large spoonful of fresh lard and one tablespoonful of flour, mix together and put it into a stew pan and let it boil one minute, then put in half a pint of hot water, the saurkraut, and as much more hot water as will cover it. When it has boiled one hour put in half a pound of fat pickled pork in the center and down on the bottom of the stew pan, cook the saurkraut two hours and a half, and if the water boils down too low replenish with boiling water, but there must be very little water in it when it is done. It is very good warmed over and makes nice salad when cold.

SAURKRAUT WITH FRESH PORK SPARE-RIBS. (THIS IS THE BEST WAY.)

Take three or four pounds of pork spare-ribs, wash them and cut them in pieces large enough to lay flat in the stew pan, cover them with water and cook them three quarters of an hour, then take them out and mix one tablespoonful of fresh lard with one tablespoonful of flour and stir it into the water that the ribs were cooked in; after the kraut, has been washed in cold water and drained, put it into the stew pan and lay the pork ribs on top. If there is not water enough in the stew pan to cover the kraut add a sufficient quantity of hot water cover the stew pan and cook the saurkraut two hours and a half. Before lifting put in salt to the taste and at table serve the spare-ribs with the saurkraut.

BOILED CABBAGE.

The best boiled cabbage is cooked with a brisket piece of sugar cured corned beef, and the best cabbage to cook is the dutch flat head. Take the smallest heads, trim off the outside leaves, cut the cabbage in two in the middle and put it into cold water for half an hour, then turn the cut side down and shake it up and down in the water to get out the sand; then put it into the pot with the corned beef and cold water enough to cover it and when it begins to boil skim it, cover the pot and boil it slowly three hours. If the water boils down too fast replenish with boiling water. The water must be boiled down low just before the cabbage is lifted.

HOT SLAW.

Two quarts of cut cabbage prepared in the following manner: Mix one tablespoonful of fresh butter with one teaspoonful of flour, and put it into a skillet and let it fry one minute, then put in one gill of cider vinegar, half a teaspoonful of salt, a quarter of a teaspoonful of pepper and one teaspoonful of my made mustard. Let it get hot, but not boil, then beat the yolks of three fresh eggs with one gill of rich sweet milk, and stir it in with the other ingredients; stir it until the egg thickens, but not to boil, then put in the cabbage and stir it until the cabbage is hot, then lift.

TURNIPS.

Pare one quarter of a peck of turnips and chip them up in thin pieces as you do apples for sauce or pies, and put them into cold water; put two tablespoonfuls of fresh butter mixed with two teaspoonfuls of flour into a saucepan and let it boil one minute, then put in the turnips with hot water enough to cover them, then two teaspoonfuls of salt. Half a pint of beef broth adds very much to the taste. If the water boils down too low replenish with boiling water; cook them slowly two hours and a half. They must be almost dry when they are done. This is the best way to cook turnips; they retain all their flavor.

Pastry, Pies and Tarts.

PUFF PASTE.

One pound of fresh butter, the salt washed out of half of it, one pound of sifted flour, with two teaspoonfuls of baking powder mixed in it, half a pint of cold water, ice cold; divide half a pound of the butter into three parts and have it soft enough to spread; mix the baking powder with the flour and rub in the half pound of butter without salt, then make it into a stiff dough and roll it out long and square at the ends, then spread on one third of the butter and set it in the coldest place, where the butter will harden in fifteen minutes, then fold over one third of the dough and turn the other on top of it, roll out again, spread on the butter, fold over and repeat the same until the butter is all in, then divide the dough into as many parts as are needed and roll out quickly. The dough must not be worked with the hands after the first butter is spread on. To be successful with puff paste in the summer time it must be made in a cool room, and mixed with ice water and rolled out on a marble slab. After the butter has been spread on put some broken ice into a long tinpan and place it over the butter, but not near enough to touch it.

PUFF PASTE.

One pound of sifted flour, with two teaspoonfuls of baking powder in it; half a pound of fresh lard, half a pint of cold water—ice cold—half a pound of fresh butter, divided into three parts and soft enough to spread. Mix the baking powder and flour together, then rub in the lard and make it into a stiff dough; roll it out long and square at the ends and spread on one-third of the butter, set in a cold place until the butter is hard, then fold over one-third of the dough and turn the other on top of it; roll out again and repeat the same until the butter is all in, then fold over, roll out quick and divide the dough into as many crusts as you want to make. The dough must not be worked after the first butter is spread on. I have made the two preceding receipts of puff paste on the same day, and the one made with half lard and half butter was the best.

PIE CRUST.

Two pounds of sifted flour, with four teaspoonfuls of baking powder in it, half a pound of fresh butter, three quarters of a pound of fresh lard, one pint, scant measure, of cold water; mix the baking powder and flour together, then rub in the butter and lard and make it into a dough just stiff enough to roll out. The quicker it is made and put into the oven the lighter and better it will be. This quantity is enough for five or six pies with lower and upper crusts. This is a very good pie crust and much more economical than puff paste.

APPLES FOR PIES.

Two quarts of sliced sour apples (pippins are the best,) half a pint of water, half a pint of sugar, two ounces of fresh butter, two tablespoonfuls of corn-starch, two teaspoonfuls of powdered cinnamon or lemon extract, put the apples and water into a saucepan and cook them until they are soft then put in the sugar and mix the corn-starch with a little cold water and stir it in, stir until it boils two minutes, then add the butter and spice and take it off the fire.

PEACHES FOR PIES.

Peaches for pies should have one quarter of a pound of sugar to one pound of peaches. Peel the peaches, quarter them and half quarter them, then put them into a saucepan with the sugar and very little water and cook them five minutes, or until they are soft, but not broken.

PEACH PIE.

Butter a deep tin pie plate and line it with puff paste then put in a layer of peaches and cover it with puff paste and bake it a light brown, then take it out of the oven and put in another layer of peaches and cover again with puff paste and bake again a light brown. It is excellent served with sweetened cream, but also good without it.

APPLE PIE

made in the same manner as in the preceding receipt is excellent.

CRANBERRY PIE.

After the cranberries are picked and washed, measure them. To one quart of cranberries allow one pint of cold water; put them into a porcelain saucepan and boil them fifteen minutes, stir them constantly with a wooden spoon until done, then measure them, and to one pint of the cooked cranberries put one pint of white granulated sugar and cook them together two minutes, then take it off the fire to cool. Butter the pie plates, line them with puff paste and put in the cranberries, cut some of the puff paste into narrow strips and lay them in cross-bars over the top of the pie.

CURD PIE.

One pint of curds after the whey has been strained out, one pinch of salt, half a pint of thick sweet cream, two tablespoonfuls of white granulated sugar, three fresh eggs beaten separately, half a pint of raspberry syrup. Put the curds, salt and cream into a bowl and rub them together with the back of a spoon against the side of the bowl until they are perfectly smooth, beat the yolks and sugar together and stir them into the curds, then stir in the raspberry syrup and beat the whites with two teaspoonfuls of white sugar to a stiff foam and stir them in last. Put it into a deep tin pie plate that has been buttered and lined with puff paste and bake about twenty minutes.

CUSTARD PIE.

One pint of rich sweet milk, one tablespoonful of corn-starch, three tablespoonfuls of white granulated sugar, three fresh eggs beaten separately, one pinch of salt, one easpoonful of vanilla extract or cinnamon; mix the corn starch with a little of the cold milk and stir it into the milk, beat the yolks and sugar together and stir them in, then beat the whites with two teaspoonfuls of white sugar to a stiff foam and stir them in, then add the salt and vanilla. Butter a deep tin pie plate, line it with puff paste, put in the custard and bake a light brown.

CURRANTS TO WASH.

Dried currants have always more or less sand mixed with them, and in order to get it out they must be treated in the following manner: Put the currants into a large pan full of cold or tepid water, make them all loose and rub them gently through the hands as quickly as possible, then pour off the water with all that floats on top, then fill two pans with clean, cold water, and put a small quantity of the currants at a time into a wire sieve and shake it up and down in the water. When they come out of the last water put them into an iron baking pan and set them into a moderate oven to dry, stir them from time to time, and when the water has all dried off take them out, they must not stay in the oven until they are hard; now pick them over carefully, for they may have some small stones among them.

LEMON PIE.

One large lemon, one pint of rich sweet milk, one pinch of salt, one tablespoonful of corn-starch, four tablespoonfuls of white granulated sugar, three fresh eggs beaten separately. Grate off the yellow skin of the lemon (that contains the oil flavoring) then peel off the white skin that is always bitter, then grate the lemon and take out the seeds. Put the milk and salt into a saucepan and set it into a pan of boiling water over the fire. Mix the corn-starch with a little cold milk and stir it in; stir it until it boils two minutes then take it off the fire, beat the yolks and sugar together and stir them in, then add the grated peel and lemon, beat the whites with two teaspoonfuls of white sugar to a stiff foam and stir them in last. Put it into a deep tin pie plate that has been buttered and lined with puff paste, and bake a light brown. It takes about twenty minutes.

MINCE MEAT.

Two pounds of beef, weighed after it is cooked and the fat, gristle and strings taken out, one pound of beef suet, weighed after it is broken up and string taken out, four pounds of apples, weighed after they are peeled and sliced, six pounds of currants, weighed after they are washed and dried, one pound of citron cut in small pieces, six pounds of white granulated sugar, four large nutmegs grated fine, two tablespoonfuls of powdered mace, two tablespoonfuls of powdered cinnamon, four large lemons grated, peel, pulp and juice, one gallon and one quart of sweet cider and one quart of brandy. Cook five pounds of lean beef five hours the day before you intend to make mince meat, it shrinks very much in cooking. Wash, dry and pick eight pounds of currants the day before they are to be used. They lose in weight by washing and picking. Mix the mince meat in a porcelain kettle, after the fat, skin and strings have been removed from the meat, pick it to pieces, weigh it, chop it up very fine and put it into the kettle, break up the suet, take out the strings, chop it up very fine and mix it with the meat. After the apples are peeled, sliced and weighed, chop them fine and put them in with the meat, weigh the currants and put them in with the meat, then put in the citron, lemon and spices and mix them well together, then put in the cider and brandy and set the kettle over the fire and let it cook five minutes, then put it hot into glass jars hermetically sealed, with a tablespoonful of hot brandy in the neck of each jar. This mince meat will keep a year.

PUMPKIN OR SQUASH PIE.

A striped long necked winter squash makes the best pies. Cut it in rings half an inch wide; take out the inside, peel off the skin and cut it up in thin chips, as you do apples for pies. Then put into a saucepan with half a pint of cold water and cook it over a slow fire until it is very soft and the water is all boiled down, then press it through a wire sieve and measure to it, one quart of pumpkin or squash, one quart of rich sweet milk, ten fresh eggs, beaten separately, twelve ounces of white granulated sugar, two teaspoonfuls of powdered cinnamon, two teaspoonfuls of grated nutmeg, one tablespoonful of ginger, two teaspoonfuls of salt. Mix the pumpkin, spices and salt together, beat the yolks and sugar together and stir them into the pumpkin, then stir in the milk and beat the whites with two tablespoonfuls of white sugar to a stiff foam and stir them in last. Put it into deep tin pie plates that have been buttered and lined with puff paste and bake a light brown. It takes about thirty minutes.

Puddings and Fritters.

ALMOND PUDDING.

Three ounces of almonds, blanched and ground fine in the mortar, with a spoonful of cold milk, one pint of rich sweet milk, two ounces of fresh butter, six ounces of white granulated sugar, five fresh eggs, beaten separately, six ounces of crushed double baked rusk or stale bread crumbs made fine, one teaspoonful of lemon extract, two teaspoonfuls of rose extract. Put the milk, almonds and butter into a saucepan over the fire and let it get warm enough to melt the butter, then take it off the fire and heat the yolks and sugar together and stir them in; then stir in the rusk and the flavoring, beat the whites with one tablespoonful of sugar to a stiff foam and stir them in last. Put it quickly into a pudding pan and set it into a pan in the oven containing boiling water and bake twenty minutes.

APPLE AND RICE PUDDING.

One pint of boiled rice, half a pint of grated apples, pippins or bellflowers, are the best; one pint of rich sweet milk, one pinch of salt, one tablespoonful of corn starch, four fresh eggs beaten separately, four tablespoonfuls of white granulated sugar, three ounces of fresh butter, two teaspoonfuls of the extract of lemon, one gill of sherry wine. First cook the rice, every grain should be separate, then measure it, peel and grate the apples, then measure them and mix two tablespoonfuls of sugar with them, beat the yolks with four tablespoonfuls of sugar and the whites with one tablespoonful to a stiff foam. Put the milk and salt into a saucepan and set it into another containing boiling water, when the milk is hot mix the corn starch with a little cold milk and stir it in, let it come to a boil, then stir in the yolks, butter, rice and apples, then take it off the fire and put in the lemon, wine and the whites last. Put it into the pudding pan, set it into another containing a little boiling water and bake it forty minutes.

APPLE DUMPLINGS.

Take sour apples of one size, peel them, take out the cores, leaving the apples whole, and fill the opening with brown sugar, then take rich pie crust (which you will find under pastry) and roll it out a quarter of an inch thick and cut it into squares, then put in the apples and close up the paste tight. Put them into a steamer and steam them half an hour, or until the apples are soft. Serve with hard sauce or custard sauce.

BATTER PUDDING.

Four ounces of fresh butter, six ounces of sifted flour, half a pint of rich sweet milk, six fresh eggs, beaten separately, four ounces of white granulated sugar, two teaspoonfuls of lemon extract, two ounces of crushed double baked rusk or bread crumbs, two teaspoonfuls of baking powder. Put the milk and butter over the fire and when the butter is melted stir in the flour, stir it until it is smooth batter and scalded through; then take it off the fire, beat the yolks with a spoonful of cold milk and stir them in, then put in the sugar, lemon, rusk and baking powder, beat the whites with one tablespoonful of white sugar to a stiff foam and stir them in last, set the pudding pan into a pan in the oven containing boiling water, and bake one hour. Serve with a sherry wine sauce or fruit sauce.

BREAD AND BUTTER PUDDING.

Four ounces of stale bread, weighed after it is cut in thin slices and the crust taken off, four ounces of fresh butter soft enough to spread, raspberry marmalade enough to spread half of the bread, one pint of rich sweet milk, four ounces of white granulated sugar, two teaspoonfuls of corn starch, six fresh eggs beaten separately, one teaspoonful of grated nutmeg, four tablespoonfuls of brandy. Butter all of the bread, then spread half of the slices with raspberry marmalade and lay the other half on top like sandwiches, then cut them with a sharp knife in pieces an inch square. Put the milk, sugar and butter that is left from the bread over the fire and when it is hot mix the corn starch with a little cold milk and stir it in, stir it until it boils two minutes, then take it off the fire. Beat the yolks and stir them in, set it over the fire again until the eggs thicken, but must not boil, then pour it into the pudding pan and stir in the nutmeg and brandy, beat the whites with one tablespoonful of white sugar to a stiff foam and stir them in, then put in the bread, carefully covering every piece with the custard, set it in a pan of boiling water in the oven and bake twenty minutes.

BREAD PUDDING.

One pint of rich sweet milk, four ounces of fresh butter, four ounces of white granulated sugar, six fresh eggs beaten together, two teaspoonfuls of vanilla extract, four tablespoonfuls of brandy and four ounces of stale bread, weighed after it is cut in slices and the crust taken off. Make the milk warm, but not scalding hot, beat the butter and sugar together to a cream and stir it into the milk, then take it off the fire and beat the eggs all together with one tablespoonful of white sugar and stir them in, then put in the vanilla and brandy, cut the bread into pieces half an inch square and stir them in last. Set the pudding pan into the oven in a pan of boiling water and bake fifteen or twenty minutes.

COCOANUT PUDDING.

One quart of rich sweet milk, six ounces of grated cocoanut weighed after it is grated, four ounces of fresh butter, twelve ounces of white granulated sugar, ten fresh eggs, beaten separately, twelve ounces of crushed double baked rusk or stale bread crumbs made fine, two teaspoonfuls of lemon extract, three teaspoonfuls of rose extract. Take out two even tablespoonfuls of the sugar to beat with the whites, and they will beat easier with a machine egg beater if put into two bowls instead of one. Put the milk, cocoanut and butter into a saucepan over the fire and let it get warm enough to melt the butter, then take it off and beat the yolks and sugar together and stir them in, then stir in the rusk and flavoring, beat the whites to a stiff foam and stir them in last. Put it quickly into a pudding pan and set it into a pan of boiling water in the oven and bake forty-five minutes.

CORN STARCH PUDDING, BOILED.

One pint and a half of rich sweet milk, four tablespoonfuls of white granulated sugar, two teaspoonfuls of lemon extract, one pinch of salt, two heaped tablespoonfuls of corn starch, one tablespoonful of fresh butter and three fresh eggs beaten together. Put the milk, sugar, lemon and salt into a porcelain saucepan over the fire; mix the corn starch with a little cold milk or water and when the milk is scalding hot stir in the corn starch, stir it until it has boiled four minutes, then set it on the side of the fire, where it will not boil. Beat the eggs all together and stir them in, then set it over the fire again till the eggs are set, then stir in the butter and pour the pudding into a porcelain mold, or what is still prettier, put it into small porcelain molds just large enough for one person. Serve it with a wine sauce, custard sauce or fruit sauce. This pudding is excellent, warm or cold.

CORN STARCH PUDDING, BAKED.

One pint of rich sweet milk, five tablespoonfuls of white granulated sugar, two tablespoonfuls of corn starch, one pinch of salt, six fresh eggs, beaten separately, three ounces of fresh butter, one teaspoonful of cinnamon and three tablespoonfuls of brandy. When the milk and sugar are hot mix the corn starch and salt with a little cold milk or water and stir it in; stir it until it boils three minutes, then take it off the fire and put in the butter and cinnamon, beat the yolks with a spoonful of cold milk and stir them in. Then beat the whites with one tablespoonful of white sugar to a stiff foam and stir them in. Then add three tablespoonfuls of brandy, set the pudding pan into a low iron pan containing a little hot water and bake half an hour.

EGG PUDDING (GERMAN EIERKÄSE.)

One quart of rich sweet milk, twelve fresh eggs, beaten together, two teaspoonfuls of vanilla extract, one teaspoonful of salt. Put the milk, vanilla and salt into a porcelain saucepan, beat the eggs well together and stir them into the milk, then set the saucepan into a pan of boiling water over a slow fire and stir it until it is thick enough to drop from the spoon, but it must not boil or it will curdle. It takes about fifteen minutes to be done. Then pour it into a tin mold that is pierced with holes to let out the whey. Set it over a stone crock, turn a wire sieve over it, put a paper over it and let the pudding stand four or five hours. When it is to be served put a china or glass plate over it and turn it out. Serve with a vanilla, fruit or wine sauce.

FARINA PUDDING.

One pint of rich sweet milk, one pinch of salt, four tablespoonfuls of farina, four tablespoonfuls of white granulated sugar, three ounces of fresh butter, six fresh eggs beaten separately, one teaspoonful of cinnamon, one teaspoonful of lemon extract, four tablespoonfuls of brandy. Put the milk and salt into a saucepan and set it into a pan over the fire, containing boiling water, when the milk is boiling hot mix the farina with a little cold water and stir it in, stir it constantly, and boil it five minutes, then put in the butter and sugar and set it off the fire, beat the yolks and stir them in, then put in the cinnamon, lemon and brandy, beat the whites with one tablespoonful of white sugar to a stiff foam and stir them in last. Put it into a pudding pan and set it into the oven in a pan of boiling water and bake thirty minutes.

FRUIT PUDDING.

Half a pint of rich sweet milk warm, but not hot, two ounces of fresh butter melted in the milk, four fresh eggs beaten separately, four ounces of sifted flour, two tablespoonfuls of white granulated sugar, five ounces of stale bread, weighed after the crust is taken off and into bread crumbs, four ounces of currants, weighed after they have been washed and dried, one teaspoonful of grated nutmeg, half a teaspoonful of salt, two teaspoonfuls of baking powder and three tablespoonfuls of brandy. Put the yolks into a pan and stir in half the milk and butter, then stir in the flour and beat it together till it is a smooth batter, then put in the other half of the milk and the sugar, then put in the bread crumbs and the currants; mix it well together and then put in the nutmeg, salt, baking powder and brandy, beat the whites with one tablespoonful of white sugar to a stiff foam and stir them in. Put it into a tin buttered mold that closes tight, set it into a saucepan cantaining boiling water, close it to keep the steam in and boil it constantly two hours. If the water boils down too low replenish with boiling water. Serve with wine sauce.

MARMALADE CRACKER PUDDING.

Five Boston crackers broken up in small pieces and soaked very soft in half a pint of boiled sweet milk, half a pint of raspberry marmalade, one pint of rich sweet milk, three ounces of fresh butter, four tablespoonfuls of white granulated sugar, five fresh eggs beaten separately, one teaspoonful of cinnamon and three tablespoonfuls of brandy. Put a layer of soaked cracker and a layer of marmalade into the pudding pan until all are in, let the milk come to a boil then take it off the fire and put the butter into it, put the yolks, sugar add cinnamon into a large bowl and beat them well together, then stir into them the hot milk, and then add the brandy; beat the whites with one tablespoonful of white sugar to a stiff foam and stir them in the bowl, then put it into the pudding pan with a large spoon or a small ladle and set it into a pan in the oven containing boiling water. Bake three quarters of an hour.

PEACH PUDDING.

Four ounces of rice, one pint of rich sweet milk, two ounces of white granulated sugar, three ounces of fresh butter, four fresh eggs, beaten separately, two teaspoonfuls of vanilla extract and one pint of canned peaches. Pick and wash the rice and put it into a tin saucepan with as much cold water as there is rice; set the saucepan into a pan of boiling water and cook the rice half an hour; then let it dry off and stir it up with a fork. Every kernel should be separate. Put the milk and sugar into a saucepan and set it into a pan of boiling water over the fire; beat the yolks with a spoonful of cold milk and stir them into the hot milk, stir it until the eggs thicken, but it must not boil; then put in the butter and vanilla and take it off the fire to cool five minutes before the whites are put in. Beat the whites with one tablespoonful of white sugar to a stiff foam and stir them in. Then stir in the rice. Now put a layer of rice custard and a layer of peaches into the pudding pan until all are in, finishing with the rice custard. Set it into an iron pan in the oven containing a little boiling water and bake thirty minutes.

PLUM-PUDDING, BAKED.

Six fresh eggs beaten separately, six ounces of white granulated sugar, three gills of rich sweet milk, six ounces of sifted flour, four ounces of beef suet chopped fine, eight ounces of crushed double baked rusk or dry stale bread crumbs, one even teaspoonful of salt, one grated nutmeg, one gill of sherry wine, six ounces of seedless or stoned raisins, six ounces of currants, after they have been washed and dried, four ounces of citron cut as fine as paper, three teaspoonfuls of baking powder. Beat the yolks and sugar together until very light, warm the milk and stir half of it into the yolks and sugar, then stir in the flour until it is a smooth batter, then put in the other half of the milk and add the suet, bread crumbs and salt; then add the nutmeg, wine and baking powder and then stir in the raisins, currants and citron; beat the whites with one tablespoonful of white sugar to a stiff foam and stir them in last. Mix it well together and put it quickly into a well buttered pudding pan and set it into a pan of boiling water in the oven and bake one hour. The oven should be hotter in the bottom than on top. Serve with a wine fruit or custard sauce.

PLUM-PUDDING, BOILED.

Half a pint of rich sweet milk, six fresh eggs, beaten separately, four ounces of white granulated sugar, four ounces of sifted flour, four ounces of beef suet chopped very fine, six ounces of stale bread crumbs stirred in dry, four ounces of stoned raisins, four ounces of currants weighed after they have been washed and dried, two ounces of citron cut as thin as paper, one grated nutmeg, half a teaspoonful of salt, two teaspoonfuls of baking powder, four tablespoonfuls of brandy. Warm the milk, beat the yolks and sugar together and then stir in half of the milk; then stir in the flour and mix it into a smooth batter, then add the other half of the milk, then put in the suet and bread crumbs and then add the fruit. Mix it well together and then stir in the nutmeg, salt, baking powder and brandy. Beat the whites with one tablespoonful of white sugar to a stiff foam and stir them in last. Put the pudding into a tin buttered mold, leaving room for it to rise; put it into boiling water and boil it two hours. The water should not be deep enough to float the mold. If the water boils down too low replenish with boiling water. Keep the saucepan or pot covered to keep in the steam. Serve with a wine sauce.

PRUNE PUDDING.

One pound of dried prunes, one gill of oat meal groats, one pint of rich sweet milk, four tablespoonfuls of white granulated sugar, one teaspoonful of cinnamon, one pinch of salt, five fresh eggs beaten separately and two tablespoonfuls of crushed double baked rusk. Wash the prunes, put them into a saucepan with cold water enough to cover them and cook them until they are soft, but not to break. Fifteen minutes before they are done put in three tablespoonfuls of white sugar; pick the oat groats, wash them in cold water and put them into a saucepan with half a pint of cold water and set them into a pan of boiling water over the fire and cook them three quarters of an hour; put the milk, sugar, cinnamon and salt into a saucepan over the fire; beat the yolks with a spoonful of cold milk and stir them into the warm milk, stir it until it thickens, but it must not boil, then stir in the warm oat meal, rusk and prunes and take it off the fire. Beat the whites with two teaspoonfuls of white sugar to a stiff foam and stir them in last. Serve warm, without sauce.

QUINCE TAPIOCA PUDDING.

Four ounces of tapioca soaked until soft in half a pint of cold water, one pint of canned quinces without the syrup, one pint of rich sweet milk, three tablespoonfuls of white granulated sugar, two ounces of fresh butter and four fresh eggs. Put the tapioca into a colander and let cold water run over it before putting it to soak. Boil the soaked tapioca in the milk until it is all dissolved. It takes from ten to fifteen minutes and must be stirred constantly. Then put in the sugar and butter, beat the eggs together, stir them in and when they are set move the saucepan to the side of the range, cut the quinces up fine then put a layer of tapioca into the pudding pan, then a layer of quinces and so on, until all are in, finishing with the tapioca. Set it into a pan in the oven containing a little boiling water and bake twenty minutes. Serve with a quince syrup sauce, made in the following manner:

SAUCE.

Put half a pint of quince syrup with two tablespoonfuls of white sugar into a saucepan and when it is hot mix one even teaspoonful of corn starch with a little cold milk and stir it in; stir it until it boils a minute then take it off the fire. Beat the yolks of two eggs with a spoonful of cold milk and stir them in. Set it over the fire again until the eggs are set, then take it off and stir in two tablespoonfuls of brandy; beat the whites with one teaspoonful of white sugar to a stiff foam and stir them in last.

RICE FLOUR PUDDING.

Four ounces of rice flour. one pint and a half of

rich sweet milk, four ounces of white granulated sugar, two teaspoonfuls of lemon extract, one pinch of salt. Put one pint of the milk, the sugar, lemon and salt into a saucepan, and set it into a pan of boiling water over the fire. Mix the rice flour and the half pint of milk together. When the milk is hot in the saucepan stir in the rice flour and milk, stir it constantly until it is thick and has boiled about fifteen minutes. Then pour it into a porcelain mold that has been dipped in cold water, and when it has cooled, turn it out. Serve with a milk sauce.

RICE PUDDING.

Three quarters of a pint of boiled rice, one pint and a half of rich sweet milk, one pinch of salt, one tablespoonful of corn starch, four ounces of butter, five fresh eggs beaten separately, four ounces of white granulated sugar, one teaspoonful of cinnamon, and tree tablespoonfuls of brandy. Put the milk and salt into a saucepan, and set it into another one containing boiling water. Mix the corn starch with a little cold milk or water, and when the milk is hot stir it in. Stir it until it boils three minutes. Then take it off the fire and stir in the butter. Beat the yolks with the sugar, and stir them in. Then add the rice, cinnamon, and brandy. Beat the whites with one tablespoonful of sugar to a stiff foam, and stir them in. Put it into the pudding pan, set it into another pan containing a little hot water, and bake it half an hour.

RUSK PUDDING.

Six double baked rusks, one pint of rich sweet milk, two tablespoonfuls of white granulated sugar, one pinch of salt, three ounces of fresh butter, five fresh eggs beaten separately, and half a glass of raspberry jelly. Crush the rusk fine with a rolling pin; put the milk, sugar and salt over the fire, and let it get boiling hot. Then take it off, and put in the butter. Put the yolks and jelly into a large bowl, and beat them together. Then stir in slowly the milk. Beat the whites with one tablespoonful of white sugar to a stiff foam, and stir them in. Then put in the rusk, and mix it well together. Set the pudding pan into another pan containing boiling water, and bake half an hour.

SAGO PUDDING.

Three ounces of sago, one pint of rich sweet milk, two teaspoonfuls of corn starch, three tablespoonfuls of white granulated sugar, four fresh eggs beaten separately, two teaspoonfuls of lemon extract, and one pinch of salt. Wash the sago in cold water and put it into a bowl with half a pint of cold water to soak until soft. Then put the sago with the water it was soaked in, and the milk into a saucepan, and set it into a pan of boiling water and boil it until the sago is all dissolved and clear. It takes from fifteen to twenty minutes, and must be stirred constantly. Then put in the sugar, salt and lemon. Mix the corn starch with a little cold milk and stir it in; stir it until it boils two minutes. Then beat the yolks with a spoonful of cold milk and stir them in. Let them cook a minute, then take it off the fire and beat the whites with two teaspoonfuls of white sugar to a stiff foam and stir them in last. Put it into a porcelain mold that has been dipped in cold water, and when cold turn it out. Serve with a raspberry, strawberry, or wine sauce.

TAPIOCA PUDDING.

Three ounces of tapioca washed and soaked until very soft in half a pint of cold water, one pint of rich sweet milk, one pinch of salt, three tablespoonfuls of white granulated sugar, one tablespoonful of fresh butter, four fresh eggs beaten together, two teaspoonfuls of vanilla extract. Put the milk, salt and soaked tapioca into a saucepan and set it into another pan over the fire containing boiling water and boil it until the tapioca is all dissolved. It takes from fifteen to twenty minutes, and must be stirred constantly, then put in the sugar, butter and vanilla, beat the eggs well together with a little cold milk and stir them in, let them cook two minutes, then put the pudding into a porcelain mold that has been dipped in cold water and when the pudding is set turn it out. Serve with a fruit, custard or wine sauce.

BATTER FRITTERS.

One pint of sifted flour, two tablespoonfuls of baking powder, one pint of sweet milk, one tablespoonful of fresh butter, half a teaspoonful of salt, four fresh eggs beaten separately. Put the flour into a pan and set it into a pan containing warm water, put the milk, butter and salt over the fire and when the butter is melted take it off and stir one half of it into the flour, stir it until it is a smooth batter, then stir in the other half; beat the yolks and stir them in, then put in the baking powder and beat the whites with one tablespoonful of white sugar to a stiff foam, stir them in and fry immediately in hot lard. Serve with a wine sauce.

APPLE FRITTERS.

Can be made by the above directions, with the addition of ripe sour apples chopped fine. Serve with a hard sauce or a wine sauce.

BREAD FRITTERS.

Three fresh eggs, three tablespoonfuls of white granulated sugar, one teaspoonful of powdered cinnamon, one pint of rich sweet milk. Beat the eggs, sugar and cinnamon together, cut the bread in slices half an inch thick, then cut them in two in the middle and leave the crust on to keep them from breaking, then lay them into the custard and let them soak through. Have ready on the fire a frying pan with a large kitchen spoonful of fresh butter in it and when it is hot enough to brown lay the bread in carefully and fry it on both sides a light brown, turn and lift it with a cake turner. Make a sauce with the custard that is left, by adding a tablespoonful of sugar and a little wine. Serve it with a wine sauce.

Sweet Sauces for Puddings.

APPLE SAUCE.

One quart of sliced sour apples, (pippins are the best) one gill of water, one gill of white granulated sugar, one tablespoonful of fresh butter, two teaspoonfuls of corn starch, one teaspoonful of lemon or cinnamon extract. Put the apples and water into a saucepan and cook them until they are soft, then press them through a wire sieve and return them to the saucepan over the fire; now put in the sugar and butter, then mix the corn starch with a little cold water and stir it in, stir it until it boils three minutes, then take it off the fire and add the lemon or cinnamon according to taste. Anise seed is a fine flavoring for apple sauce.

APRICOTS FROM CALIFORNIA.

One pint of apricots, one quart of cold water, one pint of white granulated sugar. After the apricots are washed in cold water put them into a stew pan with cold water enough to cover them, and when it is scalding hot pour the water off, then put in the quart of cold water, and when it begins to boil cook them fifteen minutes, then put in the sugar and let them simmer fifteen minutes longer.

CRANBERRY SAUCE.

Pick the cranberries, wash them in cold water and pour off all that floats on top of the water, then put them into a colander to drain, and then measure them. To one quart of cranberries allow one pint of water; put them into a porcelain saucepan and boil them fifteen minutes, stir them constantly with a wooden spoon to prevent them from sticking; then press them through a wire sieve, all but the skins. Now measure them and to one pint of strained cranberries put one pint of white granulated sugar; mix it well together before putting it on the fire, as soon as it begins to boil skim it quickly and take it off the fire. It is done in two minutes.

BUTTER SAUCE.

Three ounces of butter, five tablespoonfuls of granulated sugar, half a pint of water, two teaspoonfuls of corn starch, one teaspoonful of powdered cinnamon, three tablespoonfuls of brandy. Put the sugar, water and cinnamon over the fire, and when boiling hot put in the butter and mix the corn starch with a little cold water and stir it in, let it boil two minutes, then take it off and stir in the brandy.

CHOCOLATE SAUCE.

Cut up two ounces of chocolate and cook it in half a pint of sweet milk until it is all dissolved, then put in half a pint of sweet cream, four tablespoonfuls of white granulated sugar and one teaspoonful of the extract of vanilla; beat the yolks of two eggs with a little cold milk and stir them in, stir it until it is thick, but it must not boil; then take it off the fire and beat the whites with a teaspoonful of sugar to a stiff foam and stir them in.

CIDER SAUCE. (Very Good.)

Half a pint of cider, (Siberian crab apple is the best,) four tablespoonfuls of white granulated sugar, two fresh eggs beaten separately, one teaspoonful of flour mixed with two teaspoonfuls of cold water, two teaspoonfuls of lemon extract. Put the cider, sugar and lemon into a saucepan and set it on the side of the range where it will get warm but not hot. Beat the whites with one teaspoonful of white sugar to a stiff foam, then beat the yolks and flour together and stir them into the whites. Then stir them quickly into the cider, and set it over a quick fire; stir it fast until it begins to rise (it must not boil) then take it quickly from the fire, pour it into a sauce tureen and stir it a minute until the foam goes down a little. This sauce when made with Siberian crab apple cider is equal if not superior to any wine sauce.

CUSTARD SAUCE. (Very Fine.)

One pint of rich sweet milk, four tablespoonfuls of white granulated sugar, one tablespoonful of corn starch, four fresh eggs beaten separately, two teaspoonfuls of lemon extract, one gill of sherry wine. Put the milk, sugar and lemon into a saucepan and set it into a pan of boiling water over the fire. Mix the corn starch with a little cold milk and stir it in; stir it until it boils three minutes. Then beat the yolks with a spoonful of cold milk and stir them in; stir it until the yolks thicken, but it must not boil. Then take it off the fire and stir in the wine. Beat the whites with two teaspoonfuls of white sugar to a stiff foam and stir them in last.

CREAM SAUCE.

Half a pint of sweet cream, two tablespoonfuls of white powdered sugar, half a teaspoonfull of powdered cinnamon. Beat the cream and sugar together until it foams, then stir in the cinnamon. Serve with cottage cheese.

CREAM SAUCE.

One gill of raspberry jelly, one gill of sweet cream, one tablespoonful of brandy. Put the jelly into a small bowl and set it into a pan of hot water until it dissolves. Then take it out and put in the cream. Beat it together until it foams, then put in the brandy.

HARD SAUCE FOR APPLE DUMPLINGS.

One ounce of fresh butter, two ounces of white granulated sugar, half a teaspoonful of grated nutmeg. Rub the butter and sugar to a thick cream, then add the nutmeg.

MILK SAUCE. (Very Fine with a Boiled Corn Starch Pudding.)

One pint of rich sweet milk, four tablespoonfuls of white granulated sugar, one dessert spoonful of corn starch, one dessert spoonful of fresh butter, two fresh eggs beaten separately, one teaspoonful of powdered cinnamon, half a teaspoonful of salt and three tablespoonfuls of brandy. Put the milk, sugar, salt and cinnamon into a saucepan and set it into a pan of boiling water over the fire, mix the corn starch with a little cold milk and stir it in, stir it until it boils three minutes. Beat the yolks with a spoonful of cold milk and stir them in, stir it until the yolks thicken, but it must not boil, after the yolks are in; then take it off the fire and stir in the butter and brandy; beat the whites with one teaspoonful of white sugar to a stiff foam and stir them in, beat it together a minute before putting it into the sauce tureen.

PRUNES, STEWED.

The French and Turkish prunes are the best. Pick them, wash them in cold water and put them into a porcelain saucepan with cold water enough to cover them, cook them until they are soft, but not to break; fifteen minutes before they are done put in three tablespoonfuls of sugar. When the prunes are done take them out and stir into the juice one even teaspoonful of corn starch that has been mixed with a little cold water. Let it boil three minutes, then take it off the fire and stir in three tablespoonfuls of sherry wine and pour it over the prunes.

PEELED PEACHES FROM CALIFORNIA,

One quart of peaches, one quart of cold water, one pint of white granulated sugar. Wash the peaches in cold water and put them into a saucepan with the quart of cold water, and when they begin to boil cook them twenty minutes, then put in the sugar and let it simmer ten minutes longer.

RASPBERRY SAUCE.

Half a quart of raspberry jelly, four tablespoonfuls of cold water, one teaspoonful of corn starch, one tablespoonful of white granulated sugar, three fresh eggs, beaten separately. Put the jelly and water into a saucepan and set it into a pan of boiling water over the fire. Break up the jelly and when it is all dissolved mix the corn starch with a little cold water and stir it in; stir it until it boils two minutes, then put in the sugar and beat the yolks with a teaspoonful of cold water and stir them in; stir it until the yolks thicken, but it must not boil. Then take it off the fire to cool five minutes before the whites are put in, beat the whites with one teaspoonful of white sugar to a stiff foam and stir them in, a spoonful at a time. This sauce can be made of fresh raspberry juice with more sugar added.

STRAWBERRY SAUCE.

Half a pint of strawberry syrup, one teaspoonful of corn starch, one tablespoonful of white granulated sugar, three fresh eggs, beaten separately and one gill of sherry wine. Put the syrup into a saucepan and set it into a pan of boiling water over the fire, mix the corn starch with a little cold syrup or water and stir it in, stir it until it boils two minutes, then put in the sugar and beat the yolks with a spoonful of cold milk and stir them in, stir it until the sauce thickens, but it must not boil after the yolks are in, then take it off the fire and stir in the wine; beat the whites with one teaspoonful of white sugar to a stiff foam and stir them in, beat it well together and pour it into the sauce tureen. This sauce can be made with the juice of fresh strawberries, with more sugar added, or with the syrup of canned strawberries, or with marmalade mixed with a little water and strained.

VANILLA SAUCE.

One pint of rich sweet milk, ten ounces of white granulated sugar, six yolks of fresh eggs, one teaspoonful of vanilla extract, three tablespoonfuls of brandy. Put the milk and sugar into a saucepan and set it into a pan of boiling water over the fire; beat the yolks with a spoonful of cold milk and stir them into the hot milk, stir it until it is as thick as cream, (but it must not boil or it will curdle) then take it off the fire and add the vanilla and brandy. This sauce can be used cold or warm.

WINE SAUCE.

Half a pint of sherry wine, one gill of water, four tablespoonfuls of white granulated sugar, one tablespoonful of corn starch, one tablespoonful of fresh butter, two fresh eggs beaten separately, two teaspoonfuls of the extract of lemon. Put the water, sugar and butter into a saucepan over the fire, and when it is hot mix the corn starch with a little cold water and stir it in, stir it until it boils two minutes, then take it off the fire. Beat the yolks with a spoonful of cold water and stir them in, set it over the fire again and stir it until the eggs thicken, but it must not boil, then add the wine and lemon, and when it is hot but not scalding, take it off the fire, beat the whites with one teaspoonful of white sugar to a stiff foam and stir them in last.

WINE SAUCE (Very Fine.)

Half a pint of German wine, three tablespoonfuls of white granulated sugar, two fresh eggs beaten separately, one teaspoonful of flour mixed with two teaspoonfuls of cold water, one teaspoonful of cinnamon extract, one teaspoonful of lemon extract. Put the wine, sugar, cinnamon and lemon into a saucepan and set it on the side of the range where it will get warm, but not hot, beat the whites with one teaspoonful of white sugar to a stiff foam, then beat the yolks and flour together and stir them into the whites, then stir them quickly into the wine and set it over a quick fire and stir it fast until it begins to rise, (it must not boil) then take it quickly from the fire and pour it into a sauce tureen. This sauce can be made with sherry or Madeira wine, with half wine and half water.

Custards.

ALMOND CUSTARD.

One pint of rich sweet milk, two ounces of almonds blanched and ground fine, with two dessert spoonfuls of cold sweet milk, four ounces of white granulated sugar, one tablespoonful of corn starch, five fresh eggs beaten separately, two tablespoonfuls of vanilla extract, one teaspoonful of lemon extract. Put the milk, almonds and sugar into a saucepan and set it into another pan over the fire containing boiling water and let it come to a boil, mix the corn starch with a little cold milk and stir it in, stir it until it boils two minutes; beat the yolks with a spoonful of cold milk and stir them in, stir it until it thickens, but it must not boil, now take it off the fire and add the flavoring; then beat the whites with one tablespoonful of white sugar to a stiff foam and stir them in. Put it into custard cups and serve with jelly cake.

APPLE CUSTARD.

One pint of rich sweet milk, four tablespoonfuls of white granulated sugar, one heaped tablespoonful of corn starch, five fresh eggs beaten separately, half a pint of grated apples, one teaspoonful of cinnamon. Put the milk and sugar into a saucepan and set it into another containing boiling water, mix the corn starch with a little cold milk and stir it in, stir it until it boils two minutes. Beat the yolks with a spoonful of cold milk and stir them in, stir it until they thicken, but it must not boil, then take it off the fire and stir in the apples and cinnamon; beat the whites with one tablespoonful of white sugar to a stiff foam and stir them in, then put it into a custard dish or cups and set it into a pan in the oven with a little boiling water in it and bake twenty-five minutes. It can be served warm or cold.

CHOCOLATE CUSTARD.

Two ounces of chocolate, one pint of rich sweet milk, four ounces of white granulated sugar, one tablespoonful of corn starch, five fresh eggs beaten separately, two teaspoonfuls of vanilla extract, one teaspoonful of cinnamon. Scrape the chocolate up fine and put it into a saucepan with four tablespoonfuls of cold water and set it into a pan of boiling water over the fire, stir it until it is dissolved into a smooth paste, which will be in five minutes, then stir in the milk and sugar, then mix the corn starch with a little cold milk and stir it in, stir it until it boils two minutes, then beat the yolks with a spoonful of cold milk and stir them in, stir it until it thickens, but it must not boil; now add the flavoring and take it off the fire to cool five minutes before the whites are put in; beat the whites with one tablespoonful of white sugar to a stiff foam and stir them in last. Put it into custard cups and serve with sponge cake.

COCOANUT CUSTARD.

One quart of rich sweet milk, four ounces of fine grated cocoanut, eight ounces of white granulated sugar, ten fresh eggs, beaten separately, two tablespoonfuls of corn starch, two teaspoonfuls of rose extract, two teaspoonfuls of vanilla extract. Put the milk, cocoanut and sugar into a saucepan and set it into a pan of boiling water and let it come to a boil. Mix the corn starch with a little cold milk and stir it in; stir it until it boils two minutes, then beat the yolks with two spoonfuls of cold milk, and stir them in; stir it until it thickens, but it must not boil. Now take it off the fire and add the flavoring, then beat the whites with two tablespoonfuls of white sugar to a stiff foam and stir them in. Put it into a custard cups, sprinkle a little cocoanut on top and serve with white cake.

CORN STARCH CUSTARD.

One pint of rich sweet milk, two tablespoonfuls of white granulated sugar, one tablespoonful of corn starch, one dessert spoonful of fresh butter, two fresh eggs, beaten separately, one pinch of salt, one teaspoonful of lemon or cinnamon. Put the milk, sugar, cinnamon and salt into a saucepan and set it into a pan of boiling water over the fire. Mix the corn starch with a little cold milk and stir it in; stir until it boils two minutes then put in the butter, beat the yolks with a spoonful of cold milk and stir them in. Then take it off the fire and beat the whites with one teaspoonful of white sugar to a stiff foam and stir them in last.

SNOW BALL CORN STARCH CUSTARD.

One quart of rich sweet milk, four fresh eggs beaten separately, four tablespoonfuls of white granulated sugar, two tablespoonfuls of corn starch, one tablespoonful of fresh butter, one saltspoonful of salt, and two teaspoonfuls of vanilla extract. Let the milk get scalding hot, but not to boil. Beat the whites with two teaspoonfuls of white sugar to a stiff foam. Then form them with a spoon into balls and put them into the hot milk without touching each other. Turn them over and they are poached in a minute. Then lay them on a platter till the custard is made. Then put the sugar and salt into the milk and mix the corn starch with a little cold milk and stir it in ; stir it until it boils two minutes. Beat the yolks with a spoonful of cold milk and stir them in. Then put in the butter and vanilla, and take it off the fire. Pour it into a custard bowl and put the snowballs on top. Serve it with sponge cake.

PUMPKIN CUSTARD.

One quart of stewed pumpkin pressed through a sieve, twelve ounces of white granulated sugar, ten fresh eggs beaten separately, two quarts of rich sweet milk, one teaspoonful of mace, one teaspoonful of cinnamon, and one teaspoonful of grated nutmeg. After the pumpkin has been pressed through a sieve, beat the yolks and sugar together and stir them into the pumpkin. Then add the milk, mace, cinnamon and nutmeg, and then beat the whites with three teaspoonfuls of white sugar to a stiff foam and stir them in last. Put it into a custard dish and bake it light brown.

RASPBERRY CUSTARD.

One pint of rich sweet milk, one heaped tablespoonful of corn starch, three tablespoonfuls of white granulated sugar, five fresh eggs beaten separate, one gill of raspberry syrup. Put the milk and sugar into a saucepan and set it into another containing boiling water, mix the corn starch with a little cold milk and stir it until it boils two minutes; beat the yolks with a spoonful of cold milk and stir them in, stir it until they thicken, but it must not boil, then take it off the fire and stir in the raspberry syrup, then beat the whites with one tablespoonful of white sugar to a stiff foam and stir them in and then put it into custard cups and serve it warm or cold.

SNOW BALL CUSTARD.

One quart of rich sweet milk, twelve fresh eggs, separated yolks from the whites, eight ounces of white granulated sugar, two teaspoonfuls of the extract of vanilla, two teaspoonfuls of the extract of cinnamon. Put the milk into a porcelain kettle over the fire, beat the whites with two tablespoonfuls of white sugar to a stiff foam. When the milk is hot enough to scald, but not to boil, take rather more than half of the whites that have been beaten and form them into balls with a tablespoon and dessertspoon. Then put them into the hot milk, turn them over. They are done in a minute. Then lay them on a porcelain plate until the custard is ready. Put the sugar into the milk and when it is dissolved beat the yolks with a little cold milk and stir them in; keep stirring it until it is thick, but it must not boil. Take it off the fire and add the vanilla and cinnamon and when it has cooled a little, stir in the rest of the whites. When it is cool enough put it into a glass bowl, place the snowballs on top and ornament each one with a piece of bright colored jelly.

WINE CUSTARD.

One gill of sherry wine, one gill of rich sweet milk, three tablespoonfuls of white granulated sugar, one tablespoonful of corn starch, four fresh eggs, beaten separately, one teaspoonful of lemon extract. Put the milk, sugar and lemon into a saucepan and set it into a pan over the fire containing boiling water. Mix the corn starch with a little cold milk and stir it in, stir it until it boils two minutes, then beat the yolks with a spoonful of cold milk and stir them in; stir it until they thicken, but it must not boil, then take it off the fire and stir in the wine. Beat the whites with two teaspoonfuls of white sugar to a stiff foam and stir them in last. Serve it with sponge cake.

Creams, Syrups and Ice Creams.

ALMOND CREAM. (Delicious and a beautiful color.)

One pint of sweet cream, two ounces of sweet almonds blanched and pounded fine with two dessert spoonfuls of sweet milk, eight ounces of white granulated sugar, six fresh eggs beaten separately, one ounce of red gelatine,(light weight,) two teaspoonfuls of rose extract. Cut the gelatine up fine with a pair of scissors and put it into a saucepan with one gill of cold water and set it into a pan of boiling water, let it stand in the warm water until it has to be used. Put the cream, almonds and sugar into a saucepan and set it into a pan over the fire of boiling water; beat the yolks with a spoonful of cold milk and stir them in, stir it until they thicken, but it must not boil, then take it off the fire and stir in the gelatine and rose extract, set the saucepan into a pan of cold water to cool, while the whites are beaten with one tablespoonful of white sugar to a stiff foam, then stir them in and put it into small molds that have been dipped in cold water.

CHOCOLATE CREAM. (Very Fine.)

Two ounces of chocolate, one pint of sweet cream, eight ounces of white granulated sugar, six fresh eggs beaten separately, one ounce of gelatine, (light weight,) two teaspoonfuls of vanilla extract. Cut the gelatine up fine with a pair of scissors and put it into a small saucepan with one gill of cold sweet milk and set it into a pan of boiling water. It will dissolve in ten or fifteen minutes; let it stand in the warm water until you are ready to use it. Scrape the chocolate up fine and put it into a saucepan with four tablespoonfuls of cold water and then set it into a pan of boiling water and stir it until it is a smooth paste, then stir in the cream and sugar and beat the yolks light and stir them in, stir it until they thicken, but it must not boil, then take it off the fire and stir in the gelatine and vanilla; set the saucepan into a pan of cold water to cool while you beat the whites with one tablespoonful of white sugar to a stiff foam, then stir them in and put it into small molds that have been dipped in cold water.

CINCINNATI CREAM. (Very Fine.)

One pint of sweet cream, eight ounces of white granulated sugar, five fresh eggs separated, half an ounce of gelatine, two teaspoonfuls of vanilla extract and one gill of sherry wine. Cut the gelatine up fine with a pair of scissors and put it into a small saucepan with one gill of cold sweet milk, then set it into another pan containing boiling water. It will be all dissolved in fifteen minutes; let it stand in the warm water until you are ready to use it. Take out one tablespoonful of the sugar to beat with the whites, then put the cream and the rest of the sugar into a porcelain saucepan and stir it into another one containing boiling water; beat the yolks very light and stir them in, stir it until they thicken, but it must not boil, then take it off the fire and stir in the gelatine and vanilla, set the saucepan into a pan half full of cold water and stir it until it is lukewarm, then beat the whites with the tablespoonful of sugar to a stiff foam and stir them in, then stir in one gill of sherry wine and put it into a porcelain mold and set it on ice. Before serving turn it out onto a china plate.

RASPBERRY CREAM. (Very Fine.)

Put three pints of ripe red raspberries and one pint of ripe red currants into a porcelain kettle and mash them a little to keep them from sticking, stir them with a wooden spoon and boil them two minutes, then strain through a linen cloth and measure, to one pint of juice, ten ounces of white granulated sugar, one tablespoonful of corn starch and six fresh eggs separated, the yolks from the whites. Put the juice and the sugar into a porcelain saucepan over the fire and mix the corn starch with a little of the cold juice; when the juice is hot, but not boiling, stir in the corn starch, stir it fast and let it boil two minutes, then take it off the fire to cool a little; beat the yolks with a little of the cold raspberry juice and stir them in, set it over the fire and stir it fast until the yolks are set, but it must not boil after they are in, then take it off the fire and stir it five minutes to cool; beat the whites with one tablespoonful of white sugar to a stiff foam and stir them in, a little at a time, beat it well together and put it into a glass dessert dish that has a cover to it, or it can be put into a mold and frozen.

STRAWBERRY CREAM.

Hull the strawberries, put them into a porcelain kettle, mash them with a wooden beetle and boil them two minutes, then strain through a linen cloth and measure. To one pint of juice allow nine ounces of white granulated sugar, one tablespoonful of corn starch and six fresh eggs separated. Put the juice and sugar into a porcelain saucepan and set it into another one over the fire, containing boiling water. Mix the corn starch with a little cold juice or water and stir it in; stir it until it boils two minutes. Beat the yolks with a little cold juice and stir them in; stir it until it thickens, but it must not boil after they are in. Then take it off the fire to cool five minutes before the whites are put in. Beat the whites with one tablespoonful of white sugar to a stiff foam and stir them in, a little at a time. Mix it well together, set it in a cold place and when cool enough set it on ice.

VANILLA CREAM.

One pint of sweet cream, two tablespoonfuls of corn starch, four tablespoonfuls of white granulated sugar, two fresh eggs and three teaspoonfuls of vanilla extract. Put the cream into a small saucepan and set it into another containing boiling water. Mix the corn starch with a little cold milk and stir it in until it boils two minutes. Then put in the sugar and then beat the yolks and stir them in. Stir it until they thicken, but it must not boil; then take it off the fire and beat the whites with one teaspoonful of white sugar to a stiff foam and stir them in; then add the vanilla.

WINE CREAM. (Very Fine.)

Half a pint of sherry wine, one gill of water, three tablespoonfuls of white granulated sugar, one gill of sweet cream, one teaspoonful of corn starch four fresh eggs beaten separately, one teaspoonful of lemon extract. Put the wine, water and sugar into a saucepan and let it get warm enough to dissolve the sugar; put the cream into a small saucepan and set it into a pan of boiling water over the fire, mix the corn starch with a little cold milk and stir it into the cream, stir it until it boils two minutes, then take it off the fire and let it stand in the hot water until needed; beat the whites with two teaspoonfuls of sugar to a stiff foam, beat the yolks and stir them into the whites and then stir them into the wine, set it quickly over a hot fire and stir it fast, and as soon as it begins to rise (it must not boil) take it off the fire;

now stir a little of the wine in with the cream and mix it well together, then stir the cream into the wine and add the lemon. Put it into glasses or custard cups and serve with white or sponge cake.

FREEZING ICE CREAM.

First the ice must be broken up very fine and there must be plenty of coarse salt on hand; then place the freezer in the center of the bucket and put on the covers, fasten them on tight, put on the crank and turn it to see if it runs smoothly. Then put a folded cloth on the cover to keep the salt and ice water from getting in; now put into the bucket a layer of ice and a layer of salt thick enough to cover the ice, then another layer of ice and salt and so on until it is within half an inch of where the cover closes; then wipe off the cover and edge of the bucket, open the freezer, put in the cream, close tight and turn the crank slowly at first. If it is Gooch's patent freezer the cream will be frozen in thirty minutes. When the cream has been in fifteen minutes fill up the bucket again with ice and salt.

CHOCOLATE ICE CREAM.

One ounce of chocolate, one pint of rich sweet milk, eight ounces of white granulated sugar, one teaspoonful of corn starch, one fresh egg beaten separately, one pint of sweet cream, three teaspoonfuls of vanilla extract. Scrape the chocolate up fine and put it into a saucepan with four tablespoonfuls of cold water and set it into a pan of boiling water and stir it until it becomes a smooth paste, then stir in the milk and sugar and mix the corn starch with a little cold milk and stir it in, stir it until it boils two minutes, then beat the yolks with a teaspoonful of cold milk and stir it in, stir it until it thickens, but it must not boil, then take it off the fire and strain it through a fine cloth and then set it into a pan of cold water to cool; beat the white with half a teaspoonful of sugar to a stiff foam and stir it in, then add the cream and vanilla and if it is not cold enough put it into the freezer.

STRAWBERRY ICE CREAM.

Half a pint of rich sweet milk, one teaspoonful of corn starch, two fresh eggs separated, half a pint of strawberry syrup, one pint of sweet cream. Put the milk into a saucepan and set it into a pan containing boiling water, mix the corn starch with a spoonful of cold milk and stir it in, stir it until it boils two minutes; beat the yolks with one tablespoonful of white granulated sugar and stir them in, stir it until the yolks thicken, but it must not boil, then take it off the fire to cool five minutes before the whites are put in; beat the whites with one tablespoonful of white sugar to a stiff foam and stir them in, then stir in the strawberry syrup and set it in a cold place. When the custard is cold beat the cream with the machine egg beater until it foams, then stir it in and put the whole into the freezer.

RASPBERRY ICE CREAM.

Is made in the same manner as in the preceding receipt and is excellent. In making ice cream with fruit syrups the custard must be made before the syrup is put in. If the syrup was put into the milk or cream alone it would curdle and spoil the whole.

VANILLA ICE CREAM.

One pint of rich sweet milk, half a pound of white granulated sugar, one teaspoonful of corn starch, one fresh egg separated, one pint of sweet cream and three teaspoonfuls of vanilla extract. Put the milk into a saucepan and set it into another pan over the fire containing a little boiling water. Mix the corn starch with a little cold milk and stir it in; stir it until it boils two minutes then put in the sugar and beat the yolks with a spoonful of cold milk and stir it in; stir it until it thickens, but it must not boil after the yolk is in. Then take it off the fire and strain it through a thin cloth, then set it into a pan of cold water to cool a few minutes and beat the white with half a teaspoonful of white sugar to a stiff foam and stir it in. As soon as the custard is cold stir in the cream and vanilla and put the whole into the freezer. A piece of white paper muslin with the stiffening washed out makes a good strainer, or a square of cheese cloth washed out in clear water is also good.

LEMON ICE CREAM.

Is made in the same manner as in the preceding receipt with three teaspoonfuls of lemon extract instead of the vanilla.

VANILLA ICE CREAM.
(Without Cream.)

One quart of rich sweet milk, half a pound of white granulated sugar, one tablespoonful, (not heaped) of corn starch. Three fresh eggs separated and three teaspoonfuls of vanilla extract. Put the milk and half of the sugar into a saucepan and set it into another pan containing boiling water. Mix the corn starch with a little cold milk and stir it in; stir it until it boils two minutes then take two teaspoonfuls out of the other half of the sugar to beat with the whites and put the rest of it in with the corn starch and milk. Then beat the yolks with a spoonful of cold milk and stir them in; stir it until it thickens, but it must not boil. Then take it off the fire and strain through a fine cloth, then set it into a pan of cold water whilst you beat the whites with the two teaspoonfuls of sugar to a stiff foam and then stir them in. Then add the vanilla and set it in a cool place until it is cold enough to put into the freezer. You cannot tell the difference between this ice cream and that which is made with cream.

STRAWBERRY SYRUP, FOR ICE CREAM, JELLIES AND SAUCES.

The dark red strawberries are the finest flavored, and should be gathered in dry weather. After they are hulled put them into a porcelain kettle and mash them with a wooden beetle, set them over the fire and boil them five minutes, then strain them through a linen cloth and measure. To one pint of juice allow three quarters of a pound of white granulated sugar, stir the juice and sugar well together and when it begins to boil skim quickly and boil ten minutes. When cold, bottle, cork tight and seal.

RASPBERRY SYRUP FOR ICE CREAM, JELLIES AND SAUCES.

Take the ripe red raspberries that have been gathered in dry weather and after they have been picked over, put them into a porcelain kettle and mash them with a wooden beetle, then boil them five minutes and strain them through a linen cloth and measure. To one pint of juice allow three quarters of a pound of white granulated sugar; as soon as it begins to boil skim it well and boil it ten minutes. When cold bottle, cork tight and seal.

Jellies With Gelatine.

CALF'S FOOT JELLY.

Calf's feet with the skins on make the best jelly. If they have to be dressed at home it is easily done. Have a teakettle of boiling water ready, then take one foot at a time and pour the hot water over it, removing the hair as fast as scalded, then take off the hoofs and throw the feet into cold water. Take four calf's feet, split them, unjoint them and put them into a large saucepan with cold water enough to cover them. When the water begins to boil pour it all off and cover the feet again with cold water, when it begins to boil again skim it as long as anything rises to the surface; boil it slowly four hours, then there should be one quart of the jelly. With a skimmer take out all the meat and bones, then strain the jelly through a linen cloth into a large bowl, cover it and let it stand over night. With a broad knife take off all the fat and then go over it with a small tea napkin, then turn the jelly out on to a plate, and if there is any sediment on the bottom take it off, cut up the jelly into small pieces, put it into a porcelain saucepan, cover it and set it into a larger saucepan containing a little boiling water. The jelly will be dissolved in five minutes; then set the sauce pan containing the jelly over the fire and put into it one pound of white granulated sugar, the yellow rind peeled very thinly from two lemons and the juice of three large lemons or four small ones; wash and wipe four fresh eggs, put the whites into a bowl and beat them a very little, then break the shells in with them and stir whites and shells into the boiling jelly. Skim it and let it boil fifteen minutes, then set it on the side of the range where it will not boil and stir in one pint of sherry wine, let it stand for twenty minutes, then strain through a flannel cloth, (not a bag.) Put it into molds or jelly glasses.

CIDER JELLY. (Very Fine.)

One pint and a half of cider, (Siberian crab apple is the best,) eight ounces of white granulated sugar, three quarters of an ounce of gelatine, half white, half red, two teaspoonfuls of lemon extract.

Cut the gelatine up fine with a pair of scissors and put it into a small saucepan with half a pint of the cider and set it into a pan of boiling water where it will be dissolved in ten minutes. Put the pint of cider and sugar into a saucepan and let it get warm enough to dissolve the sugar; when the gelatine is dissolved stir it into the cider and let it get hot, but it must not boil, then take it off the fire and strain through a fine cloth into a bowl, then add the lemon and set the bowl into a pan of cold water and stir it until the jelly is cold, but not set, then put it into porcelain molds that have been rubbed with olive oil and set it in a cool place. When ready to serve set the mold into warm water (not hot) for a minute, then turn it out. This jelly is beautiful in color and if made of Siberian crab apple cider is equal to any wine jelly.

LEMON JELLY. (Very Fine.)

One pint of rich sweet milk, eight ounces of white granulated sugar, three lemons, half a pint of white wine, one ounce of gelatine, half white and half red, one gill of cold water. Cut the gelatine up fine with a pair of scissors and put it into a small saucepan with the gill of cold water and set it into a pan of boiling water over the fire where it will dissolve in ten minutes. Grate the yellow peel of the lemon off very thin, then peel off the white part and squeeze out the juice; put the milk, sugar and grated lemon peel into a saucepan and set it into a pan of boiling water over the fire and let it come to a boil, then take it off the fire and put in the lemon juice, wine and gelatine, then strain it through a linen cloth into a bowl and set the bowl into a pan of cold water and stir it until it is cold, but not set, then put it into porcelain molds that have been rubbed with olive oil and set it in a cool place. When ready to serve turn it out. It has a beautiful color.

RASPBERRY JELLY WITH GELATINE.

One pint of raspberry syrup, one lemon, (the juice only) three quarters of an ounce of gelatine, half a pint of cold water. After the gelatine has been cut up put it and the water into a small saucepan and set it into a pan of boiling water where it will dissolve in ten minutes. Put the syrup and lemon juice into a porcelain saucepan and set it where it will get warm. When the gelatine is all dissolved stir it into the syrup and let it get hot, then take it off the fire and strain through a fine cloth into a bowl and set the bowl into a pan of cold water and stir it until the jelly is cold but not set. Then put it into porcelain molds that have been rubbed with olive oil and set in a cool place. When ready to serve turn it out and serve it with ice cream.

STRAWBERRY JELLY WITH GELATINE.

Is made in the same manner as in the preceding receipt.

WINE JELLY WITH GELATINE.

Three quarters of an ounce of gelatine, half white and half red, half a pint of cold water, one pint of sherry wine, eight ounces of white granulated sugar, two teaspoonfuls of lemon extract. Cut the gelatine up fine with a pair of scissors and put it into a small saucepan with the half pint of water and set it into a pan of boiling water. Put the wine and sugar into a saucepan and let it get warm enough to dissolve the sugar. When the gelatine is dissolved stir it into the wine and let it get hot, but it must not boil. Then take it off the fire and strain through a fine cloth into a bowl. Then add the lemon and set the bowl into a pan of cold water and stir it until the jelly is cold but not set. Then put it into porcelain molds that have been rubbed with olive oil and set it in a cool place. When ready to serve turn it out and serve it with ice cream.

Charlotte Russe and Blanc Mange.

ALMOND BLANC MANGE.

One pint of rich sweet milk, three ounces of sweet almonds blanched and ground fine in the mortar, six whole peach kernels blanched and ground fine, three ounces of white granulated sugar, two ounces of corn starch and five whites of fresh eggs. Put the milk, almonds, peach kernels and sugar into a porcelain saucepan and set it into another pan containing boiling water. When it has come to a boil mix the corn starch with a little cold milk and stir it in, stir it until it boils three minutes then take it off the fire to cool a little before the whites are put in. Beat the whites with one tablespoonful of white sugar to a stiff foam and stir them in, then put it quickly into a porcelain mold that has been dipped in cold water, and when it is cold turn it out. Make a sauce with the yolks that are left. One pint of sweet milk, four ounces of white sugar, one teaspoonful of corn starch, five yolks, two teaspoonfuls of vanilla extract and one gill of sherry wine or three tablespoonfuls of brandy, according to taste. Put the milk and sugar into a saucepan and set it into another containing boiling water. Mix the corn starch with a little cold milk and stir it in; stir it until it boils three minutes. Beat the yolks and stir them in; stir it until they thicken, but it must not boil. Then take it off the fire and stir in the vanilla, wine or brandy.

BLANC MANGE.

One pint and a half of rich sweet milk, four ounces of white granulated sugar, two ounces and a half of corn starch, one tablespoonful of fresh butter, three fresh eggs beaten separately, three teaspoonfuls of lemon extract. Put the milk and sugar into a porcelain saucepan and set it into another containing boiling water, mix the corn starch with a little cold milk and stir it in, stir it until it boils three minutes, then stir in the butter; beat the yolks and stir them in, stir it until they thicken, but it must not boil after they are in, then take it off the fire and beat the whites with one teaspoonful of white sugar to a stiff foam and stir them in, then stir in the lemon and put it into a porcelain mold that has been dipped in cold water. When it is cold turn it out and serve with a wine custard or fruit sauce.

CHARLOTTE RUSSE. (Very Fine.)

One pint of sweet cream, eight ounces of white granulated sugar, six fresh eggs beaten separately, half an ounce of gelatine, three teaspoonfuls of vanilla extract. Before commencing the charlotte russe get everything ready. First cut the gelatine up fine with a pair of scissors and put it into a small saucepan with one gill of cold sweet milk, then set it into another pan containing boiling water and it will be dissolved in fifteen minutes; let it remain in the warm water until you are ready to use it. Double a large sheet of writing paper, place a porcelain mold on it and mark it close around the bottom with a lead pencil, then cut it a straw's breadth inside the pencil mark and it will fit the inside of the mold; place it in the bottom, butter the paper and place a weight in the middle to keep it in place. Cut the sponge cake half an inch thick, dip the crust edges into the beaten white of an egg and place them close together around the mold. Now prepare the charlotte in the following manner: First take out one tablespoonful of the sugar to beat with the whites, then put the cream and the rest of the sugar into a porcelain saucepan and set it into another containing boiling water, beat the yolks well and stir them in, stir it until they thicken, but it must not boil, then take it off the fire and stir in the gelatine and vanilla, then set the saucepan into a pan half full of broken ice and water and stir it constantly until it is lukewarm, then beat the whites with the tablespoonful of sugar to a stiff foam and stir them in, stir it well together, then put it into the mold and set it on ice. When ready to serve place a china or glass dish over it and turn it upside down and remove the paper.

Cakes and Macaroons, Meringue.

CAKE.

The day before you intend making cake have the currants washed, dried in the oven and picked over. If you cannot get California seedless raisins stone the others and cut them in two. Cut the citron up as thin as paper and if almonds are to be used blanch, skin and grind them. It is a slow process and takes time. Before commencing the cake butter the cake pans, then sift the flour, weigh it and mix the baking powder with it. Then set the vessel containing the flour into a pan of hot water to warm and stir it occasionally until needed. Mix the fruit together and dredge it with a spoonful or two of the weighed flour. Weigh the butter and sugar and put it into the vessel you are going to make the cake in (a large earthen bowl is the best) and if the butter is too hard set the bowl into a pan of hot water for a minute until it softens but it must not melt. Then beat them together with the back of the spoon against the side of the bowl to a very light cream. Separate the eggs, beat the yolks and stir them in with the butter and sugar, then beat the whites with one teaspoonful of white sugar to every two whites, to a stiff foam. Now stir the flour in with the butter, sugar and yolks, then stir in the whites and the flavoring. If it is a fruit cake, the dredged fruit is put in last. The whites of eggs beat better in a bowl with a machine egg beater than in any other vessel and not more than six whites should be beaten at a time. A wooden skewer is necessary to ascertain when the cake is done. It should be six inches long and the size of a large knitting needle.

ALMONDS, TO BLANCH AND GRIND.

Put the almonds into boiling water and just as soon as the water begins to boil again after they are in, take them off the fire, pour off the water, slip off the skins. The sooner they are out of the water the better the almonds will be. They should be ground in the mortar as soon as the skins are off. One ounce of almonds is enough to grind at a time and after they are broken up fine put in one dessert spoonful of sweet milk to one ounce of almonds and grind them until they are white and creamy. A white porcelain mortar and pestle is the best to grind the almonds in. Bitter almonds or peach kernels are prepared in the same manner as in the preceding receipt, but they should be ground separately.

CING FOR CAKES.

Four ounces of finely powdered sugar to one white of an egg. Beat the white and sugar together two or three minutes, not longer; then spread it on the cake with a broad knife. The cake can be more evenly iced when only warm than when first taken out of the oven. The icing can be flavored with a few drops of lemon or rose extract.

CHOCOLATE ICING.

One ounce of chocolate, one tablespoonful of cold water, four ounces of finely powdered white sugar, one white of an egg. Scrape the chocolate up very fine and put it into a porcelain cup with one tablespoonful of cold water and set it into a pan over the fire that has a little boiling water in it, stir it until it is a smooth paste, which will be in two or three minutes; then take the cup out of the water and beat the white and sugar together two or three minutes, then stir in the chocolate, mix it well together and spread it on the cake with a broad knife.

ALMOND CAKE.

Eight ounces of sifted flour with three teaspoonfuls of baking powder mixed with it, six ounces of fresh butter, eight ounces of white granulated sugar, six fresh eggs beaten separately, one nutmeg, four ounces of almonds blanched and ground fine with a dessert spoonful of sweet milk to an ounce of almonds. Set the vessel containing the flour into a pan of hot water until needed, beat the whites with one tablespoonful of the sugar to a stiff foam, beat the butter and sugar to a light cream, beat the yolks and stir them into the butter and sugar, then add the nutmeg and almonds, mix it well together and then stir in half of the flour, then half of the whites, then the other half of the flour and the whites. Put it quickly into a well buttered cake pan and bake forty-five or fifty minutes. Try it with a wooden skewer and if it comes out dry it is done.

ALMOND JUMBLES.

Four ounces of sifted flour with one heaped teaspoonful of baking powder mixed with it, four ounces of white granulated sugar, two ounces of fresh butter, two ounces of almonds blanched and pounded fine, two fresh eggs beaten separately, one teaspoonful of lemon extract. Beat the whites with one teaspoonful of sugar to a stiff foam, beat the butter and sugar to a light cream, beat the yolks and stir them into the butter and sugar, then stir in the almonds and lemon and mix it evenly together, then stir in half of the flour, then the whites, then the rest of the flour. Put it into well buttered muffin pans and bake a light brown.

COCOANUT JUMBLES.

Are made in the same manner, with fine grated cocoanut.

ALMOND MACAROONS.

Four ounces of almonds blanched and pounded with two dessert spoonfuls of milk, four ounces of white granulated sugar, one white of an egg, two teaspoonfuls of corn starch, one teaspoonful of rose extract. Mix the almonds and sugar together, beat the white with one teaspoonful of sugar to a stiff foam and stir it in, then stir in the corn starch dry and then add the rose extract. Cover the bottom of a baking pan with white paper and butter it, then lay on the paper half a teaspoonful of the mixture one inch apart and bake in a slow oven for three quarters of an hour, or until they are a light brown and are hard and dry.

COCOANUT MACAROONS.

Are made in the same manner, with grated cocoanut.

ALMOND MACAROONS.

Half a pound of almonds blanched, dried and pounded to a paste, with one teaspoonful of rose water. Beat together the whites of three eggs and half a cup of white granulated sugar, adding the sugar a teaspoonful at a time, then add the pounded almonds, and if too soft to be shaped add one tablespoonful of flour, roll out, cut with a small cake cutter, place some distance apart on buttered paper and bake slowly three quarters of an hour, or until hard and dry.

ALMOND SPONGE CAKE.

Three ounces of sweet almonds blanched and ground fine in the mortar, with one dessert spoonful of sweet milk ground in with each ounce of almonds, half an ounce of peach kernels blanched and prepared in the same manner as the almonds, six fresh eggs beaten separately, nine ounces of white granulated sugar, nine ounces of sifted flour with three teaspoonfuls of baking powder mixed with it, one nutmeg grated. Beat the whites with one tablespoonful of the sugar to a stiff foam, beat the yolks and the sugar until very light, then stir in the almonds and peach kernels, then stir in half of the flour and baking powder, then the whites and then the other half of the flour. Put it quickly into a buttered cake pan and bake one hour, the time depends upon the heat of the oven. Try it with a wooden skewer when the cake has been in fifty minutes, and if it comes out clean the cake is done.

BRIDE'S CAKE. (Very Fine.)

One pound of sifted flour with four teaspoonfuls of baking powder mixed with it, one pound of white granulated sugar, ten ounces of fresh butter, sixteen whites of fresh eggs, three teafuls of the extract of lemon, six teaspoonfuls of the extract of roses, one gill of sherry wine, and eight ounces of citron cut as thin as paper; set the vessel containing the flour and baking powder into a pan of hot water and stir it occasionally until needed; take out one tablespoonful of the weighed flour and dredge the citron with it; put the whites into two bowls with one tablespoonful of the weighed sugar in each bowl and beat them with a machine egg beater to a stiff foam; beat the butter and sugar together to a light cream, then stir in half of the flour, then half of the whites, then the other half of the flour and the whites, then add the flavoring and wine, and last the citron. Mix it evenly together, put it quickly into a buttered cake pan and bake one hour and twenty minutes. Try it with a wooden skewer when it has been in the oven one hour, and if it comes out clean, it is done. The bride's and groom's cakes should be made on the same day.

CHOCOLATE MACAROONS.

Two ounces of chocolate scraped up very fine, two ounces of sweet almonds blanched and pounded very fine, with two teaspoonfuls of sweet milk, **four** ounces of white granulated sugar, one white of an egg, one teaspoonful of corn starch, one teaspoonful of vanilla extract, half a teaspoonful of cinnamon. Mix the chocolate and almonds well together then stir in the sugar and beat the white with a teaspoonful of sugar to a stiff foam and stir it in, then add the vanilla and cinnamon and stir in the dry corn starch. Cover the bottom of a baking pan with white paper and then butter it. Then put on the paper half a teaspoonful of the mixture one inch apart and put them into a slow oven and bake three quarters of an hour or until they are hard and dry.

CITRON CAKES. (Excellent.)

Half a pound of sifted flour, two teaspoonfuls of baking powder in it, half a pound of white granulated sugar, three fresh eggs beaten separately, three ounces of citron cut fine, three ounces of currants, three teaspoonfuls of lemon extract. Beat the yolks and sugar to a light cream; beat the whites with two teaspoonfuls of the sugar to a stiff foam then stir in the whites, citron and currants, then stir in the flour, baking powder and the lemon. Make them into small cakes and put them into a well buttered pan and bake them a yellow brown.

COCOANUT CAKE.

Four ounces of fine grated cocoanut weighed after it is grated, six ounces of fresh butter, eight ounces of white granulated sugar, six fresh eggs, beaten separately, one nutmeg, eight ounces of sifted flour with three teaspoonfuls of baking powder mixed with it. Set the vessel containing the flour into a pan of hot water and stir it occasionally until needed. Beat the whites with one tablespoonful of the sugar to a stiff foam, beat the butter and sugar together to a light cream. Beat the yolks and stir them into the butter and sugar, then add the nutmeg and cocoanut and mix it evenly together. Then stir in half of the flour, then half of the whites, then the other half of the flour and the whites. Put it quickly into a well buttered cake pan and bake forty-five or fifty minutes. The time depends upon the heat of the oven; try it with a wooden skewer and if it comes dry and clean the cake is done.

GRANDMOTHER'S COOKIES.

One pound of white granulated sugar, half a pound of butter, four eggs beaten separately, one pound and a quarter of flour. Beat the butter and sugar together to a cream, then add the yolks and stir in the flour. Beat the whites with one teaspoonful of white sugar to a stiff foam and stir them in last. Drop the batter from a teaspoon into large greased baking pans and bake. Put the cookies into a cake box and they will become soft in two or three days. They will keep a long time.

BERLIN COOKIES.

One pound and three quarters of flour, one pound of white granulated sugar, half a pound of butter, four eggs, beaten separately, beat the butter and sugar to a cream then add the yolks. Beat the whites with one teaspoonful of white sugar to a stiff foam and stir them in. Then stir in the flour last, make it into a soft dough and roll out thin. Cut it with a cake cutter or cut it into forms. If kept in a cake box they will become soft and nice.

SUGAR COOKIES. (Very Good.)

Half a pound of butter, one pound of white granulated sugar, three eggs, beaten separately, two pounds of flour with four teaspoonfuls of Royal baking powder in it, half a pint of cold sweet milk and two teaspoonfuls of grated nutmeg. Beat the butter and sugar to a cream then beat in the yolks and half of the flour; then add the milk and nutmeg. Beat the whites with one teaspoonful of white sugar to a stiff foam and stir them in with the rest of the flour; then roll them out thin, cut them with a small cake cutter and bake in a quick oven ten minutes. Keep them in a cake box.

CINCINNATI CREAM CAKES.

One pint of rich sweet milk, four ounces of fresh butter, one tablespoonful of white granulated sugar, one teaspoonful of grated nutmeg, half a teaspoonful of salt, six ounces of sifted flour with two teaspoonfuls of baking powder mixed with it, six fresh eggs beaten separately. Put half of the milk, butter, sugar, nutmeg and salt into an iron skillet over a slow fire and let it come to a boil, mix the flour and baking powder with the other half of the milk until it is a smooth batter, then stir it into the boiling milk and continue stirring it until it is a smooth dough, then take it off the fire to cool and beat the yolks and stir them in, then beat the whites with one tablespoonful of white sugar to a stiff foam and stir them in last. Mix it well together and put a dessert spoonful of the mixture into each well buttered muffin pan and bake them a dark yellow. It takes from fifteen to twenty minutes. When done open them at the side with a sharp pointed knife and put in one heaped teaspoonful of the cream. This quantity makes twenty-four cakes.

FILLING FOR CREAM CAKE.

Half a pint of sweet cream, one tablespoonful of corn starch, two tablespoonfuls of white granulated sugar, one fresh egg beaten separately, two teaspoonful of vanilla extract. Put the cream into a small saucepan and set it into another containing boiling water, mix the corn starch with a little cold milk and stir it in, stir it until it boils two minutes, then put in the sugar and beat the yolks with a spoonful of cold milk and stir it in, then take it off the fire and beat the whites with half a teaspoonful of white sugar to a stiff foam and stir it in, then add the vanilla and when it is cold fill the cakes. This quantity will fill twenty-four cakes. The filling should be made before the cakes are made.

CUP CAKE.

Three quarters of a cup of butter, one cup of white granulated sugar, five eggs beaten separately, three cups of flour, one cup of cold sweet milk, two teaspoonfuls of lemon extract, three teaspoonfuls of Royal baking powder, (not heaped.) Let the butter be a little soft, but not melted, beat the butter and sugar together until it is a light cream, then put in the yolks and beat them a few minutes, then stir in one cup of the flour with one third of the milk and so on until the flour and milk is all in, then put in the lemon extract and beat the whites with two teaspoonfuls of white sugar to a stiff foam and stir them in, then add the baking powder last. Let it bake one hour.

CURRANT CAKE.

Half a pound of flour with one teaspoonful of baking powder in it, half a pound of white granulated sugar, four ounces of butter, one teaspoonful of extract of lemon, five fresh eggs beaten separately, four ounces of currants. Beat one half of the sugar with the butter and the other half with the yolks, then mix them together and stir in the flour and the lemon; beat the whites with one tablespoonful of sugar to a stiff foam and stir them in, then dredge the currants with flour and stir them in last.

FRUIT CAKE. (Very fine.)

Twelve ounces of sifted flour with four teaspoonfuls of baking powder mixed with it, twelve ounces of white granulated sugar, six ounces of fresh butter, six fresh eggs, beaten separately, one teaspoonful each of cinnamon, nutmeg and cloves, eight ounces of seedless California raisins, eight ounces of currants, six ounces of citron cut as thin as paper, one gill of brandy. Put the fruit all together into a deep dish and dredge it with two tablespoonfuls of the weighed flour. Set the vessel containing the flour into a pan of hot water until needed. Beat the whites with one tablespoonful of the sugar to a stiff foam. Beat the butter and sugar together to a light cream. Beat the yolks and stir them into the butter and sugar. Then add the spices and stir in half of the flour, then half of the whites, then the other half of the flour and the whites then add the brandy and stir in the fruit last. Mix it well together and put it quickly into a well buttered cake pan and bake one hour and a quarter. When it has been in one hour, try it with a wooden skewer and if it comes out dry and clean it is done.

FRUIT CAKE.

Four ounces of California seedless raisins, four ounces of currants after they have been washed and dried, four ounces of citron cut in thin chips as thin as paper, ten ounces of sifted flour with three teaspoonfuls of baking powder mixed with it, four ounces of fresh butter, eight ounces of white granulated sugar, six fresh eggs separated and one grated nutmeg. Dredge the raisins, currants and citron out of the weighed flour. Take out one tablespoonful of the sugar to beat with the whites. Beat the butter and the rest of the sugar to a light cream; beat the yolks and stir them in with the butter and sugar, then put in the nutmeg and stir in the flour and baking powder. Beat the whites with the one tablespoonful of sugar to a stiff foam and stir them in, and last add the fruit, mix it well together, put it quickly into the oven and bake.

GOLDEN CAKE.

Twelve ounces of white granulated sugar, six ounces of fresh butter, twelve yolks of fresh eggs, twelve ounces of sifted flour, with four teaspoonfuls of baking powder mixed with it, two nutmegs grated, one gill of brandy, six ounces of currants, weighed after they have been washed and dried. Dredge the currants with one tablespoonful of the weighed flour. Warm the flour by setting the vessel containing it into a pan of hot water, beat the butter and sugar to a light cream; beat the yolks with a spoonful of cold milk and stir them in with the butter and sugar, beat them together until very light, then add the nutmeg; then stir in the flour and baking powder, then add the brandy and last the currants. Mix it well together and put it quickly into a buttered cake pan and bake one hour.

GROOM'S CAKE.

One pound of white granulated sugar, ten ounces of fresh butter, sixteen yolks of fresh eggs, one pound of sifted flour, with four teaspoonfuls of baking powder mixed with it, two nutmegs grated, one gill of brandy, one gill of sherry wine, eight ounces of currants, weighed after they have been washed and dried. Dredge the currants with one tablespoonful of the weighed flour, warm the flour by setting the vessel containing it in hot water. Beat the butter and sugar together to a light cream, beat the yolks with a spoonful of cold milk and stir them into the butter and sugar, beat them together until very light, then add the nutmeg; then stir in the flour and baking powder. Then add the brandy and wine and last the currants; mix it well together and put it quickly into a buttered cake pan and bake one hour and twenty minutes.

SOFT GINGER BREAD.

Eight ounces of fresh butter, one pint of the best sugar house molasses, seven ounces of brown sugar, six fresh eggs beaten separately, two tablespoonfuls of ginger, one tablespoonful of powdered cinnamon, half of a grated nutmeg, one quart of sifted flour, with four teaspoonfuls of baking powder mixed with it. Put the molasses and butter into a saucepan and let it get warm enough to melt the butter, then take it off the fire, beat the yolks and sugar together to a light cream and stir them into the molasses and butter, then stir in the ginger, cinnamon and nutmeg and then add the flour and baking powder, beat the whites with one tablespoonful of white sugar to a stiff foam and stir them in last. The whites should be beaten and ready to put in as soon as the flour is in. Put it into an iron baking pan and bake three quarters of an hour.

WHITE GINGER BREAD.

One pint of rich sweet milk, eight ounces of fresh butter, eight fresh eggs, beaten separately, two tablespoonfuls of white ginger, one tablespoonful of powdered cinnamon, one grated nutmeg, one large lemon, grated, peel and juice, one quart of sifted flour with four teaspoonfuls of baking powder mixed with it. Melt the butter in the milk, beat the yolks and sugar to a light cream and stir them into the milk and butter. Then put in the ginger, cinnamon, nutmeg and lemon; then stir in the flour and baking powder. Beat the whites with one tablespoonful of white sugar to a stiff foam and stir them in last. The whites should be beaten and ready to put in as soon as the flour is in. Put it into an iron baking pan and bake three quarters of an hour.

JELLY CAKE.

Eight ounces of white granulated sugar, four ounces of fresh butter, six fresh eggs, beaten separately, eight ounces of flour with two teaspoonfuls of baking powder in, three teaspoonfuls of lemon extract. Beat the whites with one tablespoonful of sugar to a stiff foam. Beat the butter and sugar to a light cream; beat the yolks and stir them into the butter and sugar, then stir in half of the flour, then half of the whites, then the other half of the flour and the whites. Then add the lemon and put the mixture half an inch deep into well buttered jelly cake plates and bake in a quick oven. Spread them with strawberry or raspberry marmalade and lay them one above another, or roll them, trim off the ends and cut them in slices half an inch thick.

MARBLE CAKE.

THE WHITE PART.

Whites of five eggs beaten to a stiff foam, half a pound of white granulated sugar, four ounces of butter, half a cup of sweet milk, half a pound of flour, half a teaspoonful of baking powder.

THE BROWN PART.

Yolks of five eggs, half a pound of brown sugar, half a pound of flour, four ounces of butter, half a cup of sweet milk, half a teaspoonful each of cinnamon, cloves, pepper, nutmeg, ginger and baking powder. Stir the butter in separate bowls, the white part in one bowl and the brown part in another. When it is well stirred grease your pan and put in a large spoonful of brown batter, then a spoonful of white batter beside it and so on until all is used, always putting a white over a brown part. Bake one hour in a moderate oven.

MERINGUE.

Two ounces of white powdered sugar, two whites of eggs beaten to a stiff foam with one teaspoonful of white sugar to every two whites, then stir in the sugar and add the flavoring according to taste.

POUND CAKE.

One pound of sifted flour with three teaspoonfuls of baking powder mixed in it, one pound of white granulated sugar, twelve ounces of fresh butter, ten fresh eggs beaten separately, and two middle sized nutmegs grated. Take out two tablespoonfuls of the weighed sugar to beat with the whites to a stiff foam, beat the butter and sugar together to a light cream, beat the yolks with a spoonful of cold milk and stir them in with the butter and sugar, beat them together until very light, then add the nutmeg; then stir in half of the flour, then half of the whites, then the other half of the flour and the remainder of the whites last. Put it quickly into a buttered cake pan and bake one hour.

SILVER CAKE.

Twelve whites of fresh eggs, six ounces of fresh butter, twelve ounces of white granulated sugar, twelve ounces of sifted flour with four teaspoonfuls of baking powder mixed with it, two teaspoonfuls of the extract of lemon, four teaspoonfuls of the extract of roses, one gill of sherry wine, six ounces of citron cut thin as paper. Take out one tablespoonful of the weighed flour and dredge the citron. Set the vessel containing the flour and baking powder into a pan of hot water and stir it occasionally until needed. Put the whites into two bowls with one tablespoonful of the weighed sugar in each bowl and beat them with a machine egg beater to a stiff foam. Beat the butter and sugar together to a light cream, then stir in half of the flour then half of the whites, then the other half of the flour and the whites, then add the flavoring and wine, and last the citron. Mix it evenly together, put it quickly into a buttered cake pan and bake one hour.

SNOW CAKE.

Whites of twelve fresh eggs, six ounces of fresh butter, twelve ounces of white granulated sugar, twelve ounces of sifted flour with three teaspoonfuls of baking powder mixed in it, three teaspoonfuls of lemon extract. Put the whites into two bowls with one tablespoonful of the weighed sugar in each bowl and beat them with a machine egg beater to a stiff foam. Set the vessel containing the flour into a pan of boiling water and stir it occasionally until needed. Beat the butter and sugar together to a light cream, then stir in half of the flour, then half of the whites, then the other half of the flour and the whites, then add the lemon and put it half an inch deep into well buttered jelly cake plates and bake a light brown. It takes it about ten minutes. Then put a layer of cake and a layer of grated cocoanut and raspberry mixture, then a layer of cake, and so on, finishing with cake and an icing with cocoanut sprinkled over the top whilst the icing is wet.

COCOANUT AND RASPBERRY MIXTURE.

Eight ounces of grated cocoanut, mixed with half a pint of raspberry syrup.

SPONGE CAKE. (Very Fine.)

Six fresh eggs beaten separately, eight ounces of white granulated sugar, six ounces of sifted flour, with two teaspoonfuls of baking powder mixed with it, three teaspoonfuls of lemon extract. Beat the whites with one tablespoonful of the sugar to a stiff foam, beat the yolks with the rest of the sugar until very light, put the sugar in with the yolks a spoonful at a time. It is easier beaten than if the whole was put in at once, then stir in half of the flour, then the whites, then the other half of the flour and the lemon. Put it quickly into a well buttered cake pan and bake forty minutes. If baked in small cakes, twenty minutes. Try it with a wooden skewer, and if it comes out clean and dry the cake is done.

SPONGE MUFFINS. (For Tea.)

Five fresh eggs beaten separately, six ounces of white granulated sugar, five ounces of sifted flour, with one heaped teaspoonful of baking powder mixed in it. Beat the whites with one tablespoonful of the sugar to a stiff foam, beat the yolks with the rest of the sugar, then stir half of the flour into the yolks and sugar, then the whites, then the other half of the flour. Put it quickly into well buttered muffin pans and bake twenty minutes. Serve them hot, split them open and butter them. They are excellent.

WHITE SPONGE CAKE.

Twelve whites of eggs, eight ounces of white granulated sugar, six ounces of sifted flour, with three teaspoonfuls of baking powder mixed with it, three teaspoonfuls of lemon extract. Beat the whites with one tablespoonful of the sugar to a stiff foam, then beat the rest of the sugar into the whites and then add the lemon and stir in the flour last. Put it quickly into a well buttered cake pan and bake forty minutes. Try it with a wooden skewer and if it comes out dry and clean it is done.

WHITE CAKE. (Excellent.)

Whites of six fresh eggs, three ounces of fresh butter, six ounces of white granulated sugar, six ounces of sifted flour, with two teaspoonfuls of baking powder mixed with it, two teaspoonfuls of lemon extract. Beat the whites with one tablespoonful of the sugar to a stiff foam, beat the butter and sugar to a light cream and then stir in half of the flour, then stir in half of the whites, then the other half of the flour and the whites; then add the lemon and put it quickly into a well buttered pan and bake thirty minutes.

Beverages.

CIDER, TO KEEP SWEET.

As soon as the cider begins to ferment bore a small gimlet hole through the bung of the barrel and put in a wooden plug. Once a day this plug must be taken out to let the gas escape, otherwise the barrel would burst. Then take one pint of yellow English mustard seed, divide it into four parts and put it into four small thin muslin bags, one gill in each bag; tie the mouth of the bags with a cord and drop them into the cider through the bung hole, make the bung tight, put in the plug, turn the barrel on end, put in the faucet tight and place the barrel high enough to allow the cider to be drawn off without moving the barrel. Cider prepared in this manner will keep sweet a long time

SIBERIAN CRAB APPLE WINE.
(Very Fine.)

Prepare the crab apple cider in the same manner as in the preceding receipt, and after the mustard seed has been in the cider four or six weeks it is ready to bottle. Ten gallons of cider will fill fifty wine bottles. Put the corks to soak in warm water. Clean the bottles inside with shot and warm water and have a ball of thick twine ready. Then put one large raisin into each bottle and fill with cider. Pound in the corks with a wooden mallet, tie them in with twine and lay the bottles on their side in a cool place.

CIDER, KEPT SWEET.

The following is a scientific method of treating cider to preserve its sweetness: When the saccharine matter, by fermenting, is being converted into alcohol, if a bent tube be inserted air tight into the bung with the other end into a pail of water, to allow the carbonic acid gas evolved to pass off without admitting any air into the barrel a beverage will be attained that is a fit nectar for the gods. A handy way is to fill your cask nearly up to the faucet, when the cask is rolled so that the bung is down. Get a common rubber tube and slip it over the end of the plug in the faucet, with the other end in the pail of water. Then turn the plug so the cider can have communication with the pail. After the water ceases to bubble, bottle or store it away.—*Farm, Field and Fireside.*

EGG NOG, WARM.

One quart of rich sweet milk, half a pint of brandy or whiskey, six ounces of white granulated sugar, one teaspoonful of grated nutmeg, three fresh eggs, beaten separately. Put the milk, brandy, sugar and nutmeg into a saucepan and set it on the side of the range, where it will get warm but not hot. Beat the whites to a stiff foam then beat the yolks and stir them into the whites, then stir them into the warm milk and set it over a quick fire, stir it fast and as soon as it begins to rise (it must not boil) take it off the fire and pour it into a bowl or pitcher and serve it in glasses. It is a very refreshing drink on a cold day.

EGG NOG, COLD.

Four fresh eggs, beaten separately, six ounces of white granulated sugar, one teaspoonful of grated nutmeg, half a pint of brandy or whisky, one quart of rich sweet milk. Beat the whites with two teaspoonfuls of the sugar to a stiff foam. Beat the yolks and sugar together to a light cream, then put in the nutmeg and the brandy, then add half of the milk and stir in the whites, then add the other half of the milk.

LEMONADE.

Three large lemons, five tablespoonfuls of white sugar, three pints of ice water. Wash and wipe the lemons, then peel off the yellow part of the rind very thin (that contains the oil) and put it into a porcelain pitcher. Then peel off the white part (which is always bitter) and cut the lemon in two in the middle; put them into the lemon squeezer and squeeze the juice into the pitcher. Then take out the seeds and put the squeezed lemon into the pitcher. Now put in the sugar and beat the whole together a minute or two, then add the water and stir it until the sugar is dissolved. It is then ready to use.

LEMON PUNCH.

Half a pint of lemon syrup and half a pint of sherry wine put into one quart of ice water. It makes a refreshing summer drink.

RASPBERRY SHRUB.

Three pints of ice water, half a pint of raspberry syrup, one gill of brandy, one large lemon. Peel the lemon and squeeze the juice into a porcelain pitcher, then put in the water and raspberry syrup. Then add the brandy and stir it well together. It makes a pleasant summer drink.

LEMON SYRUP.

Wash and wipe the lemons, then grate the yellow rind very thin off of one half of the lemons, then peel off the white part and throw it away, it is always bitter. Then peel the other half of the lemons and cut them all in two in the middle and put them into the lemon squeezer and squeeze out all the juice, then take out all the seeds and throw the squeezed lemon into a bowl of hot water, a good deal of the acid remains in the lemon after it is squeezed. When the lemons are all squeezed measure the juice in a pint and mark it down on paper, then strain the lemon and water through a wire sieve and measure one pint of the water to each pint of the lemon juice and mark it down beside the juice, keep the water separate and weigh the sugar. To each pint of the water and juice allow one pound and a quarter of white granulated sugar. Put the sugar and grated lemon peel into a porcelain kettle and mix it together, then put in the water and boil it five minutes, then add the lemon juice, take it off the fire and strain through a linen cloth. Bottle it, and when it is cold cork tight and seal. Half a pint of lemon syrup to one quart of ice water makes a delightful drink in warm weather. Three tablespoonfuls of lemon syrup is the right quantity for a goblet of ice water. One tablespoonful of lemon syrup is enough for one lemonade glass of ice water.

MILK PUNCH.

Five lemons, six ounces of white granulated sugar, one pint of rich sweet milk, one pint of water, one grated nutmeg, one pint of rum or brandy and the juice of the lemon. Grate the yellow skin off the lemons and mix it with the sugar, put the milk, water, grated lemon and sugar into a saucepan and let it come to a boil, then take it off the fire and put in the nutmeg, rum and lemon juice; strain the whole through a jelly cloth and serve when cold.

MULLED CIDER.

One quart of good cider, six ounces of white granulated sugar, four fresh eggs, beaten separately. two teaspoonfuls of grated nutmeg. Put the cider, sugar and nutmeg into a saucepan and set it on the range where it will get warm, but not scalding hot. Beat the whites with three teaspoonfuls of white sugar to a stiff foam, then beat the yolks and stir them into the whites, and then stir them into the cider. Set it quickly over a hot fire and stir it fast until it begins to rise (it must not boil) then take it off the fire and pour it into a pitcher. Serve it warm.

MULLED WINE.

One pint of sherry wine, one pint of water, six ounces of white granulated sugar, four fresh eggs, beaten separately, two teaspoonfuls of cinnamon or nutmeg, according to taste. Put the wine, water, cinnamon and sugar into a saucepan and set it on the side of the range where it will get warm, but not hot. Beat the whites with three teaspoonfuls of white sugar to a stiff foam, then beat the yolks and stir them into the whites, then stir them into the wine and set it over a quick fire and stir it fast until it begins to rise (it must not boil) then take it quickly off the fire and pour it into a pitcher. Put it into glasses and serve it warm.

ROMAN PUNCH.

Four lemons, half a pound of white granulated sugar, two quarts of boiling water, half a pint of Jamaica rum. After the lemons have been washed and wiped, peel off the yellow skin very thin and put it into the vessel the punch is to be made in, then peel off the white skin, which is bitter, and throw it away; then cut the lemons in two and squeeze the juice into the vessel, then take out the seeds and put the squeezed lemon in with the juice, then put in the sugar and rub the sugar and lemons together a few minutes, then pour in the boiling water and let it stand until it is cold, then place a fine sieve over the punch bowl and pour it through, then add the rum and slice two lemons into the punch bowl.

RASPBERRY VINEGAR.

Put four quarts of ripe red raspberries into a porcelain preserving kettle and mash them with a wooden beetle, then boil them five minutes and take them off the fire. Then stir into them one quart of strong cider vinegar, then strain through a linen cloth and measure. To one pint of the juice allow three quarters of a pound of white granulated sugar, set it over the fire, and when it begins to boil skim it well and boil it ten minutes. When cold bottle, cork tight and seal, when it is to be used put two tablespoonfuls of the raspberry vinegar into a goblet two thirds full of ice water.

Canned Fruits, Marmalades, Jellies and Preserves.

JELLY, TO MAKE.

To make fine jelly of the small fruits, the fruit must be boiled ten minutes with the skins, cores and seeds. The skins increase the flavor and the cores and seeds contain the gluten which makes the jelly. For a strainer I use a jelly cloth instead of a jelly bag. I find it more convenient and much quicker done. I take a piece of fine Russia linen crash three yards long and wring it out of warm water. Place a wire sieve over a flat stone crock and put one end of the linen over the sieve, then put in a ladle full of the fruit, fold the two sides together and twist the two ends in opposite directions. It takes two persons to do it. Then remove to another part of the linen, and so on, until all is strained. If the linen is right the jelly will be perfectly clear. I have never failed to have fine jelly although I never have used gelatine.

MARMALADE.

To make the finest marmalade the fruit must be boiled ten minutes before the sugar is put in with it. The marmalade will be smoother, finer flavored and quicker made than according to the old method. Sugar always hardens the fruit and prevents it from mashing easily.

STRAWBERRIES, CANNED.

The dark red Wilson strawberries are the best for all purposes. They should be gathered in dry weather and be fresh from the vines. After they are hulled, weigh them, and to one pound of strawberries allow half a pound of white granulated sugar. Spread the strawberries on porcelain plates, strew the sugar thickly over them and let them stand in a cool place until the next morning. The sugar will extract the juice and harden the fruit. Use a silver knife or spoon to take them off the plates into the kettle. Use a wooden spoon in the kettle. Let them heat very slowly and when they come to a boiling heat (they must not boil) they are ready to put up. Put them into glass jars hermetically sealed.

STRAWBERRY MARMALADE.

To one pound of strawberries, three quarters of a pound of white granulated sugar. Put the strawberries into a porcelain preserving kettle and mash them with a wooden beetle until there is juice enough to cover the bottom of the kettle. Let them boil ten minutes then add the sugar and cook them thirty minutes, stirring them constantly with a wooden spoon to prevent it from sticking. Put it warm into jelly glasses, cover with double writing paper, cut to fit the inside, dipped in brandy, and close with metal covers, or put it into glass jars hermetically sealed.

STRAWBERRIES, PRESERVED.

To one pound of Wilson strawberries allow one pound of white granulated sugar, spread the strawberries thinly on porcelain plates and strew all the sugar over them and let them remain in it over night, in the morning the plates will be full of juice. With a silver knife or spoon take all from the plates into a porcelain preserving kettle, set it over a slow fire until it comes to a boiling heat, but not to boil, then take the kettle off and with a skimmer take the strawberries out, a few at a time, and spread them on the same plates to cool; strain the syrup through a linen cloth and return it to the kettle, boil it two minutes, skimming it well. Take it off the fire, put the strawberries into the syrup, cover the kettle and set it in a cool place until the next morning. The strawberries must not be taken out of the syrup again until they are done. In the morning set them over the fire and as soon as they are hot take them off, cover them, and put them in a cool place until the next morning. Repeat this for four mornings and the strawberries will be perfectly clear and not one broken. Put them into pint or half pint, wide mouthed, glass jars, cover with double writing paper cut to fit the inside, dipped in brandy, cork and seal them.

RED RASPBERRY JELLY.

To three pints of raspberry juice put one pint of currant juice, and one pound of white granulated sugar to each pint of juice. The raspberries and currants must be ripe and gathered in dry weather. Mash the raspberries with a wooden beetle in a porcelain preserving kettle and boil them ten minutes; then strain them through a linen cloth and measure. Put the currants into a preserving kettle, stems and all; mash them and boil ten minutes, then strain and measure; mix the currant and raspberry juice together in the kettle and stir in the sugar, as soon as it begins to boil skim it as quick as possible, for it often jellies in five minutes. Put it hot into jelly glasses with double writing paper cut to fit the inside, dipped in brandy. Use jelly glasses with metal covers, and the jelly should be cold before the covers are made tight.

RED RASPBERRY MARMALADE.

To three pounds of raspberries put one pound of currants and three quarters of a pound of white granulated sugar to each pound of fruit; mash the raspberries and currants together in the kettle and boil them ten minutes; then add the sugar and boil twenty minutes longer, stir it all the time with a wooden spoon to prevent it from sticking. Put it hot into small glass jars or jelly glasses with double writing paper cut to fit the inside, dipped in brandy. Close the marmalade when cold, if put in jelly glasses.

BLACK RASPBERRIES, Canned for Pies Tarts and Sauce.

To three pounds of raspberries put one pound of ripe currants, and two pounds of white granulated sugar to four pounds of fruit; after the currants are picked and weighed mash them with a wooden beetle and put them in the bottom of the preserving kettle and sprinkle a handful of sugar over them, then put in a layer of raspberries and a layer of sugar until all are in; set the kettle on the side of the range where they will heat slowly for one hour, or until the juice is extracted; then stir them up from the bottom, let them get hot and they are ready to put up. Put them into glass jars, hermetically sealed.

CURRANT JELLY.

To one pint of currant juice put one pound of white granulated sugar. Pick the leaves out from the currents, then mash them stems and all together, with a wooden beetle and put them into a porcelain preserving kettle and boil them ten minutes; then strain through a linen cloth, measure and return the juice to the kettle. Mix the sugar and juice together before the juice is hot and stir it with a wooden spoon until it begins to boil, then skim it as quickly as possible, for it will be jelly in about five minutes. Put it hot into jelly glasses, cover with double writing paper cut to fit the inside, dipped in brandy. Close with metal covers when the jelly is cold.

CHERRIES, CANNED.

After the cherries are stemmed and stoned, weigh them, and to each pound of cherries allow half a pound of white granulated sugar. Put them into a porcelain kettle, a layer of cherries and a layer of sugar until all are in. Then add one quart of water to six pounds of cherries. Put the water in at the side of the kettle, set them over a slow fire and let them heat gradually for two hours, or until the juice is extracted, then let them come to a boiling heat and they are ready to put up. Put them into glass jars hermetically sealed.

GREEN GAGE PLUMS, PRE-SERVED.

To one pound of plums allow one pound of white granulated sugar, and one-half a pint of water to each pound of sugar. Take large fine green gage plums that are not fully ripe but have turned a little yellowish, pick them, weigh and wash them in two waters. Put the sugar and water into a porcelain preserving kettle, and as soon as the sugar is dissolved put in the plums, turn them over with a skimmer, that they may heat evenly. As soon as the skins are curled and cracked move them to the side of the range, where they will not boil. Let them stand for one hour, or until the juice is extracted; then cover the kettle and set it in a cool place over night. In the morning set them on the fire and when they are at a boiling heat take the plums out onto large porcelain dishes. Boil the syrup, skim it and return the plums to the kettle; let them get hot, but not to boil, cover the kettle and set it away until the next morning, when they are ready to put up. The syrup must cover the plums. Put them into glass jars hermetically sealed.

GREEN GAGE JELLY.

The plums for jelly should be fully ripe. Wash them or wipe them off with a wet cloth, take off the stems and cut out the spots, weigh them, and to one pound of plums allow half a pint of water. Put the plums and water into a porcelain preserving kettle and boil them twenty minutes, then strain them through a linen cloth; after they are all strained, strain the juice over again; measure it and to each pint of juice allow one pound of white granulated sugar. Put the juice and sugar into the preserving kettle and stir it until the sugar is all dissolved, as soon as it begins to boil look at your watch, skim it well and let it boil ten minutes. Put it hot into the jelly glasses with double writing paper cut to fit the inside, dipped in brandy. When it is cold close up with metal covers.

GREEN GAGE PLUMS, CANNED.

Plums for canning should not be fully ripe. To four pounds of plums allow two pounds of white granulated sugar and half a pint of water; pick the plums carefully, taking out all the spotted ones and those that are fully ripe, for jelly. Weigh them and wash them in two waters, put the sugar and water into a porcelain preserving kettle and as soon as the sugar is dissolved put in the plums, set them over a slow fire and turn them over carefully from the bottom of the kettle with a large skimmer that they may heat evenly and not break. This must be done as soon as they are put on the fire and continued until they are done. As soon as the skins curl and split open and they are scalding hot they are ready to put up; they must not boil nor break. If there is not syrup enough add a little hot water and mix it well together. The quantity of syrup depends a great deal on the ripeness of the plums. Put them into glass jars hermetically sealed.

WHITE HEATH FREE-STONE PEACHES, CANNED.

To four pounds of peaches, one pound of white granulated sugar. In putting up peaches for the table I prefer the White Heath. They are rich in flavor and delicate in color. They should not be over ripe. Pare them and cut them in halves, or if they are very large, quarter them and take out the stones. Put into the preserving kettle a layer of peaches and a layer of sugar until all are in, then put in one pint of water to one bushel of peaches, sprinkle the water over the top of the peaches, set them on the side of the fire where they will heat very slowly. They should stand one hour and a half before they are put over the fire, or until the juice is extracted. Crack one quarter of the peach stones and put the kernels into a small saucepan with water enough to cover them and boil them thirty minutes; then strain off the water and mix it with the peaches. It gives them a fine flavor. As soon as the juice is extracted set the kettle over the fire, and when they are at boiling heat (but not to boil) they are ready to put up. Put them into glass jars hermetically sealed. Peaches for pies are put up in the same manner.

WHITE HEATH CLING-STONE PEACHES, CANNED.

Take cling-stone peaches that are ripe and after they are pared, divide them into quarters and cut them from the stones. To four pounds of peaches allow one pound of white granulated sugar and one pint of water. Put the peaches into the preserving kettle with a layer of sugar between each layer of peaches, then put in the water at the side of the kettle and set them on the side of the fire where they will heat slowly. Crack one quarter of the peach stones and put the kernels into a small saucepan with water enough to cover them and boil them thirty minutes. Then strain the water off and mix it with the peaches. Cook the peaches until they are tender, but they must not break. Try them with a fork and when they are soft they are ready to put up. Put them into glass jars hermetically sealed.

PEACH PRESERVES.

To one pound of free-stone peaches one pound of white granulated sugar and half a pint of water.

Pare the peaches, cut them in halves and take out the stones, put them into a porcelain preserving kettle, the cut side uppermost, with a layer of sugar and a layer of peaches, finishing with a layer of sugar. Then put the water in at the side of the kettle; set them on the side of the range where they will heat slowly for one hour and a half; crack one quarter of the stones, take out the kernels and boil them in one pint of water for thirty minutes, then strain off the water and put it in with the peaches, set the kettle of peaches over the fire, and as soon as it comes to a boiling heat, but not to boil, take it off, cover it and let it stand over night. In the morning let it get boiling hot, but it must not boil; then take the peaches out with a skimmer onto large porcelain dishes; boil the syrup long enough to skim it well and then return the peaches to the kettle, set it over a slow fire and as soon as the peaches look clear they are ready to put up.

PEACH MARMALADE.

To one pound of peaches allow three quarters of a pound of white granulated sugar and one pint of water to four pounds of peaches. Take ripe, juicy free-stone peaches; pare them, take out the stones and crack one quarter of them, put the kernels into a saucepan with water enough to cover them and cook them thirty minutes, then strain off the water, cut the peaches into thin slices and put them into a porcelain preserving kettle with one pint of water to four pounds of peaches and cook them ten minutes from the time they begin to boil; then add the sugar and the water from the kernels, stir it well with a wooden spoon and cook it twenty minutes longer. Put it into glass jars or jelly glasses with double writing paper cut to fit the inside, dipped in brandy.

BRANDY PEACHES.

White Heath "clings" are the best for brandy peaches. Weigh them before they are skinned and mark it down on paper with a pencil. To one pound of peaches allow half a pound of white granulated sugar, one gill of water and half a pint of white brandy. Put eight ounces of cooking soda with two quarts of cold water into an iron pot and let it get scalding hot, then put in one dozen of the peaches at a time and let them stay in just five minutes, then take them out with a skimmer into a colander. Rub off the skin with a dry, coarse linen cloth and put the peaches into a large pan full of cold water. Put the sugar with one gill of water to half a pound of sugar into the preserving kettle and when it is dissolved take the peaches out of the water into a colander, let them drain a minute and then put them into the syrup, turn them over from time to time and skim when anything rises. Cook them slowly until they are soft enough for a silver fork to go easily through, then take them out onto flat porcelain dishes and boil the syrup down to one half, skim it as long as anything rises to the surface, and then take it off the fire and let it cool ten minutes. Then put in the brandy and return the peaches to the brandy syrup. Set the kettle over the fire again and when it is hot (but not to boil) take it off the fire and fill the glass jars first with the peaches and then with the brandy syrup. The syrup must cover the peaches. Close the jars hermetically.

SECKEL PEARS, CANNED.

To four pounds of pears, one pound of white granulated sugar, two quarts of water, one ounce of whole cinnamon, two large lemons and one pint of red wine. Wash the lemons, slice them and take out the seeds. The pears must not be over ripe. Pare them, leaving on the stems and taking out the blossom end. Put them into the preserving kettle with the water, cinnamon, lemons and sugar and boil them one hour, or until they are tender; try them with a fork; it depends upon the size and ripeness of the pears. Then take them out onto large porcelain dishes and strain the syrup through a linen cloth; return the syrup and pears to the kettle and put in the wine. When it comes to a boiling heat they are ready to put up. It must not boil after the wine is put in. Put them into glass jars hermetically sealed. They are excellent.

SIBERIAN CRAB APPLE JELLY.

There are two kinds of crab apples. The largest size is mellow and has very little juice, the smaller size is juicy and the best for jelly. They are ripe the latter part of August. Wash the crab apples in two waters and spread them on a table that is covered with a cloth, select the finest, cut off the stems, take out the blossom end and slice them in three pieces, skins, cores and seeds all together. Weigh them, and to four pounds of apples put one quart of cold water and one lemon; wash the lemons, wipe them, slice them and take out the seeds; put the whole into a porcelain preserving kettle and boil it thirty minutes, then strain through a linen cloth. Put a small quantity of the apples in at a time, it will be quicker done; after they are all strained, strain the juice over again. To one pint of the juice allow one pound of white granulated sugar, put it into the preserving kettle and stir it well together; when it begins to boil skim it and boil five minutes. I have had it jelly in that time. Put it into jelly glasses with double writing paper cut to fit the inside, dipped in brandy, and when the jelly is cold close with metal covers.

QUINCE JELLY.

After the quinces have been washed, wiped and the blemishes and blossom end removed, pare them, quarter them and cut out the cores; put them with the cores, seeds and skins from the canned quinces. Weigh them, and to one pound of skins and cores, allow one pint of water. Boil them twenty minutes; put them into a wire sieve, and when the juice has run through strain it through a linen cloth. Cut the quartered quinces in thin slices and to one pound of quinces put one pint of the juice; cook them until they are soft, but not to break; strain through a linen cloth. To one pint of the juice put one pound of white granulated sugar, mix the juice and sugar well together before putting it on the fire. As soon as it begins to boil skim quickly, it is jelly in five minutes. Put it into jelly glasses with double writing paper cut to fit the inside, dipped in brandy. This jelly can be colored beautifully with cranberry juice, one pint of cranberry juice to four pints of quince juice, but there must be one pound of sugar to a pint of juice.

DAMSON PLUMS FOR SAUCE OR TARTS.

Take ripe damson plums, pick them carefully and wash them in two waters, measure them and to three quarts of plums, allow one pint of water. Put them into a porcelain preserving kettle and boil them twenty minutes; then put them into a wire sieve, a small quantity at a time, and press all through excepting the skins and stones. Then measure them and to one quart of the strained plums put one pint and a half of sugar; mix it well together and set it over a slow fire and boil it thirty minutes, stir it with a wooden spoon all the time it is on the fire.

DAMSON PLUMS, CANNED.

Wash the plums in cold water and drain them through a colander, then pick them carefully, taking out all the blemished ones, then weigh them. To eight pounds of plums, allow six pounds of sugar and one pint of water, put the sugar and and water into a preserving kettle, and when it comes to a boil put in the plums and keep turning them over with a skimmer until they begin to boil. Then let them boil just five minutes, put them hot into glass jars hermetically sealed.

CRANBERRY JELLY.

Pick and wash the cranberries and then measure them. To one quart of cranberries put one pint of water and boil them fifteen minutes, stirring them with a wooden spoon to prevent them from sticking, then rub them through a wire sieve, all excepting the skins. To one pint of the cranberry juice put one pint of white granulated sugar; mix it well together before putting it on the fire. As soon as it boils skim it as quick as you can, it is jelly in two minutes. Put it into jelly glasses or jars. It moulds beautifully.

QUINCES, CANNED.

The pear shaped quinces are the best for all purposes. Wash the quinces, wipe them, remove the blemishes and blossom end, pare them, cut them in halves and divide each half in three pieces. Take out the cores and save them and the skins for jelly. To one pound of quinces allow half a pound of white granulated sugar and half a pint of water, mix the sugar and water together in the preserving kettle and put in the quinces. The water should be even with the quinces; cook them over a low fire until they are soft enough for a fork to go easily through them, but must not break them. Put them hot into glass jars hermetically sealed.

QUINCE PRESERVES.

To one pound of quinces put one pound of white granulated sugar and half a pint of juice. Take large, yellow, ripe, pear shaped quinces, and after they are washed, wiped, blemishes and blossom end removed, pare them, quarter them and take out the cores. To one pound of skins, cores and seeds, put one pint of water. Boil them twenty minutes, then put them into a wire sieve and then strain the juice through a linen cloth. If there is not juice enough add some water; put the quinces and juice into the preserving kettle with half of the sugar and cook them until they are soft enough for a fork to go through them, then put in the other half of the sugar, and when it is all dissolved and begins to boil take them off the fire, cover them and let them stand two days, then set the kettle on the fire and when it is boiling hot take the quinces out onto large plates, boil up the syrup and skim it well, return the quinces to the kettle and when they are hot again put them into glass jars with double writing paper cut to fit the inside, dipped in brandy.

QUINCE MARMALADE.

To one pound of quinces, put three quarters of a pound of white granulated sugar. Wash and wipe the quinces after the blemishes and blossom end are removed, pare them and cut out the cores. To one pound of skins and cores put one pint of cold water and boil them twenty minutes, then put them into a wire sieve, and when the juice is all through, strain it through a linen cloth; cut the quinces in thin slices and to one pound of quinces put one pint of the juice. If there is not juice enough add some water. Cook them until they are soft but not broken, and then rub them all through a coarse wire sieve; mix the sugar and quinces well together and cook it thirty minutes, stir it all the time with a wooden spoon to prevent it from sticking. Put it into jelly glasses or glass jars with double writing paper, cut to fit the inside, dipped in brandy.

Canned Vegetables.

ASPARAGUS, CANNED.

The best cans for putting up asparagus are flat and square and just as long as the asparagus and deep enough to hold three or four bunches, with a cover as large as the can, that has an opening in it the size of a half dollar. Wash the asparagus in cold water and place it in the cans, heads together, until the can is full, then put on the cover and solder it tight with lead, then fill the cans with cold water and put one teaspoonful of salt into each can, then solder the opening in the covers and put the cans into a large boiler with cold water enough to cover them, and boil them slowly thirty minutes. After they begin to boil then take out the cans and puncture a small hole in the top of each can, to let out the steam, then solder them quickly and return them to the boiler, and let them boil slowly thirty minutes longer. When the asparagus has to be used pour off all the water in the can, then put half a pint of rich sweet milk into a stew pan over the fire and mix two tablespoonfuls of fresh butter with two teaspoonfuls of flour and stir it into the hot milk and let it boil two minutes, then put in the asparagus and let it come to a boil and simmer a few minutes.

CAULIFLOWER, CANNED.

Is put up in the same manner and boiled the same length of time and prepared for the table in the same manner as asparagus.

GREEN CORN, CANNED.

Select young sugar corn that is in the milk, and after it is husked, silked and the blemishes taken out, cut it off the cob and scrape out what is left in the cob, it is the best part of the corn. Then fill the cans full with the corn and the milk that came out of it and put one teaspoonful of salt to each pint of corn and solder the cans tight with lead and put them into a large boiler with cold water enough to cover them, and let them boil slowly two hours; then take the cans out and puncture a small hole in the top of each can to let out the steam, then solder them quickly and return them to the boiler and boil them two hours longer.

STRING BEANS.

The yellow wax beans are the best. String them with a knife, break them into two or three pieces and throw them into cold water for half an hour, then wash them and drain them in a colander and fill the cans, then put in cold water enough to fill the cans with one teaspoonful of salt to each pint can and solder them tight with lead, then put them into a large boiler with cold water enough to cover them, and boil them one hour and a half.

GREEN PEAS, CANNED.

The best peas are those which have flat pods. After the peas have been shelled, picked over and put into cold water, pour off all that floats on top of the water; then put them into a colander to drain, and then fill the cans full and pour in cold water enough to just cover the peas, then put in one teaspoonful of salt to each pint, cover the peas and solder the cans tight with lead. When all are ready put them into a large boiler with cold water enough to cover them and heat them slowly and boil them thirty minutes. Then take the cans out and puncture a small hole in the top of each can to let out the steam, then solder them quickly and return them to the boiler and boil them thirty minutes longer.

LIMA BEANS, CANNED.

Take young lima beans and after they are picked over and washed in cold water and drained in a colander, fill the cans and pour in cold water enough to cover the beans, and put in one teaspoonful of salt to each pint of beans; then solder the cans tight with lead, and when all are ready, put them into a large boiler with cold water enough to cover them and boil them one hour, then take the cans out and puncture a small hole in the top of each can to let out the steam, then solder them quickly and return them to the boiler and boil them one hour longer.

TOMATOES, CANNED.

Tomatoes that are a dark red are over ripe and unfit to use for canning or any other culinary purpose. They should be pale pink red, and should be put up the last week in August, they are the best at that time. Have a kettle with boiling water over the fire and put in a small quantity of tomatoes at a time, and let them remain in it about two minutes, or until the skins begin to crack, then take them out quickly with a large skimmer into a colander and put them onto waiters to cool. After they are all peeled and cut up put them into a large kettle with one gill of salt to one bushel of tomatoes; let them heat slowly and boil them twenty minutes. They must be boiling hot, but not boil, while the cans are filling, or there will be air bubbles in them. Hold the covers down tight with a knife while the hot wax is poured around them.

Diet for the Sick.

BROTH AND MILK.

Dr. Pulte says there are cases where the mother's milk is too poor to nourish the babe, even when there is plenty of milk. In such cases he prescribes warm beef broth or mutton broth with warm cow's milk, half and half.

PAP.

Mix one full teaspoonful of flour with one tablespoonful of cold milk, and then stir it into half a pint of boiling milk that has a pinch of salt in it. Boil it five minutes and then stir in one teaspoonful of white sugar.

PANADA.

Grate half of a double baked rusk, or half of a Boston cracker into half a pint of cold new milk that has one teaspoonful of white sugar in it; boil it three minutes from the time it begins to boil, stir it constantly from the time it is put on the fire until it is done.

BEEF BROTH.

The leg of beef makes the best broth, and four pounds will make one quart. After the leg has been cut up into four or five pieces, wash it in cold water and put it into the soup kettle with cold water enough to cover it, and just when it begins to boil skim it as long as anything rises to the surface. Cover the kettle and boil it slowly five hours; if the water boils down too low replenish with a little boiling water. When it is done take out all the meat and bones, skim off all the fat, and season only with salt; then strain it through a wire sieve and serve it in a china cup and saucer with double baked rusk or crackers. A cup full of this broth, with a double baked rusk is very refreshing to a patient, as I can speak from experience. If rice is permitted in the broth it must boil one hour. When cold this broth will become a jelly.

CHICKEN BROTH.

An old chicken makes the best broth, and it is

much clearer and nicer by cooking the chicken whole. After the chicken is dressed, light a paper and singe it off, then wash it in cold water and put it whole into the soup kettle, with cold water enough to cover it, and when it begins to boil skim it, keep the kettle covered and cook it slowly five hours. When it has cooked two hours turn it, and if the water boils down too low replenish with a little boiling water. When it is done lift the chicken, skim off the fat and season only with salt. There should be only one pint and a half of broth. Serve it with double baked rusk or crackers. If rice is permitted in the broth it must cook one hour. This broth when cold will become a jelly.

MUTTON BROTH.

Old meat makes better broth and soup than young. Four pounds of the leg of old mutton will make one quart of good broth. After it has been cut up into three or four pieces wash it in cold water and put it into the soup kettle with cold water enough to cover it, and just when it begins to boil skim it as long as anything rises to the surface. Cover the kettle and boil it slowly five hours then take out all the meat and bones and skim off all the fat and season only with salt. If pearl barley is permitted in the broth, one tablespoonful is enough for one quart of broth, and it must cook two hours.

MILK PORRIDGE.

Half a pint of rich sweet milk, two teaspoonfuls of flour mixed with a little cold milk and a pinch of salt. Put the milk into a small saucepan and set it into another one containing boiling water and let it get boiling hot, mix the flour with a little cold milk until it is very smooth; then add a little more milk to make it thin enough to stir into the boiling milk, stir it until it boils three minutes, then take it off. If the physician permits, and the patient desires it, sugar and sherry wine or brandy can be added according to prescription and taste.

OAT MEAL PORRIDGE.

Pick one gill of oat groats carefully, seeing that all the hulls are taken out; then wash them in cold water and put them into a tin saucepan with one pint of cold water and half a teaspoonful of salt; cover it close and then set it into a larger saucepan containing boiling water and boil it one hour. The water in the larger pan must not stop boiling until the porridge is done.

BARLEY BOILED.

One gill of pearl barley, one pint of cold water and one saltspoonful of salt; after the barley has been washed in cold water put it and the pint of cold water and salt into a small tin saucepan that has a steam pipe through the cover and set it into another saucepan containing boiling water and boil it two hours. The water must not stop boiling until the barley is done. It may be served with sugar, cream or milk.

OAT GROATS.

Wash half a pint of the groats in cold water and put them into a tin saucepan with one pint of cold water and a saltspoonful of salt. Cover the saucepan and set it into another pan containing boiling water. Don't stir it nor put any more water in it and boil it three quarters of an hour; then set it on the side of the range until the groats are about as thick as mush. Serve it with white powdered sugar and sweet cream or rich sweet milk. It is a very healthy diet, and is considered by some a remedy for dyspepsia and constipation of the bowels. In such cases it must be taken in the morning on an empty stomach before breakfast.

RICE BOILED.

cold water into a small tin saucepan that has a steam pipe through the cover and set it into another saucepan containing boiling water. Put a pinch of salt in with the rice; cover it and boil it three quarters of an hour, then set it on the side of the range for a few minutes until the water is all dried out, then stir it up with a fork. It will be soft and every kernel separate. Serve it with a milk sauce that has a little brandy in it.

ARROWROOT GRUEL.

Mix one tablespoonful of arrowroot with three tablespoonfuls of cold water; then put one pint of cold water and a salt spoonful of salt into a porcelain saucepan and stir in the arrowroot; stir it and boil it five minutes from the time it begins to boil. With the permission of the physician it can be made of milk, and if preferred wine and sugar can be added.

SAGO GRUEL.

Put two tablespoonfuls of sago to soak over night in one pint of cold water. In the morning put the sago and the water in which it was soaked into a porcelain saucepan, with one salt spoonful of salt in it, and boil it slowly five minutes from the time it begins to boil. If permitted it can be made with sweet milk and sugar and flavored with lemon or wine, if desired.

TAPIOCA GRUEL.

Soak one tablespoonful of tapioca over night in one pint of cold water or milk, then put the tapioca and water or milk in which it was soaked into a small porcelain saucepan with one salt spoonful of salt in it and boil it slowly ten minutes, that is from the time it begins to boil. Lemon, wine and sugar can be used, with the consent of the physician.

FARINA GRUEL.

Put one quart of boiling water over the fire, with one teaspoonful of salt in it. Mix three tablespoonfuls of farina with three tablespoonfuls of cold water and stir it into the boiling water; stir it all the time and boil it five minutes from the time it begins to boil. This is one of the finest gruels that is made. With the permission of the physician a little wine and sugar can be put in, but patients generally prefer it seasoned only with salt.

OAT MEAL GRUEL.

One quart of cold water, one gill of oat groats and one even teaspoonful of salt. Pick the groats carefully, taking out all the hulls. Wash them in cold water and put them into a tin saucepan, with one quart of cold water and the salt. Cover it and set it into a larger saucepan containing boiling water and boil it one hour and a half. The water in the large pan must be kept constantly boiling. When the gruel is done, strain it through a fine wire sieve. If wine and sugar are used it must be by the permission of the physician. This is the best way to make oatmeal gruel.

ICELAND MOSS TEA.

One ounce of moss, soaked over night in one quart of cold water, then boil in the water in which it was soaked, for thirty minutes from the time it commenced boiling. Then strain it through a linen cloth and serve it as you would a cup of black tea, with cream and sugar or milk and sugar, to suit the taste of the patient.

BEEF TEA.

Take one pound of lean beef and make it fine by cutting it up like mince meat. First cut it in very thin slices and then it cuts easily. Put it into a tin saucepan with half a pint of cold water and a salt spoonful of salt; cover it closely and set it into a larger saucepan containing boiling water. The water must come up around the sides of the saucepan that contains the beef; set it over a brisk fire and boil it two hours; then strain it through a fine wire sieve pressing the meat with the back of a spoon, to extract all the juice.

FLAX SEED TEA.

From the whole flax seed, the best flax seed tea is made. Put five ounces of flax seed into a bowl half full of cold water, stir it up and pour off whatever floats on top. Then pour the flax seed into a tin strainer. Peel off very thinly the yellow skin of one large lemon and put it into a pitcher with three tablespoonfuls of white granulated sugar, stir it together with a spoon and then squeeze the lemon juice in with it; then put in the washed flax seed and three pints of boiling water; stir it up from time to time. Cover the pitcher with a folded napkin and when it is cool enough to drink it is ready to use.

SLIPPERY ELM TEA.

Break up four ounces of slippery elm bark and put it into a pitcher with two tablespoonfuls of white sugar; then pour in three pints of boiling water, stir it up now and then, cover the pitcher and when the tea is thick enough it is ready for the patient to take. If it becomes too thick to be pleasant add a little more water and **sugar**.

TAPIOCA JELLY.

Put one tablespoonful of tapioca to soak over night in half a pint of cold water; then put the tapioca and the water in which it was soaked into a small porcelain saucepan and boil it five minutes from the time it commenced boiling. It must be stirred constantly; then stir in two teaspoonfuls of white granulated sugar and half a teaspoonful of extract of lemon and pour it into little molds that have been dipped in cold water. Serve it with sweetened cream flavored with lemon or wine

RICE JELLY.

Mix one tablespoonful of rice flour with three tablespoonfuls of cold water, then stir it into half a pint of boiling water with two teaspoonfuls of white granulated sugar in it and boil it ten minutes, stirring it constantly; then stir in half a teaspoonful of the extract of lemon and mold it. Serve it with cream and sugar and if the patient has fever flavor the cream with lemon, but if the patient has diarrhea flavor with brandy.

ARROWROOT JELLY.

Put half a pint of cold water and two teaspoonfuls of white granulated sugar into a porcelain saucepan, then mix one tablespoonful of arrow root with two tablespoonfuls of cold water and stir it into the half pint of cold water; stir it constantly and boil it three minutes from the time it begins to boil, then stir in half a teaspoonful of the extract of lemon and put it into little molds. The molds must be dipped in cold water before they are filled. I have used small glass salt cellars for molds and they looked very nice. Serve it with cream and sugar, and wine if permitted.

ICELAND MOSS JELLY.

Soak one ounce of moss over night in one pint of cold water; then put it into a saucepan, the moss and the water it was cooked in, and boil it thirty minutes from the time it commenced boiling, then strain it through a linen cloth, wash out the saucepan and put the strained jelly into it with two teaspoonfuls of white granulated sugar and boil it twenty minutes longer. It must be stirred constantly to keep it from sticking. Put it into little molds that have been dipped in cold water, and serve it with cream, wine and sugar.

BLACKBERRY SYRUP.

The Lawton blackberry is the finest and should be gathered in dry weather. Pick them carefully, put them into a porcelain kettle, mash them with a wooden beetle and boil them five minutes, then strain through a linen cloth and measure. To one pint of juice allow three quarters of a pound of white granulated sugar and boil ten minutes; skim it well and when cold put it into small glass bottles, cork tight and seal. It is often used in children's bowel complaints.

WINE WHEY.

Put one pint of rich, sour, unskimmed milk with four tablespoonfuls of sherry wine into a porcelain saucepan, cover it and set it where it will be quite warm, but not scalding hot. When the curd has formed pour it all into a linen cloth, hang it up and let the whey run out, then put into the whey one tablespoonful of white granulated sugar and four tablespoonfuls of sherry wine. This is a very pleasant drink for a weak patient.

WINE COTTAGE CHEESE.

The curd from the wine whey makes a delicious cottage cheese. The wine gives it a fine flavor.

Put the curd into a porcelain bowl with three tablespoonfuls of rich sweet cream and rub it together with the back of the spoon against the bowl until it is very fine and smooth; then stir in one dessert spoonful of white granulated sugar. It can be served with more cream and sugar, according to taste and is very fine for a convalescing patient if permitted by the physician.

WHEY.

Put half a gallon of rich new milk into a large porcelain pitcher, then take a piece of rennet four inches square, wash it in cold water and put it into a piece of white musquito bar lace; tie it in with a small cord and put it into the milk, fastening the cord to the handle of the pitcher. Cover the pitcher and set it where it will keep warm until the curd is formed, then take out the rennet and pour off the whey. Sweeten it with white sugar and flavor it with sherry wine, if desired and permitted.

WHEY. From Wyeth's Liquid Rennet.

Put one quart of rich new milk into a tin saucepan and set it over the fire until it is warm enough to drink without burning, then stir in four teaspoonfuls of the liquid rennet and set the saucepan where it will keep at the same heat. In thirty minutes the curd will be formed, but by letting it stand one hour there will be double the quantity of whey. Serve it as desired, with or without wine. The curd will make fine cottage cheese, but must not be given to a patient.

APPLE WATER.

Take half a pound of the best dried apples and wash them quickly in cold water and put them into a porcelain pitcher, then put in three pints of boiling water; cover the pitcher and stir them up from time to time, let them draw two hours; the water is then ready to use. The best dried apples are those which are sliced and dried by steam.

APPLE WATER.

The best apples for making apple water are the bellflowers and the pippins. Take four good sized apples, wash them and without paring them, put them into a tin pie plate with one gill of cold water and roast them until they are very soft, then put them into a porcelain pitcher with the juice that is in the plate and pour in one quart of boiling water. When it is cool enough to drink it can be used.

TAMARIND WATER.

Put half a pound of tamarinds into a pitcher and pour over them one quart of cold water, stir them up from time to time; cover the pitcher and let them stand half an hour.

BARLEY WATER.

Put one ounce of pearl barley into three pints of cold water, with one salt spoonful of salt in it, and boil it one hour and a half. There should be one pint and a half of water when it is done, then strain it through a fine wire sieve. If the patient desires it, sweeten it with sugar and flavor it with lemon.

RICE WATER.

Put two tablespoonfuls of rice into a quart of cold water that has a salt spoonful of salt in it and boil it slowly one hour. When it begins to boil the rice lays on bottom of the saucepan and will stick fast, if it is not stirred for a minute. When it is done strain through a fine wire sieve; there should be one pint of water. Rice water can be taken cold or warm, sweetened with sugar or seasoned with salt, just as the patient desires.

TOAST WATER.

Cut two slices of bread half an inch to three quarters of an inch thick the whole length of the loaf and with the crust on, toast it on both sides a dark brown, but be careful not to let it get black. That would spoil it entirely. When it is done break it in two and put it warm into a porcelain pitcher and pour three pints of boiling water into it; cover the pitcher and when it is cool enough to drink it is ready to use.

RASPBERRY WATER.

This is a very cooling and refreshing drink for a fever patient. Put one tablespoonful of raspberry jelly that is made with one-fourth currant juice into a goblet of cold water and let it dissolve. If the jelly is made with raspberries alone it is too sweet and insipid; then take one tablespoonful of raspberry jelly and one teaspoonful of currant jelly.

CURRANT JELLY AND CRANBERRY JUICE.

Are both made in the same manner as in the preceding receipt, and make a very pleasant drink for a patient.

ICE, ITS PRESERVATION AT THE BEDSIDE.

A piece of flannel about nine inches square is secured by a cord about the mouth of an ordinary tumbler, so as to leave a cup shaped depression of flannel within the tumbler to about half its depth. Small pieces of ice placed in this flannel cup and loosely covered with another piece of flannel may be preserved for hours. Cheap flannel with comparatively open meshes is preferable, as it allows the water to drain through and the ice is thus kept quite dry. The ice should be broken in pieces suitable for sucking.

RASPBERRY VINEGAR.

Put two tablespoonfuls of raspberry vinegar into a goblet two-thirds full of ice water. This makes a refreshing drink for a fever patient.

MULLED WINE.

Half a pint of German wine, one tablespoonful of white granulated sugar, half a teaspoonful of lemon extract, one fresh egg beaten separately. Put the wine, sugar and lemon into a small saucepan and let it get warm, but not hot; beat the yolks with one teaspoonful of sugar, beat the whites with one teaspoonful of sugar to a stiff foam and stir it into the yolks. Then stir it all into the wine and set it over a quick fire and beat it with an egg beater until the foam begins to rise, (it must not boil,) then take it off the fire, stir it a minute or two and then pour it into a goblet and serve it warm. This is a very refreshing drink for a consumptive patient. If mulled wine is made of sherry or Madeira wine it must be half wine and half water. If made of German wine no water.

MILK PUNCH.

Put half a pint of rich sweet milk and one tablespoonful of white granulated sugar into a small saucepan and let it get boiling hot; then take it from the fire and stir in three tablespoonfuls of brandy or rum and half a teaspoonful of lemon extract.

EGG NOG.

Put a little less than half a pint of rich sweet milk into a tin pint and let it get warm, but not hot; put the yolk of one fresh egg and two teaspoonfuls of white granulated sugar into a goblet and beat it well together, then stir in one tablespoonful of brandy and the warm milk. Beat the white with one teaspoonful of white sugar to a stiff foam and stir it in last. This is a very refreshing drink for a weak patient.

WARM LEMONADE.

Wash three large lemons and wipe them, then peel off the yellow part very thin (that contains the oil,) and put it into a porcelain pitcher, then peel off the white part, which is always bitter, and cut the lemons in two in the middle; put them into the lemon squeezer and squeeze the juice into the pitcher, then take out the seeds and put the squeezed lemon into the pitcher, then put in five tablespoonfuls of white granulated sugar and beat the whole together a minute or two; then add three pints of boiling water; stir it until the sugar is dissolved, then cover the pitcher with a napkin and when it is cool enough to drink it is ready to use.

COLD LEMONADE.

Is made in the same manner, and with the same proportions as in the preceding receipt, with one exception only, that of using cold water instead of hot.

KOUMISS.

A very nourishing and nutritious drink. Ingredients: One quart of rich sweet milk, two ounces of white granulated sugar and one half of a quarter of a two cent cake of compressed yeast. Put the milk and sugar over a slow fire and stir it until the sugar is dissolved and the milk is only lukewarm; then take it off the fire and cut up the yeast in a cup with two tablespoonfuls of the warm milk. When the yeast is all dissolved stir it into the milk, then put it into bottles, not quite full, and leave them uncorked for twenty-four hours, or until it has fermented. Then cork the bottles tight and tie the corks in with a strong twine. Lay the bottles on their side in a cool place for eight days, by which time the koumiss is ready for use.

ROASTED APPLES.

Bellflowers or pippins are the best apples for roasting; their tartness and sweetness being sufficiently blended to make them agreeable without the addition of sugar. Wash them, wipe them and put them into a bright tin pie plate with one gill of cold water in it. Put them into the oven and roast them very soft. Some apples take half an hour, others again take three quarters; it depends in some measure upon the size of the apples.

MILK TOAST.

Cut a slice half an inch thick from a loaf of wheat bread and then cut it in two. Toast it on both sides a yellow brown and whilst it is still hot spread a little fresh butter on both sides, lay it into a small toast dish and pour over it as much boiling milk (that has a pinch of salt in it) as the toast will absorb. Set it in a warm place until the toast is very soft.

DRY TOAST.

Is made in the same manner as in the preceding receipt, with the exception of the milk. If the the patient desires it a little boiling water can be put on the toast to soften it.

CRISPED HAMS.

When patients are convalescing they generally want something salt and tasty. A nice relish is prepared in the following manner: Cut some very thin slices from the lean part of a sugar cured ham, put them into a skillet that is hot enough to brown and not burn; brown them on both sides and fry them until they are crispy; serve them without any fat or gravy. Let the patient chew the ham, suck out the juice and then put the ham out of the mouth. The patient must be watched at such a time; the ham creates such an appetite there is danger of its being swallowed.

RUSK PANADA.

Take two double baked rusk that are well baked and break them into pieces about an inch in size and put them into a bowl, then pour over them half a pint of boiling water and then stir in one tablespoonful of white granulated sugar and four tablespoonfuls of sherry wine.

CRACKER PANADA.

Boil half a pint of new milk one minute, just to take off the raw taste; break up two Boston crackers in small pieces into a bowl and then pour the boiling milk over them. Then stir in one tablespoonful of white sugar and two tablespoonfuls of brandy. It is ready to use as soon as it is cool enough.

TEA.

Black tea only should be used for the sick and should not be drawn in a teapot. When drawn in a teapot the aroma escapes through the spout and half the strength is lost by not having a uniform heat. Tea should be drawn in a bright tin cup that is used only for that purpose and has a close cover to it. Put three teaspoonfuls of the best black tea into a tin cup with one pint of boiling water, cover it close and set it on the side of the range where it will keep hot for half an hour, but it must not boil. When it is to be served, set the tea strainer into the teapot and pour in the tea.

COCOA. (Baker's.)

Put half a pint of cold milk and half a pint of cold water into a saucepan, then stir in one tablespoonful and a half of cocoa and set it over the fire, stir it all the time and boil it fifteen minutes from the time it commenced boiling, serve it with milk and sugar, as desired.

Plasters and Poultices.

MUSTARD PLASTER.

Put the ground black mustard into a small bowl and stir in boiling water until it is thick enough to spread without running, then take a piece of thin book muslin more than double as large as the plaster will be and spread the mustard in the middle of one half, leaving an inch all around of the muslin clear, then turn over the other half of the muslin and lay the plaster onto a bandage and apply it warm.

MUSTARD POULTICE.

A mustard poultice is made in the same manner and applied in the same way as in the preceding receipt, with the exception that you take one-half mustard and one-half corn meal.

BREAD AND MILK POULTICE.

A small milk poultice is made with one gill of sweet milk and three tablespoonfuls of stale bread that has been made fine. Put the cold milk and bread into a tin cup over the fire, stir it and boil it two minutes; spread it between book muslin that is more than double as large as the poultice. Fold a piece of old linen, four thicknesses and lay the poultice on it, apply it warm and put a bandage over it.

SLIPPERY ELM POULTICE.

If a small poultice is wanted, one tablespoonful of slippery elm flour is enough. Put it into a small bowl and stir in boiling water until it is thick enough not to run, then spread it between thin book muslin that is more than double the size of the poultice and lay it onto a piece of folded linen; apply it warm and cover it with a bandage to keep it warm.

Remedies.

ARNICA TINCTURE.

Arnica tincture is an article that every family should keep in the house to use in case of accidents. The ingredients can be bought at the drug store very cheap. Put two ounces of arnica flowers into a clear glass bottle that you can see through, then put in one pint of pure alcohol and one pint of clear soft water. Cork the bottle tight, shake it up and let it stand forty-eight hours before using it. When using it dilute it with water in the proportion of one teaspoonful of arnica tincture to half a pint of water.

REMEDY FOR SPRAINS.

Bathe the parts affected with arnica and water in the proportion of one teaspoonful of the tincture of arnica to half a pint of water; fold a cloth into four thicknesses and saturate it with the mixture and put it on the parts affected; put a bandage around the whole to keep it in place and moisten it from time to time with the arnica water and take a teaspoonful internally. If it is a sprained ankle, the foot should be kept elevated. If it is an arm it should be put in a sling.

FOR A COUGH FROM A COLD.

Wash whole flax-seed twice in cold water and pour off whatever floats on the top; then put it into a strainer to drain. Measure it, and to one gill of the flax-seed put three tablespoonfuls of white granulated sugar and one quart of boiling water. Peel one large lemon, cut it in two and squeeze the juice in with the flax-seed; take the seeds out of the lemon, cut it up and put it in with the other ingredients, stir it up from time to time and when it is cool enough to drink it is ready for use.

TO CURE A FELON.

As soon as you feel the pain apply aconite tincture to the part affected. Apply it every time you feel the pain; if it is a thumb or a finger put a cloth around it and keep moist with the tincture.—*Dr. Pulte.*

TO CURE SCALDS AND BURNS.

Castile soap is the best, but any other good hard soap that has no rosin in it will do. Dip the soap in to hot or cold water to soften it and then rub it onto linen cloth until the cloth is all covered, or shave the soap up fine and moisten it with water until it is very soft and then spread it on, whichever way can be done the quickest. The burn or scald must be all covered with the soaped linen and then a bandage put around whole. If the burn is a large one it is best to cut the linen into smaller pieces after the soap has been spread on, they can be handled better. They must not be removed until they fall off; moisten the outside of the soaped linen with a sponge dipped in cold water from time to time as long as the burn pains. —*Dr. Pulte.*

TO HEAL A CUT.

If the cut is long and deep, wash it off in cold water that has a few drops of the tincture of arnica in it and close up the wound with sticking plaster. Put the sticking plaster on in strips, leaving spaces between in case it should suppurate. Cover the wound to keep out the air and it will heal in a short time. If it is a small cut, or if the skin is broken in any other way, cover it with a piece of court plaster.

TO CURE A BRUISE.

If you have bruised yourself by falling or running against something until you are black and blue, bathe the parts affected with arnica and water in the proportion of one teaspoonful of the tincture of arnica to half a pint of water; fold a linen cloth into four thicknesses and saturate it with the mixture and bind it on to the parts affected; keep the cloth moistened with the arnicated water from time to time, and take a teaspoonful internally.

Household Receipts.

HOUSE CLEANING. (Chambers.)

Before I commence house cleaning I buy a web of low priced yellow muslin and tear it off in yard lengths and hem it on the sewing machine, then have it boiled and rinsed, and it is ready to use for wiping cloths. Just before the fires are put out and whilst it is raining I light two newspapers and push them up each chimney; this burns them out clean. It must be done whilst there is a little fire in the grate to create a draught. When the chimneys are done burning and the fires are out in the grate take some coarse linen or tow cloth and make bags of it and fill them with paper and cork the chimneys up tight; this keeps everything nice and clean during the summer. Now take up the carpet, and the right way to do it is to fold it, according to the breadths until you come to the middle, then fold the other side until you come to the middle then fold the ends until you come to the middle, then put one end on top of the other and tie a string around it. The carpet is now ready to have the dust taken out of it. If you have pictures on the walls put them on the beds, glass side down, then cover up the beds and have the ceiling whitened, then take the covers off the beds, shake them and then have the floor scrubbed up. If the walls are painted, clean them. Take a piece of a woolen blanket and fold it the size that you can hold comfortably in your hand, wet it in warm water, soap it and rub the wall as far as you can reach. Then take a sponge with clean water and go over it, then dry it with a clean cloth. Now clean the pictures with a sponge dipped in soapy water and squeezed out, and then with a sponge in clear water, then dried with a clean cloth and hung on the walls. Now clean the window frames, windows and doors. Then spread a large counterpane on the floor and put the beds and bedclothes on it and wash the bedsteads with soap and water, and dry them off, then apply the corrosive sublimate with a small brush or goose quill to all the cracks and crevices and you will never be troubled with bed bugs. Now make up the bed and take all the clothes out of the wardrobes and dressing bureaus and lay them on it. Then clean the furniture, inside and out with soap and water, and when it is dry enough put the clothes back again. Now if there is a sofa in the room take it out and beat the dust out of it.

and if it is covered with haircloth take a sponge and clean it with soap and water. Now wash off the rest of the furniture in the same manner and you are ready to put down the carpet.

PARLOR.

After the carpet has been taken up, take the ornaments off the mantels into another room, then take the globes from the chandeliers and take them out, then take a sheet and cover the chandelier and pin it close up to the ceiling; then cover up the mirrors in the same manner. Now take the paintings down, the large ones first, dust them off with a feather duster and stand them on the floor against the wall, then cover them with a cloth, cover the piano with a thick cloth and the furniture that cannot be taken out of the room, place lengthwise in the middle of the room and cover it. Now have the ceiling whitened, then take off the covers, shake them and then scrub up the floor; now clean the painted walls and then clean the paintings and hang them up.

HOW TO CLEAN PAINTINGS.

I have a bar of old castile soap which is thirty years old which I use for cleaning my paintings, and this is the way I do it: I place a painting on a table and at the end of the table I place two chairs with a bucket of warm water on each one and into each one a soft sponge, with one I apply the soap quickly and with the other rinse off, then dry off with a fine linen cloth that has no starch in it, and then go over it with a silk handkerchief, which puts a gloss on it.

HOW TO RESTORE PAINTINGS.

When paintings have hung for a long time the paint cracks and they look badly; this was the case with mine. I thought perhaps it was the heat from the furnace and they needed a coat of varnish, so I sent for an artist to come and see them. He said paintings should never be varnished, and that all mine needed was a coat of poppy oil, so I sent to the druggist and got it. After the painting is clean and dry place it on a table, then pour some of the poppy oil into a saucer, then take a small, soft, loose sponge and dip it into water and squeeze it out tight, then put it into the oil and squeeze it out tight; then go over the painting gently and not a crack will be seen. The poppy oil should be applied every four years, not oftener.

HOW TO COOL A HOUSE IN SUMMER.

Rise at five o'clock in the morning and open all the windows in the house and leave them open for one hour; then close them and shut the shutters. A darkened room is always cooler than a light one. Light gives heat. At six o'clock in the evening open up the house and leave it open until bed time. Now when you open the windows don't raise one six inches, another one foot and another two feet, for it has a ragged look from the street. When I see a house in this condition I say to myself, the mistress of that house has not the bump of order fully developed.

HOUSEKEEPING.

A systematic housekeeper has a place for everything and everything in its place, a time for everything and everything done in its time. Monday, wash day; Tuesday, ironing day; Wednesday, kitchen and laundry cleaned, ironed clothes mended, folded and put in the drawers; rest in the afternoon. Thursday, windows cleaned, rest in the afternoon; Friday, sweeping day and cleaning of silver; Saturday, baking and preparing for Sunday; Sunday, go to church.

CLOTHES, TO SOAK.

A piece of washing soda the size of an egg to ten gallons of water is enough for one tub full of clothes. Dissolve the soda in one gallon of boiling water, then pour it into the tub containing the other water, which should be just warm enough to put the hands in; assort the clothes, the fine from the coarse, and put them to soak (in separate tubs) over night.

CLOTHES, TO WASH.

When the clothes are wrung out of the soak, wash them through two tubfuls of warm soapsuds, rubbing them carefully on the washboard, then rub them with soap and put them into the wash bag and boil them twenty minutes; then wash them out of the boiling suds and rinse them through three waters, the last one having a little bluing in it; put them through the clothes wringer and shake them out well before hanging them up to dry.

TO CLEAR WATER.

As much powdered alum as will lay on a dime, stirred into a bucket of water, will clear it in five minutes.

STARCH, TO COOK.

Half a gallon of boiling water, half a tablespoonful of salt, half a tablespoonful of lard, one piece of alum the size of a five cent piece, half a pint of starch. Put the boiling water, salt, lard and alum into a kettle over the fire; put the starch into a bowl with half a pint of cold water and stir it until it is all dissolved, then stir it into the boiling water and let it boil ten minutes from the time it begins to boil again, stirring it constantly; then strain it. Now it is ready for use. This starch is thick enough for collars, bosoms and wristbands. The alum gives a fine gloss to the clothes and makes them stiff even in wet weather.

COLD STARCH.

Take two tablespoonfuls of starch and two tablespoonfuls of cold water and mix them well together, then stir it into a pint of clear cold water and add a few drops of indigo water. Put the articles into it, squeeze them out and iron them while wet, with a hot iron. Rub the iron on a greased cloth to keep it from sticking.

FLANNELS, TO WASH.

Prepare three tubs, each half full of warm water, in two of the tubs make a strong soapsuds by rubbing the soap on the hands in the water, or by rubbing it on a small piece of cloth. The soap must not be rubbed on the flannels; the water in the third tub must only have a very little soap in it. Don't begin to wash the flannels until you have the three waters ready; flannels must not lay wet any time, and must not be washed with other clothes, nor in the same water that other clothes have been washed in. Wash the flannels with the hands, never on a wash board, that shrinks them and makes them hard. When they are wrung out of the water shake them out well before hanging them up to dry. Don't dampen them before ironing them; iron them dry.

BLANKETS, TO WASH.

Blankets should be washed on a warm sunny day, and two pounds of hard soap is enough to wash twelve blankets. Cut up two pounds of good hard soap very fine and put it into an iron pot with two quarts of cold water and let it soak over night, then set it over the fire and stir it until it is as smooth and thick as honey. Then prepare three tubs of warm water; in two of them make a strong soapsuds and in the third tub put a very little soap and a little bluing. After the blankets have been washed out of the second suds and wrung out of the third water, shake them out well and stretch them before putting them on the line. When blankets are to be put away for the summer, if the chest they are to be kept in is measured and the blankets folded according to the measurement, you can pack away double the quantity that you could if they were laid in in disorder.

CARPET CLEANING.

Olive soap, one pound; soda, one quarter pound; borax, two ounces; alum, two ounces; alcohol, eight ounces. Cut the soap up fine and put it into an iron pot with one gallon of cold water, and let it stand over night. In the morning set it over a slow fire and put in all the other articles; stir it until all are dissolved, then boil it five minutes. Pour it into a tub and add four gallons of cold soft water; it is then ready to use. After the carpets have been shaken and tacked down the wash is applied with a hair scrubbing brush that has a handle on the back and a strip of india rubber inserted in one side of the brush. Have two buckets, one containing the wash and the other clear water and a large sponge. Scrub the carpet gently with the brush, then with the rubber draw the dirty water towards you and take it up with the sponge then squeeze the sponge out of the clear water and go quickly over the carpet and then dry it with a clean cloth. This quantity will clean forty yards of velvet or brusseis carpeting, and if it is done right it will look as bright as when it was new.

TO REMOVE WHITE SPOTS FROM FURNITURE AND RESTORE ITS LUSTRE.

Alcohol, ten and a half ounces; linseed oil, seven ounces; gum benzoine, one ounce; gum shellac, one ounce; oxalic acid, half an ounce. white rosin, one ounce. Dissolve all the gums and acids in alcohol and let it stand twenty-four hours, then add the linseed oil and mix it well together. After the furniture has been washed with soap and water and dried with a clean cloth, then apply the varnish with a piece of white canton flannel. It will remove all the white spots from furniture and restore it to its original lustre.

VARNISH FOR FURNITURE.

Four ounces of alcohol, two ounces of gum shellac, one ounce of yellow beeswax, one ounce of boiled linseed oil. Put the alcohol and gum shellac into a large wide mouthed bottle and let it stand twelve hours, then melt the beeswax and all together. Shake it up well and it is ready to use.

WHITEWASH.

The following is the receipt for the preparation used in whitewashing the White House: Take a half bushel of unslaked lime and slake it with boiling water, covering it during the process. Strain it and add a peck of salt dissolved in warm water and three pounds of ground rice boiled to a thin paste and put in boiling hot half a pound of Spanish whiting and a pound of clear glue dissolved in hot water, mix and let it stand for several days, then keep it in a kettle and apply it as hot as possible with a paint or whitewash brush.

WHITENING FOR CEILINGS.

Fourteen pounds of Paris whitening and half a pound of transparent glue. Put the glue into cold water at night and the next morning heat it over the fire until it is all dissolved; stir hot water into the Paris whitening until it is as thick as cream, then stir in the glue. If the ceiling has been whitened with lime then it must be wet and all scraped off, If it has been done with whiting wash it off with a sponge.

AN EFFICIENT DISINFECTANT.

Nitrate of lead, one half teaspoonful; salt two tablespoonfuls. Dissolve the lead in a quart of hot water and let cool. Dissolve the salt in two buckets of cold water; mix the two solutions. Directions—Sprinkle the carpet, or room, with it, or wring out cloths in it and hang up in the room. Pour down closets and sinks.

TO CLEAR A SINK PIPE.

How often the waste pipe of a sink is filled up with grease and the plumber has to be sent for to open it. Now, to avoid this expense and keep everything sweet and clean about the sink, take a can of concentrated lye, open it, set it into a pan under the hot water faucet in the sink and let the water run slowly on it until half of it is dissolved and gone through the waste pipe. If this is systematically done once a week, say every Saturday, it will save a plumber's bill.

TO CLEAN WATER CLOSET BASINS.

One pound and three quarters of oxalic acid dissolved in two quarts of hot water. Apply it with a small stiff broom with a short handle to it. If the basin has not been cleaned for a long time it will take hard rubbing. After rubbing it with the oxalic acid dip the broom into coarse sand, and scrub it well; then let the water on. After the sand has been washed down apply the oxalic acid again and then take a cake of Sapolio and go over it again. If this is done twice a year you will always have clean water closets.

TO DESTROY BED BUGS.

Put four ounces of corrosive sublimate into a bottle with one pint of whiskey, cork the bottle tight and put a label on it marked poison, and let it stand twenty-four hours, before using it; then shake it up and apply it with a goose quill or a small paint brush, going into all cracks and crevices. It is certain death to bed bugs, but it must be carefully used, for it is a dangerous poison. When not used the goose quill or brush should be tied to the neck of the bottle and both put in a safe place.

TO GET RID OF COCKROACHES.

Take the powdered borax and put it between and around all the water pipes, and in the cracks and corners of the closets and drawers. This is an effectual way to rid the house of these troublesome insects.

TO DESTROY RATS AND MICE.

Take two ounces of arsenic and mix it with one quarter of a pound of lard, (it must be mixed well together,) then take a five cent loaf of bread and cut it in slices not quite half an inch thick, and spread on the lard generously, so that every part of the bread is covered; then cut it into pieces an inch and a half square and put the larded sides together like sandwiches, then put it into the rat holes and close them up. It must be carefully done and carefully disposed of, for arsenic is a dangerous thing to handle.

BUTTER KEPT SWEET.

Half an ounce of white granulated sugar; one pound of fresh butter. The butter must be fresh and have all the milk washed out of it and be salted; then mix in the sugar evenly and pack the butter into stone crocks, then make a brine strong enough to bear an egg, strain it and put it two inches deep over the butter, cover the crock close and when the butter is to be used cut it out without removing the brine.

HOW TO KEEP EGGS FRESH.

To two gallons of water add one pint of salt, one pint of air-slaked lime and two tablespoonfuls of tartaric acid. Let it stand twelve hours, stirring it occasionally before putting in the eggs, then cover the eggs with a lid and keep the eggs well below the liquid.

RANCID OIL RESTORED.

If hair oil or any other oil has become rancid, it can be restored in the following manner: Take half a teaspoonful of soda and dissolve it in four tablespoonfuls of cold water, and stir it into one ounce of rancid oil. Put it into a large vial, and shake it together for five minutes. Then pour it into a vessel that contains one quart of cold water. Stir it together, then let it stand until the oil rises to the top of the water when it can be easily removed.

RANCID BUTTER RESTORED.

Rancid butter can be restored by putting one teaspoonful of cooking soda into one pint of clear, cold, soft water, and working the butter in it until every particle comes in contact with the soda water. Then pour the water off and work the butter in clear, cold water three times. Two teaspoonfuls of salt is enough for one pound of butter.

LARD KEPT SWEET.

Put one pound of white granulated sugar to twenty-five pounds of lard. After the lard has been tried out and strained, let it get cool enough to congeal until it is just stiff enough for a stick to stand upright in it, then stir in the sugar and mix it evenly together. Put it into stone crocks or wooden firkins that have covers, and it will keep sweet for a year.

SPERMACETI AND STEARINE REMOVED.

To remove spermaceti and stearine spots from woolen goods and carpets, place a piece of brown paper over the spots and set a hot iron on them, don't let the iron remain on them more than a second, then place a clean part of the paper over the spots, and replace the iron and repeat this as long as there is a spot on the paper.

GREASE CAN BE REMOVED

From woolen goods and carpets with turpentine. Saturate a piece of woolen cloth or canton flannel with turpentine, and rub the grease spots with it.

FRESH PAINT

Can be removed in the same manner with turpentine as in the preceding receipt.

TO CLEAN BUSTS OF PLASTER OF PARIS.

Take a piece of the finest sand paper and rub the bust gently all over with it. This will restore it to its original whiteness without injuring it if done carefully. A fine stiff brush will restore it in the same manner.

TO CLEAN MARBLE.

Take a piece of canton flannel, wet it in warm water, and rub Sapolio on it until it lathers, then rub the marble all over with it. Sponge it off with clear water and dry it off with a clean soft cloth.

HOW TO CLEAN BRASS CHANDELIERS, BRASSES, ETC.

Put one ounce of oxalic acid into one pint of cold water. Apply it with a brush, or if the surface is even apply it with a piece of canton flannel.

HOW TO CLEAN A BRASS OR COPPER KETTLE.

Take salt and vinegar and a piece of canton flannel and wash the kettle with it.

SATIN AND SILK RIBBONS CLEANED.

Satin and silk ribbons of the most delicate colors can be cleaned beautifully with the spirits of turpentine without changing the color in the least.

Fold a linen towel lengthways, four double, and lay it on a press-board, then place the ribbon on it right side uppermost, then take a piece of an old fine linen pocket handkerchief that has no starch in it, and saturate it with turpentine. Rub the ribbon gently all over with it, then place it on the ironing table, spread a gentleman's linen pocket handkerchief over it and iron it, then hang it in front of an open window until the odor of the turpentine is gone.

GREASE SPOTS ON LIGHT COLORED SILKS.

Can be taken out with magnesia. If the dress is lined make an opening in the lining and rub the magnesia on the under side of the silk and let it remain there. At the drug stores they have it made in squares and put up in small boxes for this purpose. It is very convenient to have in the house, or in traveling in case of an accident.

BLACK SATIN AND SILK.

That is soiled and has grease spots on it can be cleaned with spirits of turpentine; to look bright and new. Apply the turpentine with a soft linen cloth, rubbing gently all the parts that are soiled and greased, then hang it in the open air until the the odor is gone.

FLOUR PASTE.

Mix one pint of flour with one pint of cold water. Pour the water in slowly and work it with the back of the spoon until it is perfectly smooth. Then stir it into a pint of boiling water over the fire and keep stirring it until it begins to boil, then take it off the fire and it is ready to use.

This is the paste that is used for putting on wall paper.

MUCILAGE.

Fill your mucilage glass not quite full with gum arabic, then fill up with cold water and it will dissolve in a few hours when it will be ready to use.

GLOVE PASTE.

Take one pound of old white castile soap and cut it up fine, then put it into an iron pot with one pint of clear soft water, and boil it fifteen minutes or until it is perfectly smooth, stir it all the time it is boiling to keep it from sticking. Then pour it into a wooden bowl and stir it with a wooden spoon until it cools five minutes; then put in one tablespoonful of alcohol and beat it well together, then add three tablespoonfuls of cold water and beat it together until it is a stiff fine paste. Put it into gallipots, and if it becomes too dry for use moisten it with a few drops of water, beat it up and it will be just as good as when first made. This paste will clean the most delicate colored gloves to look just like new.

KID GLOVES, TO CLEAN.

Stretch the fingers of the glove on a wooden pin that is made for that purpose, and apply the paste with a white woolen cloth. Turn the cloth over the end of the forefinger of her tight hand, and take a small quantity of the paste on it at a time. Rub it on gently, and take a clean part of the cloth every time that you apply the paste.

LISLE GLOVES CLEANED AND COLORED.

Lisle gloves always fade in washing. After the gloves have been washed, clean with soap and water, rinse them in two waters and wring them out tight. Then take half a pint of strong black coffee (if you want a dark shade of cream color) and put the wet gloves into it and wring them out quick. Then put them wet onto your hands and dry them. If you want them a light cream color, dilute the coffee with water. Remember the gloves must be wet when they are put into the coffee, and they must be dried on your hands.

GRAY GLOVES.

Gray gloves, the color can be restored by putting one tablespoonful of ink into half a pint of water, or two tablespoonfuls of strong indigo water.

RENEWING BLACK LACE.

Take two bowls and put half a pint of whisky into each one. Then take two teaspoonfuls of dissolved gum arabic and stir it into two tablespoonfuls of cold water. Then stir it into the last bowl of whisky that you are going to use. Now put the lace into the first bowl and squeeze it gently two or three minutes. Then put it all into the second bowl at one time, otherwise one part would be stiff and the other not. If you have a large quantity of lace, you must double the quantities.

LAWN DRESS WASHED WITHOUT FADING.

Wash the dress quickly in two and a half gallons of tepid water with half a pint of cider vinegar in it; rinse it in two and a half gallons of tepid water with half a pint of salt in it, then rinse it again in tepid blue water and dry it in the shade.

TO WASH A MAROON WOOLEN TABLE COVER, EMBROIDERED IN SILK.

Make a strong suds with Ivory Soap and hot water. Let the soap lay in the hot water until it is soft. The soap must not be rubbed on the table cover. After it is washed clean, rinse it in two waters that are warm. When it is half dry, iron it on the under side until it is dry.

WHITE DRESSES AND LAWNS WITH A WHITE GROUND

Can be kept white in the following manner: Have the starch all washed out of them, and into the last rinsing water put one-third more indigo bluing than you have formerly done. This will keep the dresses white as snow until they are used again.

TO PREVENT HANDS FROM CHAPPING.

Take a two-ounce bottle and fill it half full of glycerine, then fill up with cold water to within half an inch of the top and shake it well, then fill up with water.

Just before going to bed wash your hands clean in soap and water, then rinse them and dry them; now shake up the bottle and pour not quite a teaspoonful into your left hand and rub it over both hands. Rub them for two or three minutes and the glycerine will all disappear, leaving the hands smooth and soft.

TO PREVENT HAIR FROM TURNING GRAY AND FALLING OUT.

Take a half pint bottle and put into it one-fifth glycerine and fill up with bay rum. Shake it well together and cork it tight; pour a little of it into a small vessel and apply it with a hair brush until you can feel it on the the scalp.

I have used it for several years, and it has prevented my hair from turning gray and falling out.

There must not be more than one-fifth glycerine.

INK SPOTS IRON RUST, STAINS AND MILDEW

Can be removed from white cotton and linen goods with lemon juice. The goods must be dry when the lemon juice is applied; then rub the juice into the spots with the fingers and lay the goods in the sun. As soon as they are dry wet them again rubbing the juice in until the spots disappear.

HOW TO KEEP WHITE GOODS FROM TURNING YELLOW.

Table linen, muslin, linen for beds and underclothes when laid away for any length of time will become yellow. Now to prevent this: the last time they are washed before putting them away, put a little more indigo bluing into the last rinsing of water than you have formerly done. This will keep the clothes white as snow until they are used again.

FRUIT STAINS ON THE HANDS

Can be removed by rubbing the hands with strong cider vinegar before the hands have been washed in soap and water.

TO RAISE THE PILE ON VELVET.

Hold the velvet side over the steam of a tea-kettle. It must not be held long enough over the steam to become wet; then shake it.

TO TAKE THE WRINKLES OUT OF VELVET.

Take a hot smoothing iron and turn it upside down and place it so it will stand firm; then take the velvet and put the under side on the iron and move it back and forth until the wrinkles are out.

HOW TO CLEAN A VELVET CLOAK.

In a city where coal is used for fuel, a velvet cloak will become soiled and rusty looking in one winter's wearing. Now to clean velvets and make it look new it must be done in the following manner: In the first place you must have half a dozen old fine linen pocket handkerchiefs that have no starch in them; gentlemen's handkerchiefs are the best for this purpose. Then half a gallon of the spirits of turpentine that is fresh from the drug store. Place a pine table or skirt board near a window where you have the light on your left hand. Spread the cloak on the table and stick pins through it into the table to keep it in its place; then tear one of the handkerchiefs into four pieces and put one of them into the turpentine and squeeze it out, then rub the velvet with it a small part at a time, rub it gently both ways; then take a clean handkerchief and rub it lightly until the turpentine is all out, as the cloths become soiled change them for clean ones. After the cloak is cleaned, hang it in the open air until the odor of the turpentine is gone; then brush it with a clean soft clothes brush, and you will have a new cloak. It is best to clean velvet two or three weeks before you want to use it.

TO WASH A CASHMERE SHAWL OR DRESS.

Take one pound of white castile soap, cut it up fine and put it with one quart of soft water into a stone pan to stand over night; then put it in an iron pot and boil it until it is very smooth; then set it off the fire, and whilst it is hot put in half a pint of alcohol; stir it and pour it into a larger vessel, and add five quarts of hot water; then put in half a pint of alcohol and one quart of spirits of turpentine; it must be used warm. Have the irons hot and the ironing table ready before you begin to wash. Wash it as quick as possible and wring it tight. Spread it on the ironing table underside up, and iron it while it is wet. Iron only a small part at a time, but iron it perfectly dry; don't let the iron come on the upper side of the shawl. If you want to crease it as it was when new, fold it, spread a cambric handkerchief on the fold and iron on it. Let it hang on the clothes-horse an hour or so before you put it away. If there is a great deal of white in the shawl, put in a small quantity of indigo water before the shawl is put in the wash.

INDEX.

BREAD AND BREAKFAST CAKES.

Baking,	1
Bread,	1
Yeast,	2
Bread,	3
Biscuit,	3
Biscuit,	3
Buckwheat,	4
Buckwheat, Harrison's,	4
Buckwheat,	5
Cinnamon Cake,	5
Coffee Cake,	6
Doughnuts,	6
Doctor's Cake,	7
Corn Griddle Cakes,	8
Corn Mush,	8
Corn Mush, Fried,	9
Corn Bread,	9
Corn Muffins,	10
Flannel Cakes,	10
Graham Gems,	11
Muffins,	11
Muffins,	12

BREAD AND BREAKFAST CAKES.—Continued.

Pan Cakes,	12
Pan Cake Rolls,	13
Puff Balls,	13
Potatoe Cakes,	14
Rolls,	15
Rusk,	15
Strawberry Short Cake,	16
Waffles,	17

EGGS AND OMELETS.

Eggs in Stand,	18
Eggs, Soft,	18
Eggs, Hard,	19
Eggs, Poached,	19
Eggs, Scrambled,	19
Omelet,	20
Omelet, Souffle,	21
Omelet,	21
Omelet, with Cheese,	22
Omelet, with Ham,	22
Omelet, with Herbs,	22

COTTAGE CHEESE—OAT GROATS—WHEAT AND RICE.

Cottage Cheese,	23
Cottage Cheese Wine,	24
Oat Groats,	24
Hulled Wheat,	25
Rice to Boil,	25

INDEX.

COFFEE AND CHOCOLATE.

Coffee Pot,	26
Coffee, to Make,	26
Coffee, the Best,	27
Chocolate,	27
Cocoa, Baker's,	27
Cocoa,	28
Tea,	28
Mock Cream,	29

SOUPS.

Beef,	30
Beef, clear,	31
Bean	47
Bouillon,	32
Chicken	43
Corn,	41
Crab,	40
Dumplings for Beef,	31
Dumplings for Chicken,	44
Dumplings for Oysters,	44
Gumbo,	44
Mock Turtle,	35
Mutton,	38
Noodles,	33
Noodles to make,	33
Noodles as a vegetable,	33
Noodles as a vegetable,	34
Ox tail	37
Oyster Veal,	39

SOUPS.—Continued.

Oyster,	45
Pea,	46
Pea without Meat,	47
Tomato,	42
Veal,	48
Vegetable,	36

FISH.

Codfish, boiled,	49
Codfish Cakes,	49
Eels, stewed,	50
Eels, boiled,	50
Eels, fried,	51
Halibut, smoked,	52
Herring, Dutch pickled	52
Mackerel, fresh broiled,	53
No 1, Mackerel, salt boiled,	53
No 1, Mackerel, salt boiled,	53
Perch and Bullheads, fried,	54
Salmon, canned,	55
Salmon, boiled,	55
Shad, fresh baked,	56
Stuffing for Shad,	58
Shad, fresh boiled,	57
Shad, fresh fried,	58
Trout, boiled,	58
White Fish, baked,	58
Stuffing for White Fish,	59

SHELL FISH.

Crabs, deviled,	64
Crabs, deviled,	65
Oyster Soup	60
Oysters, escaloped,	61
Oysters, fricasseed,	62
Oysters, fried,	62
Oyster Patties,	63
Oysters, raw,	63
Shrimp Salad,	132
Shrimps, stewed,	65
Terrapin,	66

BEEF.

Beef Roast,	67
Beef Steak,	68
Beef Steak and Onions,	68
Beef, a la mode,	69
Beef, Corned and Cabbage,	70
Beef Tripe, stewed,	71
Beef, Corned Hash,	70
Spiced Pickle for Beef Venison and Rabbits,	72
Beef, spiced	72
Beef Tongue, spiced,	73
Beef Tongue, fresh,	74
Sauce for Beef Tongue,	75

VEAL.

A la Mode Veal,	76
A la Strasburgh Veal,	77

VEAL.—Continued.

Cutlet Veal,	78
Fricassee Veal,	79
Fricandeau Veal,	79
Fricassee with Sweet breads,	80
Hash Veal,	82
Roast Veal,	81
Sweet Breads, Fricassee,	83
Sweet Breads, Fried,	83
Liver, Calf's,	84

LAMB AND MUTTON.

Lamb and Turnips Stewed,	86
Leg of Lamb, Roasted,	87
Leg of Lamb, Roasted,	87
Lamb Chops, Fried,	88
Leg of Lamb, Boiled,	88
Mutton Chops, Broiled,	89

PORK.

Ham, Boiled,	90
Ham, Roasted,	90
Pig, Roasted,	91
Pig Stuffing,	91
Pig's Feet, Soused,	92
Pork and Beans,	93
Sausage,	94
Spare Ribs,	94

POULTRY.

Chicken Boiled,	99
Chicken Fricasse,	100
Chicken Fricasse,	100
Chicken Pie,	101
Chicken, Spring,	102
Ducks, Roasted,	103
Duck Stuffing,	103
Goose, Roasted,	104
Goose Stuffing,	105
Turkey, Boiled,	98
Turkey, Roasted,	96
Turkey Stuffing,	97
Turkey and Chicken Stuffing,	98
Turkey, How to Know a Young One,	96

GAME.

Hasenpfeffer,	106
Quails, Roasted,	107
Quail and Bird Stuffing,	107
Rabbit, Spiced,	108
Venison, Saddle, Roasted,	109
Venison, Saddle, Spiced,	110
Venison Steak,	111

SAUCES FOR FISH, FOWLS AND MEAT.

Caper,	116
Drawn Butter,	115

SAUCES FOR FISH, FOWLS AND MEAT.—Continued.

Egg,	116
Hollandish Fish,	112
Horseradish,	114
Mayonaise,	113
New Mayonaise,	113
Oyster,	114
Parsley,	115
Pickles,	116
Tomato,	116
Tomato,	117

PICKLES, CATSUP AND MUSTARD.

Beans,	118
Beets,	119
Cabbage,	120
Cucumbers,	121
Onions,	119
Tomato Catsup,	122
Mustard,	123

SALADS.

Bean,	127
Cabbage, Cold Slaw,	125
Celery,	128
Chicken,	131
Corn,	127
Cucumber,	127
Dressing, No. 1,	124

SALADS.—Continued.

Dressing, No. 2,	124
Endive,	126
Fish,	133
Fish Dressing,	133
Herring,	135
Italian,	130
Lettuce,	126
Oyster,	129
Oyster Dressing,	129
Potato,	136
Potato Dressing,	136
Shrimp,	132
Shrimp Dressing,	132
Tongue,	134

CROQUETTES—MACARONI.

Chicken,	140
Chicken Sauce,	140
Oyster,	141
Oyster Sauce,	141
Tongue,	142
Tongue Sauce,	142
Macaroni, with Herb Cheese,	138
Macaroni, with Tomatoes,	138

VEGETABLES.

Asparagus,	150
Beans, Marrowfat,	155
Beans, Lima,	154

VEGETABLES.—Continued.

Beans, Yellow Wax,	157
Beets, Young,	153
Cabbage, White,	164
Cabbage, Red,	155
Cabbage, Curled Savoy,	154
Carrots,	158
Cauliflower,	150
Corn, Boiled,	156
Corn, Oysters,	157
Corn, Stewed,	156
Greens, Wild,	149
Kale,	148
Kale, with Bacon,	148
Kohlrabe,	152
Leek,	160
Onions, Stewed,	159
Parsnip Cakes,	161
Parsnips, Fried,	160
Parsnips, Stewed,	159
Peas; Green,	151
Peas and Carrots,	152
Potatoes, Boiled,	144
Potatoes, New,	145
Potatoes, Mashed,	145
Potatoes, Dresden,	146
Potatoes, Fried,	146
Potatoes, Baked,	147
Potatoes, Fried,	147
Potatoes, Mashed,	147

VEGETABLES.—Continued.

Saurkraut, to Make,	161
Saurkraut,	163
Saurkraut, with Pork Ribs,	163
Slaw, Hot,	165
Spinach,	149
Succatash,	158
Tomatoes,	153
Turnips,	165

PASTRY—PIES AND TARTS.

Puff Paste, No. 1,	166
Puff Paste, No. 2,	167
Pie Crust,	168
Apples, for Pies,	168
Apple,	169
Cranberry,	169
Curd,	170
Custard,	170
Currants, to Wash,	171
Lemon,	172
Mince Meat,	172
Peaches, for Pies,	168
Peach,	169
Pumpkin,	174

PUDDINGS AND FRITTERS

Almond,	175
Apple and Rice,	176
Apple Dumplings,	176

PUDDINGS AND FRITTERS.—Continued.

Batter,	177
Bread and Butter,	178
Bread,	179
Cocoanut,	179
Corn Starch, baked,	181
Corn Starch, boiled.	180
Egg, German Eierkase,	181
Fruit,	183
Marmalade,	184
Peach,	185
Plum, baked,	185
Plum, boiled,	186
Prunes,	**187**
Quince, Tapioca,	188
Quince Sauce,	189
Rice Flour, boiled,	189
Rice, baked,	190
Rusk,	191
Sago,	191
Tapioca,	192
Fritters, Apple,	194
Fritter Batter,	193
Fritter Bread	194

SWEET SAUCES FOR PUDDINGS.

Apple,	195
Apricots,	196
Butter Sauce,	197
Chocolate,	197

SWEET-SAUCES FOR PUDDINGS.—Continued.

Cider,	197
Cranberry,	196
Cream,	199
Cream,	199
Custard,	198
Hard,	199
Milk,	200
Peaches,	201
Prunes,	200
Raspberry,	201
Strawberry,	202
Vanilla,	203
Wine, German,	204
Wine, Sherry,	203

CUSTARDS.

Almond,	205
Apple,	206
Chocolate,	206
Cocoanut,	207
Corn Starch,	208
Corn Starch Snow Ball,	208
Pumpkin,	209
Raspberry,	210
Snow Ball,	210
Wine,	211

CREAMS, SYRUPS AND ICE CREAMS.

Almond,	212
Chocolate,	213

CREAMS, SYRUPS AND ICE CREAMS.—Continued.

Cincinnati,	214
Raspberry,	215
Strawberry,	216
Vanilla,	216
Wine,	217
To make Ice Cream,	218
Chocolate,	218
Lemon,	221
Raspberry,	220
Strawberry,	219
Vanilla,	220
Vanilla without Cream,	221

SYRUPS FOR ICE CREAMS JELLIES AND SAUCES.

Raspberry,	223
Strawberry,	222

JELLIES WITH GELATINE.

Calf's Foot,	224
Cider,	225
Lemon,	226
Raspberry,	227
Strawberry.	228
Wine,	228

CHARLOTTE RUSSE AND BLANC MANGE.

Charlotte Russe,	231
Almond Blanc Mange,	229
Blanc Mange,	230

INDEX.

CAKE MACAROONS MERINGUE.

Almond,	236
Almond Jumbles,	237
Almond Macaroons,	237
Almond Macaroons,	238
Almond Sponge,	230
Almonds to Blanch and Grind,	234
Bride's,	239
Cake,	233
Chocolate Macaroons,	240
Citron	241
Cocoanut,	242
Cocoanut Jumbles,	237
Cocoanut Macaroons,	238
Cocoanut and Raspberry,	255
Cookies, Berlin,	243
Cookies, Grandmother.	242
Cookies, Sugar,	243
Cream, Cincinnati,	244
Cream Filling,	245
Cup Cake,	245
Currant,	246
Fruit,	246
Fruit,	247
Gingerbread, Soft,	249
Gingerbread, White,	250
Golden,	248
Groom's,	249
Icing,	235
Icing, Chocolate,	235

CAKE MACAROONS MERINGUES.—Continued.

Jelly,	251
Marble,	252
Meringue,	252
Pound,	253
Silver,	253
Snow,	254
Sponge,	255
Sponge, Muffins,	256
Sponge, White,	256
White,	257

BEVERAGES.

Apple Wine,	258
Cider, to Keep Sweet,	258
Cider, Kept Sweet,	259
Egg-Nog, Warm,	260
Egg-Nog, Cold,	260
Lemonade,	261
Lemon Punch,	261
Lemon Syrup,	262
Milk Punch,	263
Mulled Cider,	263
Mulled Wine,	264
Roman Punch,	264
Raspberry Vinegar,	265
Raspberry Shrub,	261

CANNED FRUITS, MARMALADE—JELLIES AND PRESERVES.

Cherries,	272
Peaches, Clings,	276

CANNED FRUITS, MARMALADES, JELLIES, ETC.—Continued.

Peaches, Freestones,	275
Pears, Seckel,	279
Plums, , Damson,	282
Plums, , Green Gage,	274
Quinces,	283
Raspberries,	271
Strawberries,	267
Marmalade,	267
Peach,	277
Quince,	284
Raspberry, Red,	270
Strawberry,	268
Jellies, to Make,	266
Apple, Siberian Crab,	280
Cranberry,	283
Currant,	271
Green Gage,	273
Quince,	281
Raspberry,	269
Preserves,	
Green Gages,	272
Peaches,	276
Peaches, Brandy,	278
Quince,	284
Strawberry,	286

CANNED VEGETABLES.

Asparagus,	286
Beans, Lima,	289

CANNED VEGETABLES.—Continued.

Beans, String,	288
Cauliflower,	287
Corn,	287
Peas, green,	288
Tomatoes,	289

DIET FOR THE SICK.

Apple Water,	304
Apple Water,	304
Arrowroot Gruel,	296
Arrowroot Jelly,	301
Blackberry Syrup,	302
Barley Water,	305
Barley, boiled,	294
Beef Broth,	292
Beef Tea,	298
Broth and Milk,	291
Bread and Milk Poultice,	315
Cranberry Water,	306
Chicken Broth,	292
Cracker Panada,	312
Cocoa,	313
Crisped Ham,	311
Dry Toast,	311
Egg Nog,	308
Farina Gruel,	297
Flaxseed Tea,	299
Ice, its Preservation,	307
Iceland Moss Tea,	298

INDEX.

DIET FOR THE SICK.—Continued.

Iceland Moss Jelly,	301
Koumiss,	310
Lemonade, warm,	309
Lemonade, cold,	309
Milk Porridge,	294
Milk Toast,	311
Milk Punch,	308
Mulled Wine,	307
Mutton Broth,	293
Mustard Plasters,	314
Mustard Poultice,	314
Oat Meal Gruel,	297
Oat Meal Porridge,	294
Oat Groats, boiled,	295
Pap,	291
Panada,	291
Raspberry Water,	306
Raspberry Vinegar,	307
Rice Water,	305
Rice, boiled,	295
Rice Jelly,	300
Rusk Panada,	312
Roasted Apples,	310
Sago Gruel,	296
Slippery Elm Tea,	299
Slippery Elm Poultice,	315
Tamarind Water,	305
Toast Water,	306
Tapioca Gruel,	297

INDEX.

DIET FOR THE SICK.—Continued.

Tapioca Jelly,	300
Tea,	312
Whey 1, Whey 2,	303
Wine Whey,	302
Wine Cottage Cheese,	302

REMEDIES.

Arnica Tincture,	316
Bruises,	319
Burns,	318
Cough,	317
Cut,	318
Felon,	317
Scalds,	318
Sprains,	316

HOUSEHOLD RECEIPTS.

Blankets, to Wash,	327
Black Satin and Silk,	339
Black Lace Renewed,	341
Bedbugs Destroyed,	332
Butter Kept Sweet,	333
Cool House,	324
Cloths to Soak,	325
Cloths to Wash,	325
Carpet Cleaning,	328
Cockroaches Destroyed,	333
Chapped Hands Prevented,	343

HOUSEHOLD RECEIPTS.—Continued.

Cashmere Shawl or Dress to Wash,	347
Disinfectant,	331
Eggs Kept Fresh,	334
Flannels to Wash,	326
Fresh Paint Removed,	336
Flower Paste,	330
Fruit Stains Removed,	345
Grease Removed,	336
Glove Paste,	339
Gloves to Clean.	340
Gray Gloves Colored.	341
House Cleaning. Chambers,	320
House Cleaning. Parlor,	322
Housekeeping.	324
Hair Prevented from Turning Gray.	344
Lard Kept Sweet,	335
Lisle Gloves Cleaned.	340
Lawn Dress Washed.	342
Mucilage,	339
Paintings Cleaned,.	322
Paintings Cleaned.	323
Pile on Velvet Raised.	345
Rats and Mice Destroyed.	333
Rancid Butter Restored.	335
Rancid Oil Restored,	334
Starch to Cook.	326
Starch, Cold,	326
Spots Removed from Furniture.	329
Sink Pipe to Clear.	331
Spermaceti and Stearine Removed,	335

Satin and Silk Ribbons Cleaned,	337
Spots on Light Silk Removed,	338
Spots from Rust Removed,	344
To Clean Busts,	336
To Clean Brass and Copper Kettle,	337
To Clean Chandeliers,	337
To Clean Marble,	337
To Wash a Table Cover,	342
Varnish for Furniture,	329
Velvet Cloak to Clean,	346
Water to Clear,	325
White Wash,	330
Whitening for Ceilings,	330
Water Closet to Clean,	332
White Dresses and Lawns,	343
White Goods Kept,	344
Wrinkles on Velvet Taken Out,	345

www.ingramcontent.com/pod-product-compliance
Lightning Source LLC
Chambersburg PA
CBHW032031220426
43664CB00006B/436